Unredeemed Past:
Themes of War and Womanhood in
the Works of Post-World War II
Austrian Women Writers

Studies in Austrian Literature, Culture and Thought

General Editors:

Jorun B. Johns
Richard H. Lawson

Unredeemed Past:
Themes of War and Womanhood in the Works of Post-World War II Austrian Women Writers

By

Kirsten A. Krick-Aigner

Ariadne Press
Riverside, California

Ariadne Press would like to express its appreciation to the
Bundesministerium für Wissenschaft und Forschung, Vienna
for supporting this publication.

Library of Congress Cataloging-in-Publication Data

Krick-Aigner, Kirsten A.
  Unredeemed past : themes of war and womanhood in the works of
post-World War II Austrian women writers / by Kirsten A. Krick-
Aigner.
     p. cm. -- (Studies in Austrian literature, culture and thought)
  Includes bibliographical references and index.
  ISBN 978-1-57241-179-1 (alk. paper)
  1. Austrian literature--Women authors--History and criticism.
  2. Jews--Austria--History. I. Title.
   PT3826.W65K75 2011
   830.9'928709436--dc23
                           2011030927

Cover Design
George McGinnis
Photographs courtesy of the United States Holocaust Memorial Museum

Copyright 2011
by Ariadne Press
270 Goins Court
Riverside, CA 92507

All rights reserved.
No part of this publication may be transmitted
in any form or by any means without formal permission.
Printed in the United States of America.
ISBN 978-1-57241-179-1

For my parents, who taught me to love reading and writing, among other things, and to hope.

Contents

All translations of German passages into English are by the author unless an English text or a translation is cited.

Acknowledgments 3

Preface 5

Introduction 8

CHAPTER ONE 25
Contextualizing Women and War: Austrian Socio-Cultural Perspectives

CHAPTER TWO 53
"Forcing Ghosts into Books": Elizabeth Welt Trahan's Memoirs

CHAPTER THREE 67
"To Write a Poem on White Paper in Blue Ink": War Trauma and Memory in Hertha Kräftner's Poetry and Prose

CHAPTER FOUR 83
Speaking Her Mind or Out of Her Mind? The Older Woman in Postwar Austrian Novels by Ilse Aichinger, Elisabeth Reichart, Eva Anna Welles, and Johanna Nowak

CHAPTER FIVE 112
"As Old as I Am, I Am So Little": The Kindertransport from Austria to Britain in Memoirs by Martha Blend, Lore Segal, Helen Hilsenrad, and Mona Golabek

CHAPTER SIX 135
"A Lost World": Imagination and Identity in the Memoirs of Exiled Austrian Jewish Women in Shanghai during World War II

CHAPTER SEVEN 164
Writing about War for Children Today: Vigilance, Personal Responsibility, and Forgiveness in Novels by Christine Nöstlinger, Käthe Recheis, and Renate Welsh

Conclusion..188

Notes 192

Bibliography 258

General Index 272

Acknowledgments

I would first like to thank Wofford College for supporting my research project with three consecutive summer grants and a semester-long sabbatical that enabled me to complete research at archives in Austria, England, and the United States. I am grateful for the generous Fulbright grant to Austria that allowed me to participate in various conferences in Vienna and enabled me to do extensive research at local archives. I greatly appreciate the time and inspiration given to me by authors Ilse Aichinger, Lilian R. Furst, Elisabeth Reichart, and Barbara Neuwirth, whom I had the great pleasure of meeting and interviewing for this project. I am also very grateful for the expertise and generous assistance from the reference and research librarians of the United States National Holocaust Memorial Museum Library and the Library of Congress Main Reading Room in Washington, DC; the Leo Baeck Institute for the Study of the History and Culture of German-Speaking Jewry in New York; the Literaturhaus Salzburg; the Literaturhaus Wien, the Nationalbibliothek Wien, and the Dokumentationsarchiv des österreichischen Widerstandes in Vienna, Austria; the Wiener Library Institute of Contemporary History in London, England; and the Sandor Teszler Library of Wofford College in Spartanburg, SC. This book is the result of over seven years of research and writing, and was developed from papers delivered at national and international conferences. A preliminary version of the seventh chapter was published in *PostScript* in 2006.[1]

I also express my heartfelt thanks to family, friends, and colleagues who encouraged and supported me throughout this project. My gratitude goes to Hans Höller, who inspired my early interests in Ingeborg Bachmann and other Austrian writers, and to my dear colleagues in the field of Austrian studies for their gracious support of this book. I greatly appreciate the insight and expertise provided by Don Daviau, Jeanne Cooper, Cindy Sheffield Michaels, Lisa Silverman, and the readers and editors of Ariadne Press. Finally, I am profoundly thankful for my husband, Martin Aigner, and his unwavering understanding for my lengthy research-related travels and the countless hours I spent in my home office, and for my daughter, Lilly Sophie, who gives me hope for a more peaceful world.

it is the ghosts that haunt me. . . . Ghosts are the unresolved, unredeemed past.

– Ruth Klüger, "Kreuzfahrt" (cruise), *Unterwegs Verloren*

Preface

> You were telling a story about war
> it is our story// an old story
> and still it must be told.
> – Adrienne Rich, excerpt from "Dark Fields of the Republic:
> Six Narratives"[2]

> That's what fiction is about, isn't it, the selective transforming of reality? The twisting of it to bring out its essence?
> – Yann Martel, *Life of Pi*[3]

I am especially indebted to the authors I have had the privilege to meet, such as Ilse Aichinger and Elisabeth Reichart, who have inspired this volume, which provides a socio-historical context for reading the body of work by Austrian post-World War II women writers on the war for both English- and German-speaking readers.[4] The fictional works and the memoirs discussed consider the experiences of women in war as well as the consequences for both women and men brought on by the horrific escalation of the events of World War II in Austria. Through these crucial works, Austrian women aspire to come to terms with this past and express hope for a future where humankind will avoid wars through personal responsibility. This volume brings together narratives by both well-known and underrepresented writers and focuses on memoirs, creative nonfiction, and fiction written by women who either have experienced firsthand or have extensively researched World War II, whose sometimes poetic style and non-chronological recounting, speculation, and imagination may blur the distinction between fact and fiction. The fiction and memoirs I discuss underscore the fact that, although authors do not always lay out memories chronologically within the framework of factual and statistical accounts offered by more traditional historical documents, past experiences are contextualized within the present. Tragically, although a large number of literary works by Austrian women on World War II do exist, countless extraordinary stories were annihilated by the incomprehensible horrors committed during World War II and the Holocaust.

This body of postwar writing by women on their experiences of war reflects the unique and diverse culture of Austria, the history of which in the first half of the twentieth century is a rush of borders waxing and waning – from the fall of the Austro-Hungarian Empire to the creation of the Austrian nation-state to its annexation to the Third Reich and, finally, to its reestablishment as a democratic nation in 1955.[5] The volume considers Austrian literature as one that is transnational yet shares a critical understanding of common Austrian culture, heritage, and history. The following chapters address themes unique to Austria, such as the landscape of Austria, the influence of the culturally diverse Austro-Hungarian Empire on postwar Austrian culture, the rural and urban topography of pre-World War II Austria, war-torn and postwar Austria, and references to vocabularies from Austrian regional dialects, expressions, songs, humor, and culinary traditions. Included in this volume are fictional works and memoirs by authors who consider themselves Austrian citizens and who live and work in Austria today, by German speakers with a heritage related to the Austro-Hungarian Empire who spent their formative years in Austria, as well as by authors who spent their childhood and youth in Austria but, due to persecution and forced migration during the Holocaust, today are citizens of another nation, now writing from the vantage point of exile and from within the context of a new homeland.

Because Austria has been a primarily German-speaking country since the fall of the Austro-Hungarian Empire in 1918, its literature is often categorized and discussed under the umbrella of German literature.[6] This cultural hegemony can be explained in part by the success of postwar Austrian authors such as Ilse Aichinger, Ingeborg Bachmann, Thomas Bernhard, and Peter Handke, who published the majority of their works in Germany rather than in Austria. Sigrid Weigel, for example, argues that the German publishing houses had a significant impact on Bachmann's career and international success as a German-speaking author.⁷ Austrian literary studies have become a growing area of scholarly interest, with strong academic and intellectual following, especially in Austria, Canada, Great Britain, and the United States. Austrian literature is indeed, then, literature written by both Austrian nationals as well as Austrians in exile. The opening of the Österreichische Gesellschaft für Exilforschung (Austrian Society for Exile Research) in Vienna in March 2002 has fostered the study of Austrian exile literature and clearly embraces a transnational definition of the Austrian literary canon.⁸

While both Austrian girls and boys, women and men, were touched and transformed by World War II, this volume focuses on the situations of girls and women, whose life stories have often been underrepresented in more traditional historical accounts of war. Beyond acts of heroism, patriotism, and dates of battle, these women write of everyday struggles related to their existence, their family relationships, as well as to their survival on the home front; in concentration, forced-labor, and death camps; in hiding; and in exile. The themes addressed in these stories are those of daughters, sisters, partners, wives, mothers, grandmothers, and friends of men. Many women who came of age during World War II and the postwar period wrote of their childhoods and girlhoods and showed how the war influenced and informed their adult identities. Their novels and memoirs are the tales of World War II from the perspectives of women, but they shed light on how war affects both women and men alike. Despite the wealth of material on the subject of women and war, many more historical accounts and personal stories exist to be discovered in archives and library collections.⁹ This book is for those who courageously shared their stories, for those whose stories are still waiting to be heard, and for those whose stories will never be known.

Introduction

> I can see now that life is made up of stepping stones, each with its own importance as we step from one to another, all contributing [to] the mosaic of our experiences.[1]
> – Charlotte Shedd, *Thank You America*[2]

The fictional works and memoirs discussed in this volume were written by women socialized by the environment in which they came of age and whose adult identities were shaped by childhood experiences. The first generation of these authors endured and survived the atrocities of war on the home front, in concentration and death camps, or in exile, while both first- and second-generation authors confronted the legacy of World War II during the immediate postwar years or much later, well into the twenty-first century. While some authors wrote immediately following World War II during the difficult postwar years in Austria, in which urban life especially was marked by landscapes in ruin, food shortages, crime, and disease, others, many from the vantage point of exile, wrote of their survival while actively pursuing careers as teachers, broadcasters, writers, and journalists. Others, like Elizabeth Welt Trahan and Ruth Klüger, authors of Austrian Jewish heritage, contemplated their pasts and wrote of the war more than fifty years after it occurred. Others still, such as the author Elisabeth Reichart and the Austrian Jewish filmmaker and writer Ruth Beckermann, were children during the postwar reconstruction period and learned of the role Austria had played during World War II not firsthand but from their families and their communities.

This volume focuses on selected works of Austrian women authors whose experiences of World War II are written from a wide range of perspectives: as victims of the Holocaust, as those forced into exile, as those hiding in Vienna during the war, as girls and women on the home front, and as informed second- and third-generation chroniclers. In order to address the works of both prominent and underrepresented authors, it was not possible to do justice to the many Austrian women writers who have contributed to Austria's long-standing literary tradition.³ Although there exist many general and specific scholarly works on Austrian women writers, this study in English of the works of Austrian postwar women writers within a socio-historical context will enable English- and German-speaking readers to appreciate these works as literary responses to Austrian twentieth- and twenty-first-century history and culture.

This volume approaches literature from a socio-historical and intertextual perspective, casting the memoirs and fictional texts as individual expressions of the past, both of what took place and what could have been. While individual chapters focus on diverse genres, such as poetry, novels, and memoirs, and on specific themes, including the figure of the grandmother or children in exile, the texts intersect on many levels. The first chapter contextualizes women and war and, more specifically, women's lives before, during, and after World War II beginning with a global perspective and moving to one that is Austrian-specific. Such a socio-historical context offers readers a chronological conceptualization of historical events and experiences that are otherwise recast in nonlinear narratives and filtered through the subjective lenses of the authors. Monika Bernhold, in her essay "Representations of the Beginning: Shaping Gender Identities in Written Life Stories of Women and Men," reflects on how gender and class identities figure into popular autobiographies, or what she calls "life stories." She states that "if the primary characteristic of human existence is its potential for reconstruction in the form of a narrative, then narrative is not then merely a literary convention, but rather *an essential part of experience and consciousness themselves*."⁴ Bernhold concludes, "Such accounts should be understood as authentic rather than 'true,' since the process of bringing to mind the lived life in a written form is, of course, a selective one. Out of the endless play of experiences, the author is selecting and establishing only certain connections. Moreover, the unlived or desired experiences of a lived life are also inscribed in the autobiographical text."⁵

Bernhold reminds readers that birth and childhood years become a "frame fleshed out with myths, narrative conventions, anecdotes, and/or fictional memories" and that "how this space beyond memory is constructed illustrates the evolving modes of self-representation under the impetus of historical change."[6] This volume seeks out these various connections and constructions by Austrian women authors of fictional texts and memoirs, thereby placing historical events and the reactions and responses to those events within a larger context while at the same time offering readers an in-depth perspective.

Girls and women coming of age during World War II and the postwar years experienced events unique to their gender and social roles in Austrian society. These authors write of their childhoods, coming of age, mother-daughter and father-daughter relationships, sisterhood and sibling rivalry, their socialization as girls, creative game-playing, their education, courtship, and marriage. They also address violence against women during and after the war: rape or the fear of being raped by soldiers; topics dealing with reproduction such as menstruation, sexuality, and child birth; mental health issues such as depression; domestic work, child and elder care, and the pursuit of a profession.

Despite shared gendered experiences of women born in Austria, Austrian-Jewish women distinguish themselves from non-Jewish women. The experiences of Austrian Jews in the early 1930s through 1945 include anti-Semitic abuse and violence, persecution, deportation, the horrors of concentration and labor camps, and forced exile. The memoirs and writings of Austrian-Jewish women of the war generation discussed in this volume reflect on their victimization and survival during the Holocaust and on their ambivalence toward their Austrian-Jewish identity and heritage following the war. Theirs are Austrian stories that counter the silence of those voices extinguished in the war and Holocaust. Shaped by the multiplicity of their experiences, Austrian women authors are united in their intention to articulate the act and art of remembrance and writing, a process that filters experiences while enabling healing.

The postwar Austrian narratives addressed in this volume are drawn from novels, poetry, memoirs, and creative non-fiction.

While some novels convey an author's carefully researched response to historical events, such as Reichart's *Februarschatten* (1984; *February Shadows*, 1989), memoirs based on an author's life, such as Trahan's *Walking with Ghosts* (1998), convey autobiographical experiences through imaginative and lyrical prose. Narratives are linear by nature even if events are laid out in a chronology that addresses personal development rather than progression through time. For many authors writing about war, the act of writing offers a therapeutic means of working through the traumatic events of war and emotional suffering. Just as the author completes the process of writing and publishing from the beginning to end, the form of a book prompts readers to progress from start to finish. The reader is drawn into the emotional life of the first-person narrator of a memoir or of the protagonist of a novel, experiencing the writer's emotional response to trauma and suffering. For example, readers share in Klüger's accounts of her experiences in concentration and death camps and in the painful loss of Trahan's friends Kurt and Ilse Mezei in the war. A reader thus shares in the author's loss and grief through the reading experience. In a sense, then, the written work has for both author and reader a healing and cathartic potential that is able to impart a sense of empowerment.

The experiences of women and war in the works discussed in this book reveal how memory reshapes history as fictional texts, creative nonfiction, and memoirs. Through these narratives of war, women writers attempt to come to terms with history by portraying the emotions created by their relationships to events and the effect of history on individuals. History is rewritten as allegory, myth, legend, literary fairy tale, or dream. In this sense, history is presented as an understanding of the past that captures perceptions and truths beyond dates, statistics, and facts. History is also bound to the psyche of an author, carried through to the present and tying the individual of today to his or her experiences in the past. In creative nonfiction, imaginative elements such as dialogues and settings are used to bolster and connect events taken from oral histories, diaries, and historical documents. In a similar manner, memoirs recast memories in a cohesive narrative from a subjective perspective. By retelling history from these varied positions, fictional narratives and memoirs give life to history by sharing with readers the authors' reflections on authentic events. The investment of these memories in the reader's own mind gives rise to self-reflection, enabling a deeper understanding of the reader's role in the world, even influencing readers' personal actions in the future. The last chapter of this volume shows that this especially is the hope of writers of fiction for children and young adults, such as Christine Nöstlinger, Käthe Recheis, and Renate Welsh.

As both scholar and writer, Klüger distinguishes between fact and fiction in her published lecture from 1999, "Fakten und Fiktionen" (Facts and fictions), in which she notes an "overlap," "where history is reworked into literature," and wonders whether "history serves poetry" or whether the reverse is true.[7] She recalls that when she was a young student after the war, literature was viewed as a linguistic construct, one in which "political and historical questions had no place" when reading novels about war. She states, "We were, however, young people who would have liked to have explanations for the landslide that [we] had just barely survived."[8] Looking back, she wonders whether reading novels about war was just an "escape from history, in fact a history that one had experienced on one's almost burned flesh."[9] Klüger asserts that for historians as for writers, "History is the event, raw material that they interpret to allow them to be provided with a form."[10] All works are therefore interpreted, even if just in the thoughts of every person who orients himself or herself in the world.[11] She states that, although the autobiography belongs "clearly to history," the autobiographical novel, the historical novel, and the historical drama all intersect. Klüger concludes that literature dealing with history provides a means of coping with reality, that "neither fact nor thing is, seen in the light, without a shadow or without meaning. One should just not confuse the one with the other, the thing with its interpretation."[12] By casting Austrian women's postwar texts as a body of work, individual works gain greater depth and a broader context in which genres and topics intersect. The reader's own experiences play into the author's experiences as written in a fictional work or memoir, creating what Klüger describes as a "tension" between reader and author:

> What a beloved or an only stimulating book says to us is not the same as what "the poet wants to tell us." We each have our own language, and these languages are as different as handwriting and fingerprints. The authors speak *one* language, we another; they are saturated with theirs, we with our experiences; they throw us a rope with their books and pull on one end while we pull on the other; tension is between us.[13]

The tension that arises between author and reader nonetheless enables both to engage in the process of coming to terms with the events and experiences of World War II. The wide range of texts by first- and second-generation writers who reflect on World War II in this volume offers multifaceted yet interconnected and overlapping reflections on women's experiences of war. While some authors experienced the war firsthand, a younger generation of writers familiarized themselves with the events of the war through scholarly research, oral histories, and personal conversations with those who had experienced the war.

Among first-generation writers, some reacted to the war by writing immediately following the war while others reflected on their past through the lens of the present over half a century later. Ilse Aichinger and Ingeborg Bachmann, for example, who were among the first Austrian authors to address Austria's involvement in the war and the Holocaust in their writings, wrote of war in an abstract style directly after the war. Theirs were bold and courageous voices at a time when Austria still denied its role in the Holocaust. In her 1948 novel *Die größere Hoffnung* (*Herod's Children*, 1963), Aichinger applies surrealistic imagery, references to the fairy tale "Little Red Riding Hood," and magical realism to work through her personal war traumas, such as witnessing her grandmother's deportation by Nazis in Vienna.[14] Bachmann, who read intently about World War II and also learned about the Holocaust from surviving friends such as Paul Celan, as well as from media reports, wrote of a daughter succumbing in a gas chamber at the hands of her fascist father in dream sequences in her 1971 novel *Malina*.[15]

A further example of a novel by a first-generation writer, Graziella Hlawaty's *Die Stadt der Lieder (Broken Songs: An Adolescent in War-Torn Vienna)*, written in 1956 and published in 1995, is described by the publisher as "more authentic than any factual report" and captures the author's experiences as a young woman in Vienna during the last months of the war through the fictional character Ilse.[16] Almost fifty years after surviving the war, Klüger wrote of her experiences of Nazi persecution in Vienna during World War II and her survival during the Holocaust and its aftermath in her 1992 memoir *weiter leben: Eine Jugend* (Living on: A youth) and its translated and updated 2001 English version, *Still Alive: A Holocaust Girlhood Remembered*.[17] Trahan also wrote her memoir *Walking with Ghosts* over fifty years after the war and bolstered her own memories with excerpts from her war diary and from historical documents.[18]

Despite the intentions of authors to provide authentic accounts of their experiences during wartime, literary reconstructions of historical events and personal experiences by both first- and second-generation authors have nonetheless raised concerns among scholars about the validity and authenticity of literary representations of the Holocaust.[19] Despite the challenges of representing the Holocaust authentically, fictional literature on this subject offers readers a deeper understanding of the effects of war on an individual's future life as well as the emotional and psychological consequences of war. Such writing is a working-through of traumatic events and represents emotional residue laid bare by the author. Atrocities of war committed during the Holocaust are interpreted, reexamined, and reconstructed in literary responses – in both fictional texts and memoirs. James Young contends that the Holocaust has influenced writers of fictional works, arguing that "the Holocaust has entered public consciousness as a trope" and showing "how it informs both the poet's view of the world and her representation of it in verse."[20] Many of the fictional works dealing with war and the Holocaust discussed in this volume, such as those by Bachmann and Reichart, offer the reader a glimpse into the author's "view of the world" and demonstrate how she illustrates her perceptions in her writing. The experiences of World War II on the home front, in concentration and death camps, and in exile have entered Austria's "consciousness as a trope," the literary representations of which reveal how history and its aftermath is reconstructed by its authors. Although Young also recognizes the potentially problematic nature of fictional representation of the Holocaust, he nonetheless recognizes that "literary and historical truths of the Holocaust may not be entirely separable."[21] For Austrian postwar women authors, the literary and historical are not intended to be separable; instead, the literary seems to reveal the historical by inviting readers to approach the past while considering the consequences of war for the present and for future generations.

Efraim Sicher's *The Holocaust Novel* (2005) further examines the problematic nature of literary responses to the Holocaust, stating that the genre of the "Holocaust novel... bursts the already fuzzy generic boundaries of autobiography and fiction, memoir and fantasy, historical document and realist novel."[22] Sicher cites differing scholarly opinions regarding Holocaust literature. For instance, while David Mirsky warns that, in literature written about the Holocaust, "The dangers of trivialization and Holocaust denial are never far away," Lawrence L. Langer argues that whether representation of the Holocaust has been distorted is "the critic's task, not the writer's."[23] As such, literature about the Holocaust written by the children of Holocaust survivors, "who have been affected by the after-effects of their parents' experience of deportation, forced labor, imprisonment in a concentration camp, or other forms of persecution by the Nazis," presents a further challenge to readers.[24] Sicher reminds readers that:

> memory is always reconstructed, always mediated, and always filtered through subjective hindsight. No story can be told with any degree of coherence without being reordered, emplotted, and retold from a point of view that will allow imaginative empathy. Imagination and fantasy do not necessarily impair authenticity. Fiction and history are not exclusive. Both, in fact, are narrative constructions.[25]

While the Holocaust and other gruesome realities of war and the postwar period seem to defy representation, Sicher cites contemporary authors, such as Art Spiegelman, author of the graphic novels *Maus I* and *II*, written between 1973 and 1991, who have "self-consciously foregrounded the theme of unrepresentability in their preoccupation with the difficulties of writing about the Holocaust."[26] This also holds true for narrative works, memoirs, and novels written by contemporary Austrian-born American women authors such as Klüger and Trahan who reflect on war and the Holocaust. As authors and literary scholars, they write in the context of the literature and historical texts they have read. While they are aware of the limitations of the representation of their memories, their narratives reveal the boundless possibilities of the literary imagination.

Sicher best describes the goals of the "Holocaust novel" and for my purposes also those of war and postwar narratives: "[it] must reconcile the inhuman, the unbearable, and the unbelievable with our need for credibility, our desire for aesthetic pleasure, and our belief in humanity; indeed, it may do much to redefine the 'literary' and dispel our delusions."[27] A reader's "desire for aesthetic pleasure" is, however, highly controversial since writers, especially Austrian postwar women writers, typically seek to represent suffering in such a way that it calls for an active engagement in the unearthing of the past and empathy rather than pleasure. Sicher also cites Elie Wiesel who, although aware that writers are faced with feelings of inadequacy in conveying "the unimaginable experience" of having survived, realized that only memory could counter the silence and that a new language would be needed "to communicate the inexpressible."[28]

The creation of such a "new language" was indeed the goal of some postwar Austrian authors. Bachmann, for example, in her early short stories from the collection *Das dreißigste Jahr* (1961; *The Thirtieth Year: Stories,* 1995) explores the boundaries of language and the need to invent a new language with which to communicate and alter the course of human nature. In her short story "Alles" (Everything), Bachmann describes everyday language as a "shadow/shady" language (*Schattensprache*) or a "con/criminal" language (*Gaunersprache*), one that is unable to express truths.

Despite his attempts, Bachmann's protagonist fails in his quest to find or create a new language. Bachmann's short story collection, as well as her later writing, is evidence of an attempt to explore and cross the prescribed borders of traditional writing. Bachmann asserts in her lecture "Literature as Utopia": "Such is literature, even though and even because it is also a hodgepodge of the past and that already in existence, always the hoped for, the wished for, that we furnish out of the stock of our desires – so it is a forward-opening kingdom of unknown borders."[29] For Bachmann, writing is an exploration and a crossing of frontiers in an attempt to get at truth, as reiterated in her 1959 acceptance speech for the Radio Play Prize of the War Blind, "It Is Reasonable for Humankind to Expect the Truth," in which she asserts that readers should demand and can handle the truth.[30]

Sicher examines history as fiction, more specifically as "Holocaust fictions" or "fictional Holocausts," and, citing Wiesel, says that "art and testimony are not incompatible."[31] Sicher states that "it would, ultimately, be impossible to construct any coherent narrative without imaginative reworking, and realism must be strained when the unimaginable has to be conveyed."[32] Sicher explains why and how novels are a valuable tool for understanding the impact of historical events on individuals: they "give empathy with an unimaginable situation of daily horror, but they also benefit from hindsight of knowledge of the outcome, so that the telling of the story is informed by the novelist's own historical overview."[33] The novels discussed in this book are influenced by the "historical overview" of each author, who brings this context into her fictional work. Even the memoirs, many of which were written more than fifty years following the end of the war and the Holocaust, are infused with an overview of historical knowledge about the Holocaust, and the authors are thereby able to construct their personal narratives with linearity and chronology.

Sicher further raises concerns about literature on the Holocaust written by a second generation of writers whose mothers and grandmothers experienced the Holocaust and "who have been affected by the after-effects of their parents' experience of deportation, forced labor, imprisonment in a concentration camp, or other forms of persecution by the Nazis."[34] It is within this context that my volume addresses the 2000 film documentary and accompanying volume *Into the Arms of Strangers* by Mark Jonathan Harris and Deborah Oppenheimer, whose mother escaped to England on the Kindertransport and who only later spoke of her experiences to her children. Sicher summarizes what these second-generation children of the Holocaust often experience: "anxieties about food, fears of separation, expectancy of over-fulfillment, and constant reliving of traumatic experiences."[35] Described as "survivors of survivors," these children bear witness to the Holocaust's aftermath,[36] yet tragically are unable "to complete mourning work for the Holocaust dead."[37] A community of second-generation survivors established themselves in the United States and Canada in the 1970s, giving themselves a collective identity, "filling in gaps in the family history," and allowing them to "recover a lost heritage."[38]

Of particular note is Sicher's review of second-generation writers in Austria and Germany, whose parents "returned to the land of their family's dispossession, persecution, and murder," causing them a great deal of anguish.[39] Sicher discusses the works of German Jewish writers Lea Fleischmann, Peter Finkelgrün, Barbara Honigmann, Esther Dischereit, and Gila Lustiger. He believes that this generation, although:

> not necessarily representative of postwar German Jewish identities (which are already complicated by the differences between East and West Germany and the influx of Jewish immigrants from Eastern Europe, as well as the reassessment of the past after reunification), is clearly affected more than others by the personal repercussions of the Holocaust and of living in Germany and Austria.[40]

Within this context of German-speaking Jewish authors, Ruth Beckermann is one of the most critical and prominent Austrian Jewish writers. She examines the "personal repercussions of the Holocaust" and clearly outlines the challenges facing second- and third-generation Austrian Jews in her 1989 volume of essays, *Unzugehoerig: Oesterreicher und Juden nach 1945* (Not belonging:

Austrians and Jews after 1945). This title clearly distinguishes between non-Jewish and Jewish Austrians, drawing attention to the fact that the second and third generations of Austrian Jews feel unwelcome in Austria. Beckermann cites public statements, historical documents, oral histories, films, and books to document Austro-Fascism and anti-Semitism, as well as the nation's general refusal to deal with the past and to face up to its crimes during the Third Reich. In her opening essay, "Davor, Danach" (Before, after), Beckermann recalls her childhood in Vienna during the 1950s, when children were regarded as wondrous creatures who would be able to accomplish everything their parents had not been able to and who would, unlike their parents, "have a childhood and a youth."[41] Beckermann states that in the 1950s Austrian Jews wished their children to emigrate to Israel or to the United States where they would enjoy a future.[42] She adds that one-third of her friends from the 1950s left Austria to live elsewhere, an emigration that resulted from Austria's disregard for Holocaust survivors whose "feelings and thoughts" and whose "identity as children of survivors" have been "ignored and insulted."[43] Beckermann's essays trace how Austrian Jews have been alienated from postwar Austrian society and how the Holocaust has been memorialized in the postwar period.[44]

Beckermann enumerates several factors that have challenged Austria's ability to confront its role in the war and the Holocaust, such as "the cementing of the victim-legend," "the estrangement of and making an unreality of events," "the portrayal of a catastrophe without perpetrators and victims," and the "reversal of the historical perpetrator-victim role."[45] Within this framework, she explains that Austrians do not identify with the perpetrators because Nazis tend to be portrayed in the media as German. She also states that public figures, such as Kurt Waldheim, who was an intelligence officer in the Wehrmacht during the Third Reich, have been described as neither "criminals" nor "heroes," thus also defining most Austrians as not criminals or heroes and therefore not responsible for atrocities committed against the Jews during the war.[46] For Beckermann, any person who actively or passively supported the Nazi movement in Austria participated in the extermination of the Jews.[47]

Beckermann examines the social history of Jews in Vienna, especially those who returned immediately after the war ended. Many Austrian Jews who survived in concentration and death camps lost their will to live after the war, when they were confronted by the loss of their loved ones and their own survivor's guilt.[48] The postwar years were unwelcoming and grim for most returning Austrian Jews; 5,700 Austrian Jews returned home to discover their businesses and homes no longer existed and that their relatives and friends had been murdered.[49] Between 1945 and 1948, one hundred thousand Jewish refugees passed through Austria, housed in American and British camps.[50] In order to receive financial aid in these camps, survivors had to prove that they had been victims of the war, which, for most, meant facing insurmountable challenges through Austrian consulates abroad.[51] Beckermann reports that while most returning Austrian Jews did not stay in Vienna, 3,955 Jews lived in Vienna at the end of 1945.[52] Of those, 1,977 people had survived in Vienna in "mixed marriages," as "half-Jews," or because their deportations had been delayed, and 200 survived in hiding.[53] After the war, 1,727 Jews returned from concentration and death camps, and 251 Jews returned to Vienna from exile.[54] The following year, 1946, 6,428 Jews were living in Vienna, although the majority was in transit to countries of exile.[55] Scholar Susanne Cohen-Weisz adds "those Austrian Jews who did come back were discouraged from settling, and were either denied the right to restitution, especially of apartments, or had to engage in lengthy fights for their aryanized assets."[56]

Moreover, during the postwar period, Austria denied its involvement in the Holocaust and also allowed former Nazis to reintegrate into Austria's public service, politics, and universities by ignoring de-Nazification.[57]

Beckermann notes that while today's Viennese Jewish community of approximately 8,000 people has grown since the war, it is mostly composed of Jews from Poland, Romania, and Hungary.[58] Cohen-Weisz argues that postwar Austrian Jews have transformed from "a mainly Shoah-based Viennese-Jewish group identity to one whose focus is on the local Jewish environment, occasionally already extending to a European-Jewish vision."[59]

Cohen-Weisz, who espouses a decidedly more positive view of the situation regarding Viennese Jews than does Beckermann, believes that "the Viennese Jewry in the 21st century is characterized by a high degree of heterogeneity under a common roof and a growing unity and discipline despite a considerable pluralism and diversity."[60] Beckermann concludes her volume with the observation that today's Austrian Jews are riddled with identity problems and that children of the second and third generations perceive themselves to live in "isolation" in a "no man's land."[61] Beckermann states that, because the survival of their parents was coincidental, future generations of Austrian Jews are left to question their own existence and still feel a lack of belonging.[62] The preface to her 2005 edition cites the same challenges for twenty-first century Austrian Jews:

> Almost twenty years have passed since the writing of this text. Many books have been published about this topic, new sources have been uncovered which have enriched and expanded this slim volume, yet have not changed my fundamental analysis but rather confirmed it. I was amazed when reading through my essay that the perception of not belonging, with which I had written it – weakened at one point and then strengthened again – remains an integral part of Jewish life in this country.[63]

The resurgence of neo-Nazi activity in German-speaking countries and the sometimes conflicted public debates regarding Holocaust memorials in Austria and Germany force Austrian and German Jewish writers to continually be engaged in a dialogue regarding their Jewishness. Sicher notes that the identities of European Jews in the postwar have been "shaped by the vicissitudes and variations of official discourse on the Holocaust and the shaping of Jewish identity."[64] In his overview of specifically Austrian second-generation writers, Sicher cites the works of Doron Rabinovici, Robert Menasse, Robert Schindel, and Elfriede Jelinek. Jelinek addresses the "violation of the body" that reflects the "social violence bequeathed by fascism"[65] and carries on a tradition of unmasking violence in society, which was initiated by earlier postwar writers Aichinger, Bachmann, and Marlen Haushofer. Sicher argues that the works of second-generation novelists are "works of the imagination mediated by popular culture and the shaping of memory" and that these writers are in a "unique position" because they carry "the memories between the victims and the next generation."[66] I would like to stress Sicher's point that the second generation of survivors of World War II and survivors of the Holocaust shared their own coming of age during a time when the topics of both World War II and the Holocaust were popularized by the media. Movies, documentary films, openings of and exhibits in Jewish museums, autobiographies, memoirs, and novels about experiences during World War II and the Holocaust have shaped narratives on these subjects written in the recent past.

Recent publications of historical works, fiction, creative nonfiction, and memoirs on Austrian history, Austrians, and Austrian exiles during World War II and the Holocaust underscore the enduring relevance of this time period for twenty-first-century readers. While the works of major Austrian writers such as Aichinger, Bachmann, Haushofer, Trahan, and Reichart are available in English translation, there are few anthologies or studies in English that place these authors in a larger social and cultural context for Anglophone readers. Although numerous translations and scholarly works have been published recently on the works of Austrian women authors, such as Bachmann, Haushofer, and Hertha Kräftner, most are in the German language. Hans Höller's 1999 biography of Bachmann and Sigrid Weigel's 1999 volume on Bachmann's work were both published in German, which demonstrates that her writing is of renewed interest in German-speaking countries. More recent studies on Bachmann in English by Karen Achberger, Sara Lennox, and Karen Remmler have been published at a time of renewed interest in her work in Anglophone countries. A 2008–2010 bilingual traveling exhibit in German and English entitled "Writing against War" presented Bachmann's writings in the context of twentieth- and twenty-first-century resistance to war and to peacekeeping efforts.[67] Other recent publications in English about German-Jewish literature and volumes on Austrian women's literature, such as Dagmar Lorenz's *Contemporary Jewish Writing in Austria* (1999) and *Keepers of the Motherland: German Texts by Jewish Women Writers* (1997), show that there is a growing interest in Austrian women's literature and in the works of German-Jewish and Austrian-Jewish writers. Publications in Austria during the past fifteen years mark a heightened awareness of its unique literary culture, especially with a focus on World War II and its consequences for multiple generations of writers. Three such examples are Barbara Neuwirth's volume of prose, *Schrifstellerinnen sehen ihr Land: Österreich aus dem Blick seiner Autorinnen* (1995; Women writers see their country: Austria from the perspective of its women writers); Ursula Seeber's volume of postwar narratives, *Ein Niemandsland, aber welch ein Rundblick! Exilautoren über Nachkriegs-Wien* (1998; A no man's land, but what a view! Exile authors on postwar Vienna); and Christa Gürtler and Sigrid Schmid-Bortenschlager's volume *Erfolg und Verfolgung: Österreichische Schriftstellerinnen 1918–1945* (2002; Success and persecution: Austrian women writers 1918–1945). The 2008 volume on the lives of Austrian women after the Anschluss, *Frauen 1938* (Women 1938), edited by Evelyn Steinthaler, examines both victims and those complicit with the Nazis during the period of Austro-Fascism. The collection of essays from 2007 by Austrian, British, and German scholars on Austrian writers in exile, *"Immortal Austria"?*, focuses on the experience of emigration and exile from "an Austrian-specific standpoint."[68]

In the context of this resurgence of interest in postwar Austrian literature, the present volume contributes to the representation and appreciation of postwar narratives by Austrian women writers by addressing their work in a larger socio-historical context. In order to present cohesively these individual as well as interdisciplinary and intertextual readings of novels, narratives, and memoirs as a body of work by postwar Austrian women authors, the first chapter contextualizes the experiences of women and war from cultural, historical, and sociological perspectives. The second chapter, on Trahan's memoirs, *Walking with Ghosts* and *Ten Dollars in my Pocket* (2006), examines the prewar and wartime experiences of a young Jewish woman in Vienna and the consequences of the events of the war and the Holocaust on her coming of age and adulthood in the United States. The following chapter on the poetry and prose of Hertha Kräftner reveals how this author writes around war trauma during the postwar era, creating a poignant collection that reflects on the emotional and psychological impact of war on women. The fourth chapter examines the role of older women in postwar fiction by Ilse Aichinger, Elisabeth Reichart, Johanna Nowak, and Eva Anna Welles, in which the cautionary advice and wisdom of elders during World War II and the postwar is considered to be symptomatic of mental illness. The subsequent two chapters deal with memoirs by and about Austrian-Jewish girls and women forced into exile either to Great Britain by a Kindertransport or to Shanghai by ship. The final chapter addresses novels by popular Austrian fiction writers, Renate Welsh, Christine Nöstlinger, and Käthe Recheis, who write about World War II for a younger generation of Austrian children and young adults so that they might learn from history and thereby give counsel on the prevention of future wars and the dangers of injustice. The volume concludes with a comprehensive bibliography of primary and secondary works on postwar Austrian history and literature.

Chapter One

Contextualizing Women and War: Austrian Socio-Cultural Perspectives

You don't choose memories; memories choose you.
— Charlotte Delbo, *Auschwitz and After*[1]

The literary texts and memoirs discussed in this volume confirm that women take part in all aspects of war and peace; while some are active participants, supporters, or combatants in war, others work against war in resistance movements and in peaceful demonstrations. Often women and girls in war, however, become the victims of war and are raped, tortured, wounded, or killed. The intention of this general overview, based on studies of gender and war, is to treat the subject of women and war as an ongoing topic of observation and discussion and to provide a context for the socio-historical reading of texts by Austrian women authors on World War II.

Some General Observations on Women and War
In the introduction to her anthology of international writings by women on war, Daniela Gioseffi argues that women and children are the primary victims of war crimes. Despite the cries of "never again" following the Holocaust, Gioseffi cites post-1945 genocides in the former Yugoslavia and Rwanda;[2] today, Sudan and Darfur must be added to this list of countries in which such atrocities have occurred. While 300 million human beings died in war in the twentieth century alone, the long-term costs of war also include displacement, poverty, famine, illness, and environmental devastation.[3] Since two chapters in my volume address memoirs by refugees, it is significant that since 2002 the United Nations High

Commission for Refugees (UNHCR) has recorded 50 million or more displaced individuals.[4] However, unlike the devastating consequences of displacement by war that affects boys and girls, men and women alike, the crime of rape during and often following wartime affects mostly girls and women. Within this context, rape, or the fear of being raped, is a significant gender-specific theme discussed in the works of postwar Austrian women writers and addressed throughout my volume. Since 1994, following the estimated 20,000–50,000 reported sexual assaults on girls and women during the conflict in Bosnia-Herzegovina, rape has been considered a war crime under the Geneva Conventions.[5] The fictional texts and memoirs discussed in this volume attest to the vulnerability of girls and women on the home front and in exile.

While Gioseffi's anthology focuses on the victimization of girls and women in war from socio-cultural and literary perspectives, Joshua S. Goldstein's 2001 study, *War and Gender: How Gender Shapes the War System and Vice Versa*, explores the roles of women in war based on biological, sociological, and historical studies. Through a "multidisciplinary and multilevel engagement with the subject," Goldstein examines the constructions of masculinity and femininity in the shadow of war by arguing that gender norms shape men, women, and children to fit the needs of the war system, for example, socializing individuals to go to war as soldiers or to serve the war effort on the home front.[6] While scholars such as Gioseffi believe in the potential and need for world peace, Goldstein argues that war will always exist and that it exists "in some form" all the time in both agrarian and industrialized societies and that "the potential for war has been universal in human societies."[7] He further notes that "the universal potential for war in human society suggests that the gendering of war may matter even in relatively peaceful times and places, because even a society that is not at war may someday go to war."[8] From an Austrian literary perspective, what comes to mind is Bachmann's post-World War II and post-Hiroshima belief that war always exists – despite the fact that her writing can be read as an act of resistance to war and a way of asserting humankind's right to peace.[9] Although Goldstein's study demonstrates that "killing does not come naturally for either gender," warriors are predominantly male; less than one percent of warriors in history have been women.[10] Women's roles in war vary from culture to culture, including "roles as support troops, psychological war-boosters, peacemakers, and so forth."[11] Goldstein reports that 23 million soldiers served in uniformed standing armies in 2001, of which 97% were male and of which approximately 500,000 were women who filled more traditionally female roles such as typists and nurses. At the time, 99.9% of designated combat forces were male. Goldstein's study attempts to unravel why, although societies construct gender norms around war, most fighters are men. In his chapter on the "biology of individual gender," he concludes that despite all the scientific studies, "the problem is that none of the gender differences arising from biology is sufficient to explain the puzzle of gendered war roles. Biology provides a partial explanation by showing why war would tend to involve mostly men. It does not, however, provide a sufficient explanation to the puzzle of why war is virtually all male."[12] Goldstein's research shows that examples of women in guerilla warfare are not rare, unlike in conventional war, and that these women have "added to the military strength of their units, and sometimes fought with greater skill and bravery than their male comrades."[13] Yet Goldstein also observes: "whenever their forces seized power and become regular armies, women have been excluded from combat. Evidently, this exclusion is not based on any lack of ability shown by the women soldiers when they participated in the guerrilla phase of war."[14] Although women are less likely to engage in combat in standing, official armies, there are women guerilla fighters, which is perhaps why, despite the statistics on the number of male soldiers, the myth of the female warrior is prevalent in Western European mythology. While examining historical evidence and myths of women armies, such as the Amazon matriarchies, Goldstein argues that "as far as available evidence goes, no society exclusively populated or controlled by women, nor one in which women were the primary fighters, has ever existed."[15] He does, however, mention cases in which women have participated in combat, such as in the state armies in the Dahomey Kingdom of West Africa in the eighteenth and nineteenth centuries and the Soviet Union in World War II.[16] In both cases, he argues, "women can be organized into effective large-scale military units. In neither case were women the majority, but in both cases the mobilization of a substantial minority of women soldiers increased the state's military power."[17] Goldstein states that while women generally do not aggressively kill on the battlefield, there are examples of female Soviet snipers who shot down German soldiers and of female soldiers who "took the lead in cruelty and torture, especially of prisoners."[18] Goldstein comments that, despite the fact that women have proven that they are capable of being skilled combatants, a society must be under great threat before it will send women to combat, as was the case in the Soviet Union during World War II.[19] He also explains that, by contrast, Nazi Germany promoted a "gender division" in which women were "assigned to the home and the production of German children, while the men engaged in politics and war."[20] A later section in this chapter will specifically address the various roles that Austrian women played during World War II, such as mothers, resistance fighters, and supporters of the Nazi regime.

Like Gioseffi, Goldstein examines rape in war, although he also discusses "feminization," in which men are humiliated and tortured by "gendered massacres" (killing all male captives, raping women, and taking women and children as slaves), castration, homosexual rape, and insults and intimidations.[21] Goldstein reports that rape is "a crime of domination," one of many atrocities of war, a "'normal' accompaniment" to war. Rape is the "ultimate humiliation…the stamp of total conquest."[22] He cites scholars who state that "for its victims, rape as a 'violent invasion into the interior of one's body represents the most severe attack imaginable upon the intimate self and the dignity of a human being,' constituting 'severe torture.'"[23] Historical evidence confirms that rape is not driven by sexual desire but rather is a violent act.[24] Like Gioseffi, Goldstein refers to the 20,000 to 50,000 rapes in Bosnia, but he also refers to the 100,000 rapes in Berlin at the end of and after World War II.

Having examined feminist theories of war and peace, Goldstein concludes that feminist literatures about war over the last fifteen years have "made little impact as yet on the discussions and empirical research taking place in the predominately male mainstream of political science and military history."[25] He states that, while a single unified or *the* feminist theory on war does not exist, there are three distinct categories of feminist theories regarding women and war: 1) *liberal feminism*, which states that "women can be capable warriors," 2) *difference feminism*, in which "partly biological gender differences" are highlighted, and 3) *postmodern feminism*, which focuses on "arbitrary cultural constructions favoring those men in power."[26] Among these categories one in particular is of note for this volume on Austrian women's literature. Goldstein associates ecofeminism with *difference feminism*, in which "war is an extension of the aggressive and exploitative relationships embodied in sexism, racism, and the 'rape' of the environment."[27] Austrian literature of the twentieth and twenty-first centuries in particular demonstrates a unique body of ecofeminist texts. In literary works written not long after the end of World War II in Austria, such as Haushofer's *Die Wand* (1968; *The Wall*, 2000) and Bachmann's poems written between 1956 and 1961, such as "Erklär mir, Liebe" and "Freies Geleit (Aria II)" on the splendor of nature as well as the neo-Romantic imagery of the Warrior Princess of Kagran at one with nature in *Malina*, the environment is portrayed as a beautiful and powerful counterstate to war yet at the same time one also threatened by war and human destruction.[28] Austrian fantasy and science fiction author Barbara Neuwirth situates her protagonists in a natural setting, in which nature is often personified and mystical, such as in her short story collection *In den Gärten der Nacht* (1990; In the gardens of night) and in her short prose work *Über die Thaya* (2000; Over the Thaya). Within the context of ecofeminism, Neuwirth considers the occurrences and consequences of past historical events, such as in her short story "Bücherverbrennung" (1990; Book burning), in which a young woman joins the resistance against the militaristic dictatorship "Greyskirts" (*Grauröcke*), saves books from being burned, and plots with the other fighters to burn the propaganda materials they have found.[29] More recently, Elfriede Jelinek, who won the Nobel Prize for Literature in 2004, also comments on the destruction of nature in her 2002 play *In den Alpen* (In the Alps). Her essay "Der Wald" (1993; The forest) unmasks the paradox of the love of nature in the Austrian culture whose natural environment is being destroyed by tourism such as skiing; she calls people "blind embryos," who "insult the earth" while cross-country skiing.³⁰ This chilling perspective on the destruction of nature by humankind in Austrian ecofeminist texts complements concerns raised by Austrian postwar women authors on war, especially the victimization of women and children by violence and rape during wartime; whether destructive of each other or of nature, the fate of humankind is cast into doubt in Austrian postwar literature.

Girls, Women, and the Holocaust

A general overview of women and war that intends to provide a context for the Austrian women's literature addressed in this volume must also include the history of women in the Holocaust. Postwar Austrian texts by authors such as Ruth Klüger, as well as those who write about it not from personal experience but from historical documents, such as Reichart, prove that the Holocaust continues to inform twentieth- and twenty-first-century Austrian culture and its literary responses. Austrian women authors, such as Aichinger and Bachmann, were among the first authors after 1945 to deal with the atrocities suffered by fellow Austrians and victims from Western, Eastern, and Central Europe. Of the approximately six million Jews murdered in the Holocaust, more than 65,000 were Austrian men, women, and children.

The Holocaust impacted children and adults, boys and men, girls and women, in unique ways. More recent studies on the subject — Dalia Ofer and Lenore J. Weitzman's *Women in the Holocaust* (1998), Lawrence L. Langer's essay "Gendered Suffering: Women in Holocaust Testimonies" in his volume *Preempting the Holocaust* (1998), Elizabeth R. Baer and Myrna Goldenberg's anthology *Experience and Expression: Women, the Nazis, and the Holocaust* (2003), and Zoë Vania Waxman's *Writing the Holocaust: Identity, Testimony, Representation* (2006) — examine the diverse and complex role of gender in the Holocaust and how it plays out in memory and written testimonies.

Ofer and Weitzman summarize the suffering that affected Jewish women primarily as "the burdens of sexual victimization, pregnancy, abortion, childbirth, killing of newborn babies in the camps to save the mothers, care of children, and decisions about separation from children."³¹ Sara R. Horowitz, in her "Women in

Holocaust Literature: Engendering Trauma Memory" in Ofer and Weitzman's volume, cautions that "gender does not constitute the totality of one's experience" but outlines why women's testimonies "reveal distinctly different patterns of experience and reflection from those of men."[32] She asserts that "in recalling and grappling with memories of personal and collective loss, trauma, and displacement, and in reconstructing a sense of meaning and ethics, women may remember differently from men – or they may remember different things."[33] Memories of uniquely female experiences include:

> menarche, menstruation, and pregnancy in the concentration camps; the strategies some women devised to endure and survive; the ways other women met their deaths; the subsequent effect on women survivors in family, friendship, and civic relations; and the way women reconstruct shattered paradigms of meaning in the face of cultural and personal displacement.[34]

She adds, "In addition, examining the ways the atrocity of the Shoah affected women or men, in specific terms – in their roles as mothers, fathers, wives, husbands, daughters, sons, lovers, friends, workers, homemakers – reveals to us something of the trauma they continue to bear."[35] The desire to reconstruct "shattered paradigms of meaning" is especially evident in the writing of men and women in exile, as discussed in the case of exiled Austrian women writers in Chapters Five and Six of this volume. Horowitz concludes that women writers use "the space of their writing to think through the complexities of the Shoah for its survivors and for others" and to expand the reader's "cognitive and psychological understanding of the Holocaust, using narratives of victimization and survival to meditate on the problematics of memory, testimony, and trauma."[36] Memories remain imperfect; they are instances strung together, in which some events have been lost to time and trauma, as a result of which the imagination reconnects and propels the memories forward, to tell a story, and to retell history. The following chapter on Trahan's memoirs explores precisely this problematic nature of reconstructing memory in survivor writing. For readers of memoirs and fictional representations of war, such a "cognitive and psychological understanding of the Holocaust" will be deeply personal and therefore also a subjective experience that calls for varied reader responses.

Langer likewise explores the experiences of women during the Holocaust – this "disabling outburst of unreason," as he calls it – which "continues to assault memory and imagination with immeasurable sorrow and undiminished force."[37] Langer cites examples in which female Holocaust survivors experienced what he calls the "missed destiny of dying," in which the deaths of their women friends are forever imprinted on the survivors' memories.[38] The victim Mado, for example, recalls that despite having survived, "time does not pass over me, over us. It doesn't erase anything; doesn't undo it. I'm not alive. I died in Auschwitz but no one knows it."[39] Langer believes that especially the "phenomenon of maternity" haunts these women survivors. He cites numerous testimonies revealing that pregnant women were gassed and newborn infants were murdered. Holocaust testimony, Langer believes, "is not a series of links in a chain whose pattern of connections can be easily traced but a cycle of sparks erupting unpredictably from a darkened landscape, teasing the imagination toward illumination without ever offering it the steady ray of stable insight."[40] As this volume will show, it is the narrative itself, whether a fictional text or a memoir, that provides for a "chain," a "pattern of connections" that allows readers a glimpse of this history of women and war and women and the Holocaust. Langer asserts that gender played no role in survival or endurance during the Holocaust, citing that, in all the testimonies he has studied, he has "found no evidence that mothers behaved or survived better than fathers, or that mutual support between sisters, when possible, prevailed more than between brothers."[41] However, while gender may not have played a role once women were in the camps, gender and age surely played a role in the selection process. Pregnant women and women with small children, for example, were selected immediately for the gas chambers in killing centers such as Auschwitz-Birkenau. Langer nonetheless calls for readers to abandon "all efforts to find a rule of hierarchy in that darkness, whether based on gender or will, ..."⁴²

Baer and Goldenberg, however, counter Langer's reasoning that "gender differences," including sporadic instances of "mutual support among women in the camps" were insignificant in the larger context of ubiquitous suffering and mass death" and that "the Shoah is inexplicable and will not yield to analysis."⁴³ Instead, they argue that gendered analysis should not focus on solely traditional notions of womanhood but rather on "a perceptive articulation of how those roles have been constructed under various circumstances."⁴⁴ The goal of Baer and Goldenberg's interdisciplinary and analytical anthology, devoted to both Jewish and non-Jewish women in the Holocaust, explores "representations of women's experiences" by emphasizing the "social construction of women" and "women's construction of their own memories and experiences through various forms of representation."⁴⁵ The notion of gendered memory is explored by examining how narratives by women may differ from those by men in terms of content, language, and metaphor.⁴⁶ Pascale Rachel Bos, in her 2003 article "Women and the Holocaust: Analyzing Gender Difference," describes that, when used as a category of analysis, "gender is more complex than previously thought, and more ambiguous."⁴⁷ Bos cites Torel Moi, who reminds readers that all narratives are (re)constructions of "a confusing, multi-faceted experienced reality" and a "controversial construct at that."⁴⁸ In addition to the influence of gender, Bos feels the "process of narrating is embedded in both the cultural understanding and the linguistic capacities of the survivor."⁴⁹ Such arguments support Austrian-specific cultural readings of narratives in which Austrian culture informs identity, especially for those living outside of Austria in exile. Bos contends that survivors select "*their version* of reality ... filtered in part through the changing lens of trauma," time, and "the psychological process of self-preservation."⁵⁰ For Bos, men and women narrate differently precisely because they experience, remember, and recount events differently.⁵¹ She argues that self-perception is gendered "because belonging to a certain sex is at the heart of our self-image as human beings and thus at the heart of the desire to 'normalize' life."⁵² For Bos, this gendered self-perception is in turn caused by socialization, which becomes especially significant in light of the discussion of the socialization of women during the Holocaust in this chapter's following section. The articulation of a personal story is what Bos calls a "renegotiation of the past," which functions as a healing process, one that seems to lie at the heart of most memoirs and novels addressed in this volume. In order to "reassert their subjectivity and agency," bearing witness and articulating their stories allow survivors to "reconsider events, rethink their role in them, and create a bridge between the past and present," in an effort to make sense of their past, and "to justify and normalize it, according to Bos."[53] In order to read narratives as gendered discourses, Bos asserts that men's and women's prewar socialization and the survivors' "present-day location vis-à-vis the competing discourses of gender, class, Jewishness . . . need to be considered as central to the narratives they will produce."[54]

S. Lillian Kremer's "Women in the Holocaust: Representation of Gendered Suffering and Coping Strategies in American Fiction" also considers the gendered discourse of novels that deal with the Holocaust by presenting the characters' wartime responses as "influenced by their prewar gender and national/ethnic socialization."[55] While Kremer summarizes the gender-specific themes of Holocaust novels written about women's experiences, such as "sexual assault, maternity, fertility, amenorrhea, fear of sterilization, the 'crimes' of pregnancy and childbirth, and selection for annihilation based on maternal status,"[56] such writings also "reveal the Shoah's enduring relevance and attest to the moral imperative to remember that is a cornerstone of Jewish thinking and liturgy."[57] Within this frame of reference of gendered discourse, this volume addresses novels, poetry, memoirs, and works of creative nonfiction by Austrian women writers as unique reconstructions of memory, from either personal experiences or by way of historical research, as well as through the author's imagination, by considering women's socio-historical roles in Austria during World War II and the postwar period.

Recent research on women and war deals with the experiences of children under the age of eighteen whose childhood was replaced by the suffering and terror of the Holocaust. The child's or adolescent's experience is important to this volume, as many of its authors were adolescents or young women when they experienced the horrors of war. While some authors, such as Lore Segal and Martha Blend, survived childhood in England and wrote about their experiences in adulthood, other authors, such as Aichinger, wrote as young women about their childhood in war. The final chapter of this book focuses on women authors such as Nöstlinger, Recheis, and Welsh who write for a young readership from the perspective of children, in texts that reflect upon their own childhood in war. The narratives of Nöstlinger, Recheis, and Welsh, although categorized as fictional, straddle the definitions of fiction and autobiography. Prologues point readers to the authors' personal experiences, provided in a narrative framework that is linear, chronological, and in a language that challenges yet is appropriate for young readers.

Two volumes that focus on children in the Holocaust, Anita Brostoff's *Flares of Memory: Stories of Childhood during the Holocaust* (2001) and Laurel Holliday's anthology *Children in the Holocaust and World War II: Their Secret Diaries* (1995), provide a background for the unique experiences of children in war. Brostoff's volume gathers writings by Jewish Holocaust survivors from writing workshops during which adults wrote of their childhood survival in narratives that range in setting from the early 1930s through the end of the war. The stories in Brostoff's volume focus on the experiences of children and young adults, "their hunger, thirst, cold, exhaustion; their helplessness, despair, and terror at the constant threat of death; their grief over the loss of their families, their homes, their whole culture."[58] The stories are grouped into sections that cover Jewish life before the Holocaust, the destruction of Jewish communities and the murders of their families, hiding in order to survive, survival through the "sustaining power of family love," and the "aftermath" of remembering. The accounts can be described as what the author of "Snapshots," Malka Baran, born in 1927 in Poland, calls "snapshots of a childhood murdered."[59] Another survivor, Edith Rechter Levy, born in Vienna in 1930, recalls being asked as an adult by a child what she considered to be the "worst part of the Holocaust."[60] In her personal essay, she concludes that the "worst part of the Holocaust is what comes afterward. It is the realization that one must continue living for the rest of one's life with part of one's soul amputated."[61] Brostoff views these survivor stories as essential for readers today because they "move us to imagine a reality, a truth, which is beyond understanding" and because they "achieve a fundamental truth" in that "the essence of the experience, its meaning, is absolutely true."[62] For Brostoff, these recorded personal histories give "shape to events individually and personally experienced," which in turn help shape readers' perspectives on the Holocaust by presenting individual, personal events that challenge the enormity and incomprehensible historical figure of the six million dead, of which at least one million were children under fifteen.[63] Langer writes that the "heritage of corpses," the murder of children, is, for surviving parents, a "tainted memory," "a legacy they cannot escape."[64] He calls upon readers to take into consideration the "absence" that resides in the survivor's memories, "a never-ending struggle to reclaim some fragment of those missing lives."[65] Both memoirs and fictional works show that the act of writing enables authors to "reclaim" such "fragments" to somehow come to terms with their childhood experiences during the Holocaust.

The final chapter of my volume, on works by Nöstlinger, Recheis, and Welsh, shows that literature written by adults for children and young adults serves to warn of the horrors of war and to illustrate the imperative to protect human freedom. Unlike the diary entries, the memoirs by women, such as those by Trahan, Segal, and Blend, are written from the perspective of adulthood but often use their childhood diary entries as triggers for memories and for the reconstruction of events of childhood.[66] As Brostoff writes in *Flares of Memory: Stories of Childhood During the Holocaust*, writing of childhood war trauma as adults "allows the writers time for contemplation" and "time to reflect, revise, and dig beneath the first layer of memory," resulting in "a deeper, richer, more poignant story."[67] I would also note that autobiographical narratives written over half a century after an event include the perspective of the present and the author's examination of his or her adult identity as formed through childhood and early adult experience, as well as references to historical materials and media on the topic examined by the author.

While Brostoff's collection relates the experiences of childhood from an adult point of view, Holliday's collection of diary entries written by nine boys and fourteen girls, Jews and non-Jews, details the children's lives during World War II and the Holocaust from the immediate perspective of childhood. Despite the challenge of locating paper and writing implements during the war and the risk to their lives by writing, these children wrote to survive: out of loneliness, as a means of finding courage "in the face of inhuman conditions and torture," "as a way of testifying to the unspeakable evils perpetrated by the Nazi criminals," to resist daily "humiliation and oppression," as a "tool for self-analysis," and to "study their own maturation and how it was impacted by the war."[68] These diaries, "outlets for anger and rage," provided children with a means of finding meaning and purpose to their suffering and an "opportunity to acknowledge their pain and to try to make sense of it."[69] For Holliday, these diary entries mark a "healing sense of resistance" and share, "by their own direct experience of oppression, that nothing is more valuable than human freedom."[70] Brostoff views the process of autobiographical writing, such as that found in Holliday's examples of children's diaries, as "in many ways difficult for the survivors" since it involves "the recovery of long buried memories;"[71] "the more one recovers memories, the more one recovers the unbearable trauma of those years."[72] While some authors, despite a worsening of emotional pain, even sleeplessness, attempt to recover memories, some maintain their silence regarding their past. Brostoff observed that "there were some memories so painful, it became clear that the survivors couldn't write about them at all."[73] The memoirs and fictional narratives discussed in this volume defy this silence. The difference, however, between the diary entries of young women written as they experienced the Holocaust and the memoirs of adults written decades after the war shows that in memoirs past experiences are chronicled from the vantage point of adulthood in an attempt to put the horrors they survived into words that were impossible to say before this long period of reflection. From a more general overview of women and children in war and during the Holocaust, the following section moves to a more specific socio-historical portrayal of women in Austria during World War II and the postwar period. The historical themes discussed in the following section of this chapter provide an interdisciplinary context in which to frame the narratives discussed in the following chapters.

Women and War in Austria: A Socio-Historical Perspective
Women's societal roles and experiences in Austria during the prewar, war, and postwar periods have been the focus of numerous studies, especially during the last three decades. Two years following the fall of the Austro-Hungarian monarchy in 1918, Austrian women received public acknowledgement of political equality. This short-lived public support of women's rights was soon undermined in the 1930s, when women were urged to "return home" by the National Socialists with their motto "Women back into the home" (*Frau zurück ins Haus*). The annexation of Austria in 1938 brought with it many laws affecting women's rights, specifically those of Austrian Jews, Roma, and Sinti, as well as the rights of those politically opposed to National Socialism, taking away their right to vote, study, work, and live in their homes. This period of Austro-Fascism and Austria's annexation into the Third Reich is described in Veza Canetti's novel *Die Schildkröten* (1999; *The Tortoises*, 2001) and in Hilde Spiel's *Die hellen und die finsteren Zeiten. Erinnerungen 1911–1946* (1989; *Hilde Spiel – The Dark and the Bright: Memoirs 1911–1989*, 2008). Spiel describes Austria's politics before the Anschluss as "dances on the edge of a volcano"[74] because she felt the country was nearing a political eruption that would cause great destruction. From her place of exile in England, to which she emigrated in 1936, Spiel followed the news of the Anschluss, calling that time "horrible and unbearable" and describing her family's plight: "My parents are in the line of fire. The devil is still in charge."[75]

The study by Brigitte Bailer for the 1998 exhibit "1938: NS-Herrschaft in Österreich" (1938: NS-Reign in Austria) for the Dokumentationsarchiv des österreichischen Widerstandes (documentation archive of the Austrian resistance) shows that the propaganda of National Socialism affected the lives of women politically and socially by focusing on their roles as mothers or as potential mothers. Women were urged to produce "racially valuable" children in order to replace the population of the

German *Volk*, diminishing because of war.[76] This meant that only couples who met the criteria of the National Socialist ideal were given financial support from the state, in the form of money for children and loans. Especially for girls and women, the fascist "Ideology of the Mother" and its mandates concerning reproductive health influenced family life. In a propagandistic brochure and in the 1934 women's magazine *N.S. Frauen-Warte* (National Socialist women's observer), women were encouraged to bear at least three to four children "for the safekeeping of the *Volk*."[77] In addition, couples were coerced through a "marriage loan" (*Ehestandsdarlehen*) to produce at least four children for the Fuehrer, meaning the loan did not need to be repaid. Families with more children were awarded medals, although some mothers refused the medals as an act of resistance.[78] Advertisements for birth control were forbidden, and abortion was considered a crime and therefore severely punished.[79] Women were also urged to not pursue professions and to commit themselves to household chores and to social careers (*Sozialberufe*). During the war, however, women were forced to work in the arms industry due to a depleted male workforce.[80] They were expected to expand their roles as mothers and housewives and were urged to collect items necessary for the war effort and to take on jobs formerly held only by men since, as the newspaper *Völkischer Beobachter* stated in 1944: "to spend all day taking one or two children for a walk with a stroller is not a sufficient task in this war. A woman should at least collect healing herbs or gather wood."[81] It was made clear, however, that women were to return to their household duties as soon as the war was over: "After the war, the German woman and mother will be able to devote herself to her true (*ureigentlichen*) tasks."[82]

Women who resisted the mandates of the regime or who had relationships with political prisoners or foreign workers were persecuted and even murdered.[83] Many Austrian-Jewish, Roma, or Sinti girls and women, categorized as "non-Aryan" by Nazi authorities, fell victim to racial laws that were largely imposed by National Socialists after Austria's annexation. In Austria, at least 25,000 Austrian citizens considered to be "non-Aryan," such as Jews, Roma, Sinti, homosexuals, and those with mental or physical illnesses, were murdered under euthanasia laws put in place by the

National Socialist regime in 1939. Another approximately 10,000 victims were sterilized by force due to racial laws, for example, the approximately 400 "mixed-race" children fathered by Senegalese soldiers in the French army occupying the Rhineland in World War I. Beginning in 1938, the Nürnberg Laws (Nuremberg Laws) in the annexed Austria and Nazi Germany of the Third Reich affected the private lives of women by forbidding relationships and marriages between "Aryans" and Jews, Roma, Sinti, and those considered of "mixed race."[84] Aichinger describes these children considered to be of "mixed race" as having a "wrong set of grandparents" in *Die größere Hoffnung*.[85] Under National Socialism, young Austrian women on the home front were socialized to work as domestic aides and caretakers. Each young woman was required to fulfill a "mandatory duty year" (*Pflichtjahr*) by doing unpaid work in agriculture, by assisting large families, or by tending to the households of high-ranking officers of the National Socialist party.[86] In 1939, the author Haushofer, for example, worked for the RAD (*Reichsarbeitsdienst*) to complete a year of service in Christburg near Elbing in eastern Prussia on the German-Polish border.[87] In such a *Pflichtjahr*, during which a young woman, typically between 17 and 25 years of age, was said to have two mothers – her own mother at home and another woman for whom she worked – a RAD manual for women advised that the "host mother" be both *Hausfrau* and mother to her young assistant.[88] Scholars Irene Bandhauer-Schöffmann and Ela Hornung note that such "women's services in the 'hinterland'" were "as important for the war as those of men at the front" since the women were supporting the National Socialist cause. Perhaps not realizing that their work through the *Pflichtjahr* was supporting the National Socialist regime on the home front, many women "did not demand collective self-analysis after the war" and did not experience a "dramatic moment of reorientation."[89] Today, the scholars note that many Austrian women "are not aware of how household duties were used to serve the state through work of Nazi girls' and women's organizations such as the BDM (*Bund deutscher Mädel*, Federation of German Girls), the NSV (*Nationalsozialistische Volkswohlfahrt*, National Socialist People's Social Service), the DFW (*Deutsches Frauenwerk*, German Women's Works), and the NSF (*Nationalsozialistische Frauenschaft*, National

Socialist Women's Union).⁹⁰ Instead, they note that women's actions, responsibilities, and guilt during World War II have been overlooked and that women are instead portrayed heroically as "rubble women," or *Trümmerfrauen*. They conclude, "for a long time, it was customary in women's history to define women's power only in terms of their contributions to postwar reconstruction."⁹¹ This volume is intended to clarify such complex and often multi-faceted experiences of women's contributions to the war effort under National Socialism as well as to the resistance movement and to postwar reconstruction.

Not only young women but also children were impacted by the National Socialist propaganda, which focused primarily on their political and physical education. Following Austria's annexation in 1938, all schools fell into the hands of National Socialist functionaries and supporters, who indoctrinated children in the politics of the regime and who prepared children for their roles as "carriers of the future of the Reich."⁹² The system functioned through hierarchy, collaborative work, and blind obedience.⁹³ The mandatory Hitler greeting (right arm lifted to the height of the forehead, left hand on the upper thigh) was instituted in the school system immediately; children resisting this form of greeting were punished. Teachers had to provide proof of their "German blood," and the Catholic teachers' union and Catholic children's groups were forbidden.⁹⁴ New National Socialist textbooks and "literature" (such as Hitler's *Mein Kampf*) replaced the former textbooks and became mandatory reading in order to indoctrinate children into the party's "racial theories." Values such as "humanity, compassion, and tolerance were publicly ridiculed by the NS-regime."⁹⁵ The glorification of war was also integral to the school curriculum, in which Hitler was compared to Jesus, "to save the German Volk from doom."⁹⁶

Children were further indoctrinated by way of the Hitler Youth (*Hitler-Jugend*), which for girls meant actively participating in the Federation of German Girls, or BDM (*Bund deutscher Mädel*) or, for the younger girls, *Jungmädel* (Young Girls). Girls participated in activities involving sports, music, and games, which socialized them to uphold National Socialist ideals as future wives and mothers. During the war, girls wrote letters and sent care packages to

German soldiers on the front and provided aid to soldiers in train stations and in field hospitals, while older girls replaced teachers, the majority of whom were at the front after 1944.[97] The motto of the Hitler Youth was that "orders are to be followed without 'when' or 'buts.' Discipline and order are the National Socialist founding virtues."[98] Girls and boys were socialized to believe that "true National Socialists" could not be members of the family or of the church but rather only of the party. This new mistrust in families was further fueled by Baldur von Schirach's mandate: "The German youth belongs to the Fuehrer."[99] Reichart's novel *Februarschatten* describes such a rift between National Socialist parents and their son, who attempts to save an escaped Russian soldier through a bold act of resistance. Beginning in 1939, boys between the ages of 16 and 18 were trained for military duty, while girls and young women aged 17 to 25 had to "volunteer" in the community for "Honor-duty" (*Ehrendienst*).[100]

Of young women who had finished their secondary schooling, only ten percent were allowed to become part of the university student population, which thereby limited or denied education to the majority of women.[101] Despite this ruling, women made up half the student population in the German Reich, which included Austria in 1941, because most male students had been drafted. Not only was education limited for women, but leadership positions in the government, such as in the Reichstag or in the courts as judges or district attorneys, were closed in 1933 to women who had completed secondary schooling and were entering the workforce.[102] Women had to prove that they had completed some social work before committing to domestic married life in order to uphold the National Socialist politics concerning women because, as the propaganda press release stated, "all practical work is only a bridge between studies and real life."[103] Both authors Aichinger and Bachmann are women whose educations were derailed by these laws. Bachmann's teacher training in Klagenfurt, for example, was ended prematurely in 1945 due to the war. Having come of age amidst Nazi propaganda, it is perhaps no wonder that Bachmann claimed not to believe in emancipation but rather believed that "marriage is an impossible institution. It is impossible for a woman who works and who thinks and who wants something for herself."[104]

The end of the war brought on new challenges for Austrian and Austrian Jewish women. In March 1945, two months before the war officially ended, Soviet troops marched into Austria, an event perceived by most citizens and described during the immediate postwar period as liberation from Nazi oppression. This perception was maintained officially and publicly for almost fifty years following the Moscow Declaration of 1943, which had named Austria "the first victim of Nazi Germany."[105] More than ten years later, on May 15, 1955, the State Treaty (*Staatsvertrag*) declaring Austria's neutrality was signed in Vienna, marking the withdrawal of the Allied Forces from Austria.[106] Later that year, on October 26, 1955, Austria declared itself a neutral country, once again underscoring the myth that it had been a victim of National Socialism. It was, however, only in the mid-1980s, during the "Waldheim Affair," that Austrian citizens were confronted both nationally and internationally with Austria's role in the Holocaust.[107] Kurt Waldheim's controversial presidency became a catalyst for conversations about and a reevaluation of Austria's role in World War II and the Holocaust, especially for many of Austria's authors, such as Elisabeth Reichart and Thomas Bernhard, who confronted Austria's past in their writing. Nonetheless, it was not until 1991, in a statement made by Austrian Chancellor Franz Vranitzky, that Austria officially admitted to its collaboration with National Socialism and to the crimes committed by National Socialists in the Third Reich. Women's experiences and their perception of what they had endured during World War II and the Holocaust were shaped by Austria's postwar image as victim and its denial of its complicity in crimes committed under National Socialism.

In a study of the oral histories of Austrian women who were over eighteen years of age in 1945 and who had lived in Vienna during and after World War II, authors Bandhauer-Schöffmann and Hornung categorize the experiences of women in terms of their experiences at the end of the war, their issues with hunger and food shortages, their challenges within family relationships, and their changing roles in society.[108] Women who were interviewed detailed their fears of rape by Allied soldiers and told of their communal efforts to survive during the last days of the war, when many lived with relatives or friends in "so-called emergency communities (*Notgemeinschaften*)."[109] The authors note:

> the most resentful, and therefore strongest, memories of all Allied troops were those pertaining to the Soviets, regardless of which occupation zone the women lived in. When asked about their experiences with "occupation soldiers," the interviewees always spoke about Soviet looting and raping first, and in greatest detail.... In women's recollections, it was the Soviet troops who freed Vienna from Nazism, and who represented to them the ten years of Allied occupation.[110]

A 1980 publication about Austria's postwar history describes that Viennese women were especially at risk of being raped by the advancing Red Army. To prevent further attacks on the population, Karl Renner, the former Chancellor and founder of Austria's First Republic, is said to have approached the Russian General Sheltow to ask for his support.[111] In a specific case of such an assault by Russian "liberators," author Kräftner, who was 17 years old during the last days of war in April 1945, and other women present were attacked by a Russian soldier in her parents' home in Mattersburg, Burgenland. The consequences of this tragic event are addressed in detail in Chapter Three of this book, which also explores Kräftner's narratives in the socio-historical context of women's reactions to trauma through writing.[112]

Despite historical documentation of rapes by Russian soldiers in Eastern Austria, not all Russians are portrayed negatively in Austrian postwar literature. Nöstlinger's autobiographical novel *Maikäfer, flieg!* (1973; Junebug, fly!) paints an alternate picture of Russian soldiers, one in which the fictional Russian military cook Cohn is described as kind and fatherly.[113] Reichart's novel *Februarschatten* portrays Russian soldiers as vulnerable victims of war who attempt to escape from Mauthausen and who, as weak prisoners, become the target of xenophobia, barbarism, and finally murder by an Austrian civilian mob.

Other experiences shared by women during the postwar period in Vienna focus on the topics of famine and food shortages. At the end of the war, citizens in Vienna and in other regions of Austria experienced such extreme famine that looting was one of the only means to acquire food.[114] Scholars Bandhauer-Schöffmann and Hornung comment on the reactions of women to food shortages:

> In our interviews, the women typically contrasted the comparatively good supply situation under the Nazi regime with postwar famine, with the suggestion that the Nazi state had provided well for its citizens. In most interviews, the reasons and the background for this went unreflected and unmentioned. It was only politically aware women, primarily from the left, who saw the connection between the food supply situation and the exploitation of Nazi-occupied countries.[115]

In mid-May 1945, the Red Army distributed food so that the average consumer received two pounds of bread per week. One document states that citizens of Eastern Austria received rations of only 350 calories a day, less than needed to exist.[116] By June, "an 'ordinary consumer' was entitled to merely 833 calories per day, causing women to focus their daily energies on 'how to scrape up a meal for the family.'"[117] In the spring of 1946, the calorie ration sank to 700, and labor unions and the government fought for more food supplies. By November 1947, the rations were increased to 1700 calories a day.[118] These food shortages and periods of famine caused an influx in trade on the black market, where starvation forced people to barter, for example, gold watches for lard and potatoes.[119] One study indicates that in Vienna in "August 1945 food prices on the black market were 264 times higher than official prices."[120] However, in 1945, due to the aid of the United Nations Relief and Rehabilitation Administration and aid programs from the United States (CARE packages) and smaller European countries such as Denmark, the Netherlands, Switzerland, and Sweden, the number of fatalities due to famine decreased.[121]

American allies also secured a long-term food supply for the Austrian population, and by July 1953, food ration cards were eliminated.[122] Topics of hunger, looting, scavenging for food, and housekeeping are themes in the works of many women authors discussed in this volume, as, for example, in Nöstlinger's *Maikäfer, flieg!* and *Zwei Wochen im Mai,* which are addressed in the last chapter.[123] Women and girls had to be resourceful in order to supplement the official rations, which were barely enough for survival. Bandhauer-Schöffmann and Hornung define such work as "survival labor," explaining "that the enormously time-consuming and labor-intensive household work on the part of women assured their and their families' survival" and could only be accomplished by "inventiveness and an enormous expenditure of work."[124] Such survival labor was a public matter, which included "waiting in queues for hours, conducting hoarding tours, and dealing in the black market."[125] The authors note that housekeeping "captured a major place in women's recollections of the period and sank deep into their memories" and that as household work within families grew in importance so did women's power within their communities.[126] The roles of women and children were greatly influenced by hunger and food shortages, as both children and women had to "hustle for food,"[127] and this labor for survival as well as the increased household work changed the family dynamics during the war and postwar period.[128]

For many couples, marital conflict ensued when surviving husbands returned from the front to discover that their wives had developed a new sense of power, "a necessity-born matriarchy."[129] For most women, survival labor had laid the basis of economic recovery yet had "remained unpaid and unacknowledged, and when the labor supply situation 'normalized' again in the postwar era, household work once again vanished from public places and public discussion."[130] With 1,562 females for every 1,000 males in 1945 Vienna, there was competition between women to find a husband, and the nuclear family once again became the ideal after the war, leaving single women marginalized.[131] A 1965 Austrian handbook for women prefaces its chapter dedicated to the bachelorette, "a new concept," by stating that as of 1961, as a consequence of

World War II, there were half a million more women than men between the ages of 30 and 40 years, and that 350,000 women lived alone to "run their own household."[132] The handbook gives single women tips on fighting prejudices in society and encourages them to overcome their own "inferiority complexes."[133] The conclusion drawn from Bandhauer-Schöffmann and Hornung's oral history study is that women were not emancipated after the end of the war but rather overworked: "Women's labor in the postwar period actually overstepped gender-drawn demarcation lines, but was explicitly understood by both men and women as a limited, temporary emergency measure that would have little consequence for fundamental changes in relations between the sexes."[134] Women, however, did not settle for the traditional marriage and family patterns but instead "gave the next generation an example of viable female self-reliance."[135] It is this self-reliance that gives young women authors of the immediate postwar period, such as Aichinger and Bachmann, the impetus to write about the war and postwar period. While Aichinger examined the consequences of Fascism for children of Jewish heritage in *Die größere Hoffnung*, Bachmann wrote against private and public Fascism throughout her life, in *Malina* and in her *Todesarten* project.

Especially the second generation of women writers critically examines Austria's role in World War II, such as Jelinek in *Die Kinder der Toten* (1995; *The Children of the Dead*) and Reichart with her novels *Februarschatten* (1984; *February Shadows*, 1989), *Komm über den See* (1988; *Come across the Lake*), and *Nachtmär* (1995; *Nighttale*).

While Bandhauer-Schöffmann and Hornung state, "most women saw the end of the war more concretely as the end of wartime misery and of fears for survival," they also point out that women who had worked with the Nazi party perceived the end of the war as the end of their "basis for existence."[136] This volume does not include works written by women who actively participated in National Socialism, but women did play an active role in the development and existence of this movement, as documented in Ute Benz's *Frauen im Nationalsozialismus* (1993; Women in National Socialism) and in Anna Maria Sigmund's *Die Frauen der Nazis* (1998; *Women of the Third Reich*, 2000). Women were also the muses, partners, wives, sisters, and daughters of National Socialist party leaders (such as Eva Braun, Carin and Emmy Göring, Magda Goebbels, and Henriette von Schirach) and SS soldiers (*Schutzstaffel* or Stormtroopers); they were nurses, some by choice, others by force, at "euthanasia" centers and concentration camps; and they were soldiers, such as the 150,000 women enlisted in the *Luftwaffe* (air force) to help as anti-aircraft auxiliaries (*Flakhelferinnen*).[137] Like countless other women who supported Hitler and his regime, Henriette von Schirach supported National Socialism and its war crimes during the war, especially in Austria, and maintained her innocence or ignorance during the postwar years.[138]

Despite these various roles of women during the war, they were nevertheless foremost defined by their role as mothers and by their ability and willingness to serve the Reich by bearing children to increase the population of the Third Reich: as Hitler told women of the *NS-Frauenschaft* on September 8, 1934, in Nürnberg, having children was their most important duty because "the only point of our National Socialist women's movement is called *the child*."[139] Hitler further emphasized that women need not be emancipated since the German Reich would take care of them, arguing that the word for women's emancipation "is a word invented by the Jewish intellect."[140] That same day the female leader of the *Deutsche Frauen in Nürnberg* (German Women of Nuremberg) said that all German women would have to participate in "Mothers'school and Mothers' duty" in order to be trained to nurture children within National Socialist tradition.[141] In 1937 the *Reichsfrauenführung* (The Reich's women's command) stated the National Socialist goals to "train physically and spiritually competent mothers."[142] Even if mothers brought sons into the world to fight and die for the German Reich, they were urged to sacrifice and to grieve heroically. The propagandistic book *Das Deutsche Hausbuch* (1943; The German home book) claimed that on the night before his death a soldier had written a poem that he dedicated to his mother, writing in its conclusion that only she had had a place in his heart next to his great love for his fatherland.[143] Motherhood then became the cult of the mother, prompting later generations of women to navigate their roles within a postwar society and the feminist movement of the 1960s and 1970s. Haushofer, who examines her own roles as mother and wife in her letters and diaries, portrays women as torn by competing desires: to be mothers, to love and to be loved by their husbands, to perform household duties, and to be writers, as evident in her novella *Wir töten Stella* (1958; *We Kill Stella*, 1995) and in her novel *Die Wand*.

Austrian Girls and Women in Exile

Many Austrian women served the National Socialist regime during the war and increased the numbers of the *Volk* by devoting themselves to the cult of motherhood, but countless other Austrian women were killed in the bombings of cities on the home front or were murdered in concentration and death camps. Some girls and women deemed "non-Aryan" (Jews, Roma, and Sinti), activists for the political opposition, and members of resistance movements managed to survive the war by hiding out with family and friends, in attics, in the countryside, or with helpful strangers. Other Austrian girls and women were able to escape the war and Holocaust by going into exile. Before 1938 approximately 192,000 Jews lived in Austria, and of those, 170,000 lived in Vienna.[144] In the two years following Austria's annexation in March 1938, more than 117,000 Jewish citizens fled Austria.[145] On Kristallnacht, November 9-10, 1938, hatred escalated against Austrian Jewish citizens; atrocities included the destruction of the Viennese synagogues, the looting of Jewish businesses, and the deportation of Jews.[146] In 1941 the first transport lists were made, and by June 10,000 Jews were deported to Poland. In the fall of 1942, 7,000 Jews, some of whom were unable to flee due to poor health or lack of funds, remained in Vienna. After the Wannsee Conference of 1942, a meeting of senior officials of the Nazi party to discuss the policies toward the Jews, including expulsion and murder, 65,000 to 70,000 Jews were deported to concentration and death camps from Vienna alone.[147] Of those Jews who were able to flee between 1938 and 1942, only a limited number obtained visas to countries that would take them in and allow them to survive, even, for most, in abject poverty.

While some 10,000 children from Austria, Germany, and the former Czechoslovakia were sent by their distraught parents on organized Kindertransport ships to England, other families scraped together their last savings for passages for their families on ships to

China and South America as well as to destinations where families had sponsors, such as in North America and Canada. This volume explores some of the experiences of girls and women who spent their childhood and adolescence in exile. Chapter Five considers the lives of Austrian girls who escaped persecution to Great Britain on Kindertransport trains and ships and who wrote about their experiences in English, from the point of view of adults, as detailed in Lore Segal's *Other People's Houses* (1964; *Wo andere Leute wohnen*, 2000), and Martha Blend's *A Child Alone* (1995; *Ich kam als Kind*, 1998).[148] Chapter Six considers the experiences of Austrian girls who escaped Austria with their families to Shanghai, as described in Vivian Jeanette Kaplan's second-generation account of her mother's experience as a young Austrian Jewish exile to Shanghai, *Ten Green Bottles: The True Story of One Family's Journey from War-Torn Austria to the Ghettos of Shanghai* (2002); Ursula Bacon's *Shanghai Diary: A Young Girl's Journey from Hitler's Hate to War-Torn China* (2002); and accounts by Ernst G. Heppner of his wife Illo Heppner in his memoir, *Shanghai Refuge: A Memoir of the World War II Jewish Ghetto (1993)*.

Exile literature shows that, although both men and women wrote countless texts about their emigration and forced exile, early texts by women were rarely published. Some were published forty to fifty years after they had been written because friends, family, and editors urged the authors to publish and publicize their works. The large number of women artists, authors, intellectuals, historians, and scientists who left Austria, including many prominent names, created one of the largest "exports" of cultural and scientific resources of its time. Among the many established authors who fled and are still known today in the field of Austrian and German studies, although often underrepresented, are Vicki Baum, Veza Canetti, Elisabeth Freundlich, Gina Kaus, Stella Rotenberg, and Hilde Spiel, to name only a few. Other authors who fled into exile were silenced by their trauma, never picking up a pen or touching a typewriter again. Most exiled women were unable to work in their professions and instead became nannies, housekeepers, or nurses. Some authors shifted their interests in order to survive and became children's book authors, journalists, translators, or screenplay writers, such as the writer Gina Kaus, who achieved success in

Hollywood. Others founded Austrian-American organizations promoting literature, such as the librarian Elisabeth Freundlich, who published the magazine *Austro American Tribune*, or Mimi Grossberg, who edited anthologies on Austrian exile literature.[149]

After 1945, some of the few Jews who had survived the death camps or had survived the war in hiding or in exile returned to Austria. Of the approximately 2,000 Austrian Jews who survived the Holocaust, it has been reported that 822 male and 905 female death camp survivors returned to Vienna. Yet by 1952, only 970 Jews reportedly lived in Austria.[150] Statistics show that 8,000 Austrian Jews had returned to Austria by 1959, and as many as 12,000 to 15,000 by 1970.[151]

Seventy years after the March 1938 annexation of Austria, the underrepresented and undervalued stories of exile and emigration are being written, published, and republished as what the exile scholar Ursula Seeber calls "a cultural political duty and official remembrance work."[152] In the epilogue of her anthology of Austrian exile narratives, *Ein Niemandsland, aber welch ein Rundblick!* (1998), Seeber describes various challenges and difficulties for those exiled Austrians, especially for those who were or who became writers in exile. In October 1987, following a conference dealing with this forced Austrian emigration, one of the main radio stations in Vienna aired the segment "Vertriebene Vernunft – Emigration österreichischer Wissenschaft" (Expelled reason – The emigration of Austrian science). One caller, reacting to reports about exiled Austrians returning to their homeland, exclaimed, "The immigrants should stay home!" This statement demonstrates, according to Seeber, the "paradoxes, the mistakes and repressions" with which Austria has "so-called come to terms" regarding its National Socialist past.[153] Seeber refers to the author Hilde Spiel, who described her life in exile as a "breach of life" (*Lebensbruch*).[154] The collection of memoir excerpts, letters, diaries, poems, and prose narratives by Austrian exiles shows a variety of themes that are also addressed in my chapters on exile: homesickness in exile, the first return to Austria after the war, and "finding home and being made foreign, of loss and new beginnings."[155] For some writers, there was a fear that they had lost their mother tongue, and for other writers, there was a great shock when they realized that

English had replaced their native tongue.[156] Of the difficulty of retrieving one's *Heimat* (homeland), Hertha Pauli writes in 1961: "One goes step by step on a double ground. One foot always stays in the past, the second strives for the future, and where they cross, the present dissolves in the change of time."[157] Austrian exile writer Lili Körber writes about her strained relationship to those who again or still live in Europe in her 1949 short story "Post aus Europa" (Mail from Europe). She writes that, while exiled individuals tried not to think about relatives and friends in order to survive, the critical opinion of those living in exile "interfered" with the exile's attempt to establish himself or herself in the United States. Körber observes critically, "The fact is: They need us less now, because Europe is recovering . . . . They have roots. We are flotsam and jetsam. Not Americans, but also not European anymore. Not fish and not meat."[158] Ruth Klüger, a scholar, writer, and death camp survivor, returned to Vienna as a tourist in 1993 following the success of her 1992 memoir, *weiter leben*. Her poem "Besuch der Exil-Touristinnen in Wien" (Visit of the exile-tourists in Vienna) captures her estrangement from the city of her childhood, describing herself and other visiting exiled Austrians as "Recognizable as natives by the pronunciation/ but as strangers by the expression."[159] For Seeber, writings by exiled Austrians, such as Klüger, illustrate that multiple homelands do not exist for individuals who were exiled or forced to emigrate; for those living in exile, the country of their birth and childhood, Austria, remains a place of mourning and loss.[160]

In sum, in writing about girls' and women's experiences during World War II in memoirs or through fiction or by crafting narratives woven from historical documents and tales of their mothers and grandmothers, Austrian women and women of Austrian heritage share tales of conflict and suffering, mourning and loss, survival and resilience in an effort to revive and document experiences of the war and the postwar period for themselves and for future generations.

Chapter Two

"Forcing Ghosts into Books":
Elizabeth Welt Trahan's Memoirs

> What are facts?
> – balls in a juggler's hand?
> – stepping stones to a truth?
> – lies in the service of truth?
> – a swarm of will-o'-the wisps?
> Take your pick!
>
> – Elizabeth Welt Trahan[1]

Elizabeth Welt Trahan's memoirs, *Walking with Ghosts* (1998) (*Geisterbeschwörung: Eine jüdische Jugend im Wien der Kriegsjahre*, 1996) and *Ten Dollars in My Pocket* (2006), document her experiences of loss, survival, and resilience as a young Jewish woman in Vienna during World War II and her coming of age and adulthood as a scholar and writer in the United States.[2] The focus of this chapter is on Trahan's recasting of her childhood and youth as documented in her first memoir, written from the vantage point of adulthood more than fifty years after the war. Related issues that resurface in her second memoir, such as the painful recovery of memory, writing as a means of overcoming the trauma of war, her relationship to the English and German languages, and the significance of faith will also be addressed within the context of the first memoir as they provide a broader scope for Trahan's war and postwar experiences.

A Jewish German speaker of German and Czech heritage, Trahan's formative years were spent in Vienna living with her father where her everyday experiences during the prewar, wartime, and postwar periods, such as her friendships with Austrian Jews, her Viennese education and extracurricular life within the young Jewish community, and the last days of the war under Russian occupation, relate a uniquely Austrian experience. In her memoir Trahan details how she and her father escaped arrest and deportation by the Nazis because they were able to acquire Romanian passports in which their Jewish heritage was not marked with a "J" for "*Jude*" (Jew) as it was in Austrian and German passports. Nonetheless, since she was Jewish and had mostly Jewish friends, her father dissuaded her from visiting places Jews were not allowed to frequent, such as parks, movie theaters, and theaters. In Vienna one of the few places in which she and her friends could enjoy any freedom was in the Jewish part of the central Viennese cemetery, the Wiener Zentralfriedhof.

Trahan describes the devastating loss of her friends and family during the war and the Holocaust; of Trahan's extended family, only her father and five other relatives survived. *Walking with Ghosts* is composed of three sections of untitled, numbered chapters, using past and present tenses interchangeably, in which memories alternate between Trahan's childhood in Ostrau and her youth in Vienna, showing how this past has impacted her present life in the United States.

Written ten years after her first memoir, *Ten Dollars in My Pocket* documents Trahan's life in four parts, spanning 1947 through 1956, entitled "New York," "Sarah Lawrence," "Cornell," and "Yale." In a chronological grouping of narratives, ranging from accounts published in the postwar Viennese journal *Weltenwende* to diary entries, letters, and poems, Trahan provides commentary about these earlier writings in italicized texts. Her impetus for writing a second memoir is her desire to revisit her past and to "look for tools that might open its doors."[3] Her second memoir makes use of material that was written while Trahan was a young woman, yet she reacts to the material through the lens of her present-day identity. The intention of her second memoir is to merge past events with a present sense of self. Trahan explains she wishes "to retrace the events recorded on those pages, and to supplement them with whatever thoughts and memories have stayed with me or might surface in the process. I can't tell whether it will be a fruitful undertaking, but perhaps a pattern will emerge and make sense, even if it is not a familiar pattern, nor the expected sense."[4] For example, when Trahan cannot recall the circumstances regarding a romantic situation hinted at in a diary entry, she comments, "And since I am determined not to embellish or fabricate, the question mark will have to remain," and wonders, "Have I eradicated that memory. . .?"[5] Trahan wishes to remind herself and her readers that her diary entries and personal essays are authentic and that her experiences, although perhaps not transparent or cohesive, do make up the person she is today.

In *Walking with Ghosts*, Trahan recalls both the urban landscape of Vienna and the historical events of war that mark her coming of age. She posits both landscapes and memories as layers whose cautious unearthing reveals that the present and past are fragmented by nature but can be observed in an act of simultaneous revelation. Trahan portrays the act of writing as a means of reconstructing the past through a process that the author engages in by choice, one in which buried memories are slowly and painfully excavated. For example, while visiting Alfred Hrdlicka's monument against war and Fascism in the center of present-day Vienna, Trahan notes that, while its bronze sculpture of the kneeling Jew is forever forced to scrub the cobblestones with a toothbrush beneath the memorial's white marble sculpture columns, those victims who died in bombings during the war near this monument are now part of Vienna's buried layers. Whereas Trahan speculates that their spirits rise up to the surface, they only do so collectively as a literary memorial in her memoir:

> On March 12, 1945, over two hundred and seventy people died in the Jockey Club cellar during a devastating air raid. They too couldn't be reached, because of the fire. When I was in Vienna last summer, I went to look for the building. It had been razed and replaced by a small public park, right across from the popular Hotel Sacher and next to Alfred Hrdlicka's controversial "Monument against War and Fascism," with its crouching Jew who is forever cleaning the pavement with a toothbrush. He has been turned into bronze, but what about those still down there and in so many other spots – have they become

part of the ground Vienna stands on, part of its new buildings and gardens, does their emanation continue to permeate Vienna's soil and water, even though we can no longer detect it?[6]

By recalling past historical events, such as the bombings of Vienna, as they occurred in Austria, and in showing how these affected her own experiences as a young woman, Trahan offers her personal history as an alternative to understanding monumentalized and traditional representations of history. Trahan's memoir documents her childhood in Ostrau in Mähren (in the former Czechoslovakia), her persecution and survival in Vienna from 1939 to 1945, and her subsequent emigration to the United States, where she lived and worked for more than sixty years. Trahan wills herself to remember long-buried memories by reminding herself in an authoritative second person that these experiences are what have formed her:

> For years you have been repressing your childhood, your youth, and now that they have caught up with you, you are trying to disown them once more. They are your past, the only past you have. It has shaped you, made you what you are, so stop resisting. Welcome it, make it your own, once and for all! – Come on, nothing is once and for all. We all know that. – All the more, accept what there is and cherish it. I will try.[7]

The comment she offers, "we all know that," prompts the inclusion of the reader, to whom Trahan bears witness and who is encouraged by the author to join her in the process of coming to terms with the past (*Vergangenheitsbewältigung*). Trahan, however, not only evokes her present self to recall past events but also the dead, whose spirits are called upon and who are given a voice. The title *Walking with Ghosts* refers to an episode in the novel describing Trahan's wartime friend Lucie Ellenbogen, who believed herself capable of calling upon spirits for answers to questions related to the friends' persecution under the Nazis and their hope to survive the war. Trahan and her friends would play the game of asking spirits their most pressing questions about the war. The author recalls, "They were strange creatures, these spirits that visited us. They would answer our questions with odd and often ambiguous statements. "Will the war end soon? – "Time brings solace." "Will I be deported?" – "Think of what is close at hand."[8] Trahan would later learn that these vague answers did not prevent her friend Lucie from being deported and murdered by the Nazis.

Just as Lucie calls upon spirits during the séances to foretell their fate, Trahan's novel summons memories from her past in order to recast them in the context of her present identity. Trahan sets her memories in the framework of a long walk in an unnamed New England town, from her home to the local bank during the course of one afternoon in the present. It is during this walk that the author recalls the time of her childhood and youth in an array of complex and dreamlike images, compressed into a brief moment in the present. Trahan's memoir unfolds in a series of arranged recollections that are triggered by tangible markers found in natural and urban landscapes. Trahan shows how the visual and physical encounters with details from these landscapes, such as intertwined trees, a barking dog, a flag, or heavy rain, jar her memories of the past and force them into the material present of her walk.

Writing her memoir during a time rife with historical documentations of World War II and the Holocaust, Trahan enriches her own recollections with personal historical documents from her diaries and from friends' memoirs. Trahan's narration of her memories considers her desires to establish patterns from her past and to confirm "traces of an overall design" while realizing that the artificial construction of such "patterning" provides "a foothold in this unstable, unpredictable world of ours."[9]

Trahan's recollections are first revealed during her walk, which "unnerves"[10] her on an otherwise bright spring day:

> But there must have been more to it, for the entire landscape seemed transformed, had sharper outlines, deeper colors, more pungent fragrances. And some of its objects, sounds and scents began to talk to me, opened doors which I had not

noticed before and had no reason to suspect. And through those doors I was pulled into another landscape, one I had long thought dismissed, done with, forgotten.[11]

Trahan describes her memories as an enormous, fragmented puzzle that seems impossible to piece together. While she finds it pointless to recreate a complete picture of her past, she proceeds to allow her memories to coalesce collaboratively and naturally by way of mental association as well as by authorial intent:

> Some align themselves almost without my participation, but many are missing and others don't seem to belong. As if they were parts of different puzzles, and it would be futile to search for an overall design, for the picture on the cover. What I can do though and suddenly feel a need to do, is assemble the pieces that came to me on my walk, add to them those which I have been able to retrieve or discover later and, whether they belong together or not, let them compose whatever patterns they will.[12]

Complex and sometimes contradictory memories are sparked by her observations of nature during her walk. For example, the smell of sweet clover and the sound of buzzing bees initially bring back memories of her childhood. After her mother's death when Trahan was four years old and her father had moved to Vienna to search for work, she lived with her grandparents in Ostrau from 1929 to 1936, where she felt safe and loved. Later in the novel, however, the same scent of clover brings back a feeling of terror and the memory of discovering a war victim lying on the side of the road in Vienna. A barking dog reminds Trahan of her own dog's death when she was a young girl, which, at age seven, was her first death: "Perhaps the most real death of all."[13] Later, a picturesque Japanese bridge over a stagnant creek evokes the memory of the discovery of her friend's dead mother: "The small ravine in the Wienerwald must have smelled like that when they found the body of Renate's mother there, several months after the end of the war."[14] In this memoir, imagined horrors are laid out alongside more concrete memories and become inherent in Trahan's personal narrative. A subsequent memory recasts elements of the natural landscape as a memorial. Intertwined birch trees introduce Trahan's recollections of her best friends, the twins Kurt and Ilse, Austrian Jews who were killed by bombs at the end of the war: "Two very white birches are rising into a very dark sky from a common base. Slim and delicate, they are wrapped in the same veil of dancing silvery leaves. Twins, separate yet inseparable."[15] For Trahan, the trees embody the twins' individuality as well as their devotion to and bond with one another.

In order to create a more cohesive and chronological pattern of her memories, Trahan calls upon friends and family, who fill in her memory gaps with their own recollections of events they had previously been unable to discuss with her during the war. When Trahan returns to Vienna in the 1980s to visit with her 84-year-old Aunt Anny, she learns the details of an evening in 1943 when Anny escaped from three Nazi officers through the back door of her friend's apartment. After lamenting that no one other than Trahan had wanted to hear about her experiences, Anny asks her, "But don't you think that these things must be told? And I can tell you some unbelievable experiences." Trahan reassures her, "Yes, I want to hear everything, I will make sure it gets told,"[16] and proceeds to document the evening in the form of a transcript of Anny's oral history. In an effort to underscore the authenticity of Anny's recollections, Trahan offers up family papers and documents given to her by Anny, which cover wartime experiences of other family members. Yet, like the unknown fate of her Aunt Olga, the origins of these documents are not traceable and therefore paint an incomplete picture of events: "Since the note only came into my hands after Massimo's death, I was unable to ascertain how he had come by it."[17] Published in the memoir, the documents become public record and, by being presented alongside her personal life story, they validate Trahan's own wartime memories.

Recalling a more recent memory while visiting with her old Austrian Jewish friends Theo and Frieda, who had married and remained in Vienna after the war, Trahan realizes that their traumatic memories are also bound to the present. Theo, who hid with relatives outside of Vienna during the last three years of the war, tells Trahan about his emotional state during this time, and Trahan realizes her inability "to shake off" her own traumatic response to the past:

> When we began to talk about old times, Theo expressed what I too felt: that we had lived through the war as if it were a nightmare which one copes with by going through all the necessary motions without being all there, by accepting that it isn't real, that one day we will wake up and shake it all off. If one may judge by appearances, he seems to have shaken it off well. But as I know by now, you can't go by appearances.[18]

Theo's wife Frieda, who had survived two years of internment at the concentration and ghetto-labor camp of Theresienstadt, shows Trahan her collection of postcards that friends had sent to her at the work camp. Trahan notes that when speaking of her past, Frieda's "voice tensed up even forty-five years later."[19] Trahan's memoir voices the experiences she shares with friends and family from whom she gathers information about the past. She realizes that traumatic memories of experiences suffered in the Holocaust and in the war are not diminished by the passing of time; instead, they continue to haunt survivors into the present.

Trahan chronicles her past by identifying shared memories of family and friends and by underscoring these experiences with historical events related to her own life. This narrative process marks her work as part of a body of literature written in the 1980s and 1990s by German-speaking Jewish women writers, such as Ronnith Neumann, Esther Dischereit, and Katja Behrens, who rewrite the past as what Dagmar Lorenz calls "their personal and literary genealogy."[20] The following paragraphs contextualize Trahan's work within this body of literature, in which Lorenz also includes works by women authors of the generations born before 1945, such as Grete Weil and Klüger, who like Trahan write about persecution, exile, and survival. In defining the term "German-

Jewish" as a "linguistic and cultural rather than national and religious concept,"[21] Lorenz considers Klüger's first memoir *weiter leben* a "landmark between earlier and more recent discussions of the Holocaust and Jewish identity in the German language."[22] Lorenz further notes that Klüger's return "to the German language to discuss Jewish concerns" marks a "new beginning for the tradition of survivors' memoirs."[23] Trahan's memoir, although first written in English and then translated into German, nonetheless figures in this tradition of emerging memoirs by Austrian- and German-Jewish authors who address their experiences of gender and ethnic discrimination in the context of their personal histories. Although Lorenz notes that the literature by this body of women writers is "anything but homogeneous," they share a "concern with geography and history" and more specifically with women's history. Their focus on mother-daughter relationships and close female bonds establishes an intercultural and multilingual "motherland" in opposition to a more nationalistic and patriarchal fatherland.[24] I would note additionally that father-daughter relationships should not be overlooked since a substantial number of Austrian- and German-Jewish women writers examine the strong influence their fathers had on their personal development as girls and young women, as evident in Trahan's memoirs and in works such as Lilian Furst's *Home is Somewhere Else* and in novels by Recheis.

Within this body of literature, Lorenz also notes the authors' search for an "intellectual or spiritual anchoring point" which she views as "the examination of traditional Jewish positions and concerns – religious Judaism, Zionism, and feminism, as well as Marxism and the leftist tradition, the relationship to Israel, Europe, and the United States, and the Shoah."[25] For Trahan, the process of writing her memoir enables her to address her Jewishness and to outline her evolving relationship to her faith. As a young woman, Trahan recalls renouncing God after attending the funeral of her beloved friend Ilse, who was killed during the bombing toward the end of the war:

> If God didn't protect someone like her, I was thinking during the funeral service, and the many others who had died equally innocently and sense-

lessly, He quite obviously did not care about anybody. Whether this meant that He didn't exist or that He was an indifferent if not sadistic God made little difference. Ivan Karamazov had been right. Such a god was not wanted and you owed it to yourself to reject him. And so I did, this time definitively, on Tuesday, March 23, 1945, even though it made things even harder.[26]

The early rejection of her faith undergoes a transformation during Trahan's adult life. In her first memoir, she notes that the rediscovery of her Jewishness during a trip to Israel, almost fifty years following the war, allowed her "deeply buried Jewishness to well up" and gave her "a new sense of self."[27] Trahan further explores her relationship to her Jewish heritage and how past experiences with her faith figure in her adult identity in her second memoir. For example, rediscovered diary entries referring to prayer take her by surprise since she remembered having broken off her "ties to religion" after her friends were killed by bombs and the Nazi SS shortly before the end of the war.[28] Diary entries from her second memoir not only show her struggle regarding her faith but also her skepticism regarding humankind. She comments on feelings of bitterness evident in her personal writing: "That is only because it is so hard to believe in mankind after all those years."[29] An encounter with a Jewish-American family allowed Trahan to come to terms with her Jewishness: "The example of the Edelmuths made me more attuned to my human environment; it also restored my long-ignored Jewish heritage to me, and led to my openly professed avowal of an at least secular Judaism."[30]

Trahan's unease regarding her relationship to Judaism is related to her conflicted relationship to language and national identity stemming from her postwar emigration experience. Trahan's memoirs provide insight into her experience in the United States and her relationship to her German mother tongue, as she says in her first memoir: "Strange: To this day I don't have much trouble integrating into new cultures, perhaps because what little of my old culture there was had been contaminated almost beyond recognition, so that much could be discarded without regrets."[31]

And, of her ability to speak multiple languages, she writes:

> Though I know five languages reasonably well, I somehow find myself standing in the spaces between them, master of none. Even English, with which I have by now been living for over forty years, has remained a step-language, a tool which I can sometimes use skillfully, even imaginatively, but which at other times fights me to the finish. I don't dare take risks with it, to bend it to my will and whimsy. Perhaps because it has never been an integral part of my sight and hearing, my breath and my dreams, the way my native language was before it abandoned me.[32]

It is of note that Trahan wrote her memoir in English and not in German: while German is a language she feels betrayed her, English provides Trahan with an objective distance needed to confront her memories. She says in her first memoir that, when she occasionally returns to Vienna as a tourist, she perceives herself as an "American tourist," "a disinterested bystander."[33] When complimented on her good German, she shrugs it off, noting that "the incident seems merely amusing, even reassuring."[34] Her conflicted relationship to the German language mirrors her conflicted feelings of homelessness that she experiences when revisiting Austria as an adult tourist; what she had once considered "home" she instead experiences as "alien."[35]

Trahan's observations about "home" are further addressed in her second memoir. In diary entries written during the nine years following her emigration to the United States, she describes herself as a "stranger" in the United States and as "lonely," leading to an emotional breakdown and to suicidal thoughts.[36] These feelings of loneliness and alienation are also bound up with her conflicted emotions about both homelessness and feeling at home. Prior to her emigration to the United States, she had visited her childhood home and realized it was no longer home: "When I returned to Czechoslovakia last summer, I realized to my dismay that I was a stranger there."[37] She continued to have positive feelings toward the United States: "But now, I have found a country that accepts me warmly, without prejudice and without distrust. The prospect of eventually belonging to it makes me feel proud."[38] Only months after pulling up to shore in the United States ("our first skyscrapers!"[39]), Trahan writes, "I soon feel at home."[40] Yet, soon after, she states, "though I have adopted this country, it has not really adopted me."[41] Later yet, having visited Austria again as a tourist, she writes that she had "almost been tempted" to call Austria home but notes that Austria "was actually totally alien."[42] Such reactions of loss, alienation, and estrangement following emigration, further addressed in this book in chapters five and six on writings by exiled Austrian women, span Trahan's earlier and later memoirs.

In *Walking with Ghosts*, Trahan perceives herself as floating in a place not quite here nor there, not in Austria anymore and not yet in the United States – instead, balancing on the precarious edge that is the present. The process of writing a memoir enables her to weave together past memories in an effort to recreate a more cohesive identity that gives her a sense of belonging. Toward the end of her first memoir, she notes:

> I notice a cup of coffee on the table in front of me and realize that I am still disoriented, no longer in Vienna and not entirely here. Suspended in a no-man's land without contours or time frame. It is the same scary feeling that has often come over me, though not lately: As if the earth were pulling away from under my feet and I on the point of floating off into nothingness, like a balloon when its string has slipped out of your hand. The only way to prevent being blown away, sucked up into the void, was to tie as many knots as I could between myself and the people I felt close to, and hope that these bonds would hold fast, would keep me secured to the earth and convince me that that was where I belonged, despite everything.[43]

Trahan's memories are what bind her to the present, "despite everything," as she observes at the end of her walk through the landscape of memory. She continues this train of thought in her second memoir and wonders whether her past has shaped her "consistently, predictably" or whether she has "streamlined it in retrospect, allowing a selective memory to compose a relatively uncomplicated, successful life."[44] In rereading her diary entries included in the second memoir, she engages in "aligning" and "realigning" her past, a process that allows her to consider "who she really is" beyond what she calls the "highly emotional" and "melodramatic" tone of her earlier writing.[45] She observes her earlier self as one would make a case study and considers the impact of war on her teenage psyche by asking herself, "Were these the typical stages of a teenager's maturation, however belated, or the outcome of a very special combination of a happy European childhood scarred by a nightmarish Holocaust adolescence, then repeatedly side-tracked but eventually reoriented toward the opportunities available in a new and hospitable country?"[46] In earlier diary entries, Trahan had wondered if she could forget her war trauma: "Will I never shake off these memories?"[47] She had hoped to put the past behind her: "I need to forget Vienna and the war."[48] Her wish to forget the war is an attempt to protect herself: "During the war all reality was a nightmare, and could only be accepted as such, so that one could preserve one's sanity."[49] In a personal essay from the early 1950s, Trahan compares the nightmare of having survived the Holocaust to being the victim of natural catastrophes. She describes herself as a "pebble washed ashore by the Deluge, battered and smoothed. An insect thrust through the meshes of the net by the Whirlwind, intact even if bruised," and as "a child in a monsoon world."[50] For Trahan, the guilt of survival, although a "heavy weight," is also "the darkness of memory, the flame of memory."[51] Despite the urge to "not look back,"[52] Trahan's diary entries and personal essays, as well as their reconstruction within her second memoir, demonstrate her desire to confront this terrible past, realizing that her past has always been part of her present, as she concludes, "The past is already all around me."[53] In later diary entries from the early 1950s, seven years following the end of the war, Trahan notes that she cannot dismiss the past because it returns with full force to haunt her:

> Coming to America I had felt was enough of a break from the experiences of war.... The past had been dismissed, so entirely as if it had not been my own at any time but a story read in a novel or seen on the screen. And the present was so full, the pageant so colorful, that I did not even feel impoverished by this absence of a past, by this lack of continuity.... And now this past keeps coming back at me, with its people and problems, for the second time in a few days, and it has hit me, very low, where I cannot ward off the blow, where it makes me wince. But perhaps this wincing too was needed to wake me up.[54]

Trahan's second memoir not only allows her to bear witness to the Holocaust but to confront her post-traumatic feelings of despair and to rein them in physically, through the act of writing a memoir. Writing becomes an act of controlling and "mastering" the events of the past: "It is the written word that will be me and will transcend me, that will give me mastery over a world of my own."[55] She writes about the therapeutic effects of writing: "Only when, after retiring from teaching, I sat down to lay the ghosts of those years by forcing them into a book, did the burden begin to lift."[56] For Trahan, writing is a means of both "recognizing" and "creating" a self.[57] Her survival, whether "accidental"[58] or "predictable"[59] has enabled her to "walk with the ghosts," to "accept"[60] her past, and to become what she calls "a citizen of the world," "by looking, learning and serving."[61] The act of writing enables Trahan to trace her path of maturation from youth to womanhood, to "feel as if [she] were finally climbing the ladder out of chaos toward the light, from juvenility to maturity."[62] Through the process of writing her memoirs, Trahan establishes the continuity within her life by redirecting her past to play an intrinsic role in her present. By revealing the impact of the experiences of World War II on her present life, Trahan's memoirs exemplify the relevance of these memoirs for readers today.

Chapter Three

"To Write a Poem on White Paper in Blue Ink": War Trauma and Memory in Hertha Kräftner's Poetry and Prose

> Write – to anything – create something, new life, you start it anew, with a new sheet!
> – Dine Petrik, *Die Hügel nach der Flut: Was geschah wirklich mit Hertha K?* (The hills after the flood: What really happened to Hertha K.?) [1]

Poets, women and men, are not politicians or historians; they are not legislators for the world; but the women and men poets of World War I and World War II together have spoken as if with one voice against the monstrous evil of war, its essential barbarism and the incalculable damage it does to human life. All poets can do is warn; it is up to the rest of us to heed them.
– Joan Montgomery Byles, *War, Women, and Poetry, 1914-1945*.[2]

Unlike Trahan's memoirs, in which traumatic experiences of war are revisited more than fifty years later through reflective prose, Hertha Kräftner's postwar poetry written during and shortly after the war is an immediate reaction to the trauma of war in what can be described as a process of poetic circumvention. Kräftner encircles personal and public experiences of war by way of surreal, haunting imagery, the melancholic tone of which nonetheless reveals the enormity of her personal loss. The impact and reception of the poetic works and prose writings of this Austrian writer seemed, until recently, to have been overshadowed by her carefully planned suicide at the age of 23. Once celebrated along with the writings of other well-known twentieth-century Austrian women authors such as Ilse Aichinger, Ingeborg Bachmann, and Jeannie Ebner in the 1940s and 1950s, Kräftner's work has experienced a renaissance in Austria more than half a century following her death. The 1998 publication, *Kühle Sterne* (Cool Stars), is a collection of Kräftner's texts presented in chronological order, consisting of poetry, prose fragments from *Notizen zu einem Roman in Ich-Form* (Notes to a novel in the first person) and "Beschwörung eines Engels" (Conjuring of an angel), letters to friends and lovers, and diary entries. The linear structure of the texts allows readers to trace the evolution of Kräftner's writing but also forces them to bear witness to her worsening symptoms of depression and suicidal thoughts.[3] The topics of death and suicide in response to atrocities witnessed during World War II are common themes in Austrian literature by postwar women writers. Kräftner joins the ranks of Austrian writers such as Aichinger, Bachmann, and Marlen Haushofer, who describe the violence of everyday life during the immediate postwar era.[4]

Kräftner's writing is a collage of texts that reveal a complex constellation of imagery that embraces both life and death, Eros and Thanatos. Kräftner's texts recall the longing (*Sehnsucht*) and passion of the Romantic era, the surrealistic color imagery and spirituality of German Expressionism, thematically affected by the tragic and violent history of the war and the postwar period. Kräftner's letters and diary excerpts reveal that she was inspired by the poetry of Paul Éluard, Georg Trakl, Paul Celan, Georg Heym, and Else Lasker-Schüler. At the time of her death, she was also working on her dissertation on aspects of Surrealism in the work of Franz Kafka (*Die Stilprinzipien des Surrealismus nachgewiesen an Franz Kafka*).

Kräftner's poetry and prose are reminiscent of the "other" or "counter-"voice in Bachmann's novel cycle *Death Styles* (*Todesarten*), in which the female protagonist's voice is set in opposition to the traditional male voice, which is said to be logical, solid, and not fluid.[5] The female protagonist's voice in *Malina*, for instance, like that of Kräftner's, is mystical, lyrical, and dreamy and makes frequent references to surrealistic images of nature, love, and spirituality. Kräftner's letters and diary entries are as lyrical as her poems and are therefore integral to her complete creative oeuvre. Although Kräftner does not address specific events of World War II, the Holocaust, or the postwar period in her poetry and prose –

which in the 1950s was considered controversial in the works of other postwar Austrian writers such as Bachmann and Aichinger – it is the absence of references to these historical events in Kräftner's writing that reveal the trauma brought about by these events. As such, Kräftner's writings represent a vital contribution to Austrian postwar women's literature.

Joan Montgomery Byles, in her 1995 study of German and British women poets, *War, Women, and Poetry, 1914-1945*, explores the "creative poetic response" to war and examines "how literature, and poetry in particular, articulates perspectives on the historical, social, and cultural realities of war."[6] Montgomery Byles writes that "women writers are important recorders of women's historical experience, and they give us invaluable insight into women's lives and their reactions and feelings in these momentous times."[7] Furthermore, she comments, "War poetry seems to be the literary form that offers the most condensed and deepest insight into the human response to war."[8] In the author's examination of women's poetry between 1914 and 1945, she argues that there exist poems of "grief, mourning, and loss, mostly in elegiac form; the poetry of protest, containing strong ideological statements; and the poetry of survival, often in sonnet form."[9] Whereas Montgomery Byles argues that the British and German poems convey the lives of "mothers, wives, sisters, lovers, munitions workers, nurses, ambulance drivers, and pacifist and militant suffragists,"[10] Kräftner's poetic voice is unique: she reflects on her role as woman, daughter, and lover. Her poetry, in which her turbulent inner life is set apart from war, skirts the topic of war through poetic imagery, in which the mechanisms, events, and outward symbols of war have no place. Instead, her world of imagery is more dreamlike, surreal, and darkly gothic in nature. While Montgomery Byles states in the conclusion of her study on women's war poems that "most of the women and men poets of both world wars were, whether intentionally or not, writing peace literature,"[11] Kräftner's poetry is at home in the aftermath of war. Her verses are not peaceful, nor do they strive for the hope for peace; instead, her work invites the reader into her painful, resigned world of despair, from which her only escape would be her early self-inflicted death.

Born April 26, 1928, in Vienna to a salesman from the

Burgenland and his Viennese wife, Kräftner moved with her family to Mattersburg in 1937, turning ten years old shortly after the Anschluss. Kräftner, having skipped two grades, graduated from the *Realschule* (secondary school) with honors in 1946, a success that "didn't faze her."[12] Before graduating, however, tragic events of the postwar period would forever mark her life and her poetry and eventually seal her decision to take her life: although no exact dates are given, Kräftner witnessed her grandfather's hanging himself from a tree. She would later connect her own death to his, as explained in her suicide letters: "Sooner or later I would have done it, just like my grandfather did," and, "It is probably my grandfather's destiny that was reborn in me."[13] In April 1945, when Russian troops marched into Eastern Austria to liberate Vienna from the Nazis, a Russian officer broke into the family's home in Mattersburg, with ten people other than the family present, attacking the women, including the then 17-year-old poet Kräftner. The attack, considered rape by Kräftner scholars, was never publicly addressed by Kräftner's family or friends.[14] It is documented, however, that during this attack on Kräftner, the officer shot at the family's friend Emilie Adam and stabbed Kräftner's father with his sword. Kräftner's father died that September from the complications of those wounds. Kräftner makes very clear in a letter to Otto Hirss that these events changed her life and transformed her from a "quiet peaceful child" to one suffering from depression:

> You once described me as jumpy and unbalanced. An almost perfect description. But I wasn't always like that. I was once a very quiet and clear child. But the experiences at the end of the war (you know what I mean), the abrupt death of my father and some other things allowed me to become this way. Then came an experience that touched me deeply and violently and finally cost me my balance completely. Then I reached for that coat and closed myself off from everything. And I lived in my own world that was wonderfully rich and beautiful.[15]

There are no further references in Kräftner's writings to the traumatic experience of the sexual assault that would claim her emotional and psychological health. Dine Petrik examines the root of Kräftner's suffering in her 1997 fictional account of the author's life *Die Hügel nach der Flut: Was geschah wirklich mit Hertha K.?* (The hills after the flood: What really happened to Hertha K.?). The sexual assault on Kräftner and her consequent silence regarding this traumatic experience is summed up in the reaction of the victim in Petrik's novel: "Say nothing. Nothing to say. Unspeakable. Nothing to say of the moment where your sex burst."[16] Petrik prefaces the narrative of the attack with a summation of Kräftner's experiences of war that include a reference to her rape by a Russian soldier: "Vienna – large building site: façades bombed to smithereens from Favoriten to the university. Walk over bombs. Occupied offices. Church steps. Russians. Don't make a fuss about it! Rapist. Rotten eyes. Quickly over. Looters. The Amalien pool, a pile of rubble. Empty stores. Hunger. Repatriated prisoners of war. Black market."[17] As Petrik has expressed in her novel, Kräftner limits writing about her war experiences to her father's death; she maintains her silence regarding her rape. She chooses instead to retreat into the "wonderfully rich and beautiful" world of poetry and prose that nonetheless reveals her suffering and loss.[18]

In pursuit of her writing, Kräftner moved to Vienna in 1947 to study English, German literature, and psychology, while living in what she described as the "small bourgeois household" of her grandmother and aunt. An early diary entry indicates her desire to write poetry: "I would like to write poems continuously, but too many thoughts befall me."[19] Her will to write is coupled with her yearning to be free of all earthly desires, as in the poem "Abend" (Evening), which lends the volume *Kühle Sterne* its name: "I would like to go with the red dusk,/ deep with red of yonder/ I want to pass on in the red dusk,/ and would like to blow in the winds/ that rush on without destination/ and climb into the cool stars."[20] The word constellations from her poetry include the terms "night," "melancholy," "farewell," and "evening."[21] She realizes that the symptoms of her depression are worsening and causing a suffering that her boyfriend, Hirss, whom she calls "Anatol" after an Arthur

Schnitzler character, cannot comprehend. Her poem "An Anatol" (To Anatol) explains: "The way to your open door is heavy/ through the certainty that the return/ will never again find me like before."[22] The poem "Ein Abschied" (A farewell) recalls her wish to follow death alone: "The twilight comes from a pale country./ I feel tired: it brings along a farewell./ Farewell. . . leave my hand. . ./ No, don't turn on the light./ I want to go in darkness."[23] In her diary, she writes of her conflicted personality: "I discover that I am ambivalent. In me I am united by contrary characteristics that always stay in balance. . . . I am cold and yet burn like a red flame."[24] Much of Kräftner's lyrical writing radiates from the approximately fifty letters to Hirss, in which she writes of beautiful nights "out there on the wide ocean, under the moon – nights and morning without a coast, and also that you give them to me and just so: hours without a coast."[25] Her more intimate thoughts – such as: "What do you know about what girls think when they lie alone in bed at night? Wonderful and terrible nights. . ."[26] – hint at youthful, romantic, and sensual fantasies.

While tending to her literary pursuits, Kräftner also attended classes in psychology in 1949, taught by the well-known therapist and writer Viktor E. Frankl. She enjoyed a brief and stormy relationship with Frankl according to letters, diary entries, and a series of lyrical prose fragments dedicated to him, entitled "Beschwörung eines Engels." Himself a Holocaust survivor, Frankl wrote a scenic dialogue among prisoners in Buchenwald, "Synchronisation in Birkenwald: Eine metaphysische Conférence" (Synchronization in Birkenwald: A metaphysical conference), which appeared under his pseudonym, Gabriel Lion, in the 17th volume of the literary journal *Der Brenner*.[27] Although he never publicly revealed the nature of his relationship with Kräftner, he commented that her depression transformed itself into poetry.[28] That same year, Kräftner met Harry Redl, who would later cherish their brief relationship by noting, "If I had to relive my life, I would only take that time in which I met Hertha; everything else seems unimportant."[29] The volume *Kühle Sterne* compels readers to be voyeuristic, laying bare Kräftner's transparent soul and offering up her most intimate thoughts. Readers learn of her all-consuming love for various suitors – Hirss, Redl, Helge, her vacation-romance in Norway, her "Angel Gabriel" Frankl, and, finally, her last romantic interest, Wolfgang K. In a diary entry from 1947, she writes of her boundless love: "I feel it: when I love, then I love so much that there is nothing else for me."[30] The volume *Kühle Sterne* concludes with excerpts from her four parting letters. The first is an apology directed to her aunt, which reads, "I am hurting you with this and I am sorry, but I have to do it anyway."[31] In three further letters, to Wolfgang K., Hirss, and Redl, Kräftner professes the significant roles they played in her life. To Hirss, "I loved you;"[32] to Wolfgang, "Everything would have been so easy had I not loved you so, had not been so at your mercy, so without rescue, been so extreme;"[33] and to Redl, "I loved you very much."[34] Kräftner compares her emotional life and her vast capacity to love to an ocean, deep, endless, and "without a coast."[35] Kräftner's desire to become "nothing" is evident from the beginning of her writings; however, the certainty of her suicide is voiced in November 1951 in her notes to a novel fragment *Notizen zu einem Roman in Ich-Form*: "I don't feel sorry for anyone anymore. I am not desperate, not intoxicated. I am like a cold reptile. Veronal. Carefully collected, by way of a ruse, often looked at in the evening, sometimes holding the smooth vials between fingers, hidden among my silk underwear."[36] Her last words, "Drink poppies and dream," are not only directed to their recipient Redl but also to herself.[37]

While some imagery from nature in Kräftner's poetry and prose, such as "reptile" and "poppies," is associated with death as a source of relief and release from the trauma of life, other images, such as those of the ocean, birds, hands, and love, can be read as life-affirming. Although familiar allusions to German Expressionist poetry, such as "countenance" (*Antlitz*), "poppies" (*Mohn*), "stranger" (*Fremder*), and "fall" (*Herbst*), found in the poetry of Georg Trakl, Else Lasker-Schüler, and Georg Heym, and romantic longing resurface in Kräftner's earlier poetry, she creates "her own world" of imagery that can be read as a constellation of words and phrases that deepen in meaning and interpretation in relation to one another.[38]

References to hands, for example, pervade Kräftner's poetry; hands are spiritual beings, capable of loving, saving, and giving life. Her very first poem, "Mädchen" (Girl), calls upon hands to save her from her loneliness: "But her dreamy-pale, soft/ hands must wait long/ until someone comes who rescues her."[39] In the poem "Die Hände" (The hands) from 1947, lovers' hands express nonverbal desires: "His fingers but feel/ these almost faded girls' hands/ root in unspoken wishes."[40] Later that year, in a letter to Hirss, she describes the hands of lovers as a resting place for the soul: "I had never before felt the meaning of hands so much. The hands of lovers live their own lives. And if the mouth is the rim of the soul, then the hands of lovers are the bowl in which it rests. And when their hands touch, it is as if the contents of two bowls flow into each other. Oh, love, I love you in your hands."[41] The following year, having parted ways, only his hand remains in an untitled poem: "You are only a white scarf/ that lifted a hand that I forgot/ in parting."[42] The soul is protected by hands, as in the poem "Ein Traum" (A dream) from 1948: "I gave my soul into your hand/ that you say to it: you are in me/ and you have no door out of me./ I hold you within a safe brim."[43] But hands, despite their powers to rescue, are tardy saviors for Kräftner: "Your hands come like two ships,/ to carry me away into the ocean,/ but my inability to come with you is much more;/ because I am already a dead woman."[44]

Like Kräftner, fellow poet Paul Celan wrote of hands as the creators of poetry:

> Handiwork – that is a thing of hands. And these hands in turn belong only to one person, that is, a unique and mortal soul, who with his voice and his silence looks for a way. Only true hands write true poems. I don't see a fundamental difference between a handshake and a poem. . . . . We live under a dark sky, and there are few humans. Therefore there are probably so few poems.[45]

For Celan, who had survived the Holocaust, "true" poetry was a sign of humanity. Poets such as Kräftner and Celan expressed their longing for humanity and salvation through the writing of poetry, yet the emotional traumas experienced during World War II would lead them both to end their lives.[46]

Within Kräftner's constellation of poetic imagery, the ocean is perhaps the most striking in that it provides insight into her state of mind. In a letter to Hirss, she writes that she imagines the eternal rolling of waves of the ocean but wishes it would instead be a calm sea. She wants him to be able to see to the bottom of the calm lake in her soul but fears the impossibility of this: "Perhaps I could someday become like that but I fear you will not be patient enough to wait so long."[47] Her diary captures her first encounter with the ocean during her trip to Norway: "For the first time I saw the ocean in the distance, a light blue strip, above it red dusk. The ocean. . . I expected it to look like that."[48] This ocean, "blue, wide, cool," instills sadness in her.[49] Having parted from Redl, who emigrates to Vancouver, she writes, "I think of a ferry that takes us back and forth over a river, but we don't notice it and believe we are on an ocean that never ends. The same coasts reappear, but we don't see them, because we are looking each other in the face."[50] A year before her suicide, the image of the ocean becomes an all-consuming power that threatens to drown her: "Now [the water] almost reaches to my chin. I think often of the end. Why didn't the ark just come?"[51] Despite the evidence in her writing that she yearned for salvation, Kräftner had already inscribed her early death into her poetry and prose.

The themes of death and dying pervade Kräftner's poetry. Poetic references to Kräftner's father's violent death reveal the depth of trauma she suffered during World War II and its aftermath on her later fragile mental state. In a diary entry written in December 1949, Kräftner is first able to formulate her conflicting thoughts regarding her father's death: "How good that my father is dead. I would have not tolerated it to not love him anymore. How terrible that my father is dead. He would have never used me; he would have always loved me. And I him."[52] She writes in an untitled poem, "The face of my dead father,/ which looks similar to mine,/ wanders among the cemetery trees/ back and forth," and, after recalling autumn in October, concludes, "Then my father died again."[53] In a diary entry, in which Kräftner writes of her unrequited love for Frankl, she associates loneliness with her father's passing and her own wish to join him in death: "Now I am alone. The night is as if made of big black pieces and all of them fall on me. Somewhere a dog howls out of abandonment. My dead father calls within me."[54] In a passage written that same year, she continues this thought, "My father is dead, but I am near to him."[55] Only a year before her death, the apparition of her father visits her in the poem "Die Eltern im Herbst" (The parents in fall): "and some evenings/ my father comes to visit me."[56]

It is Kräftner's mental anguish stemming from the loss of her father, her rape, and other traumatic experiences of war that motivate her writing of poetry. She writes, "I can say perhaps: Oh, melancholy! and write a poem on white paper in blue ink (I love that very much). . . ."[57] For Kräftner, the color blue – the color of ink, her "blue book" and its "blue words" – is related to her melancholy and to mourning.[58] In a letter written in English in February 1950 to her French friend Marguerite Rebois, she speaks of her calling to write: "But my greatest love is for books. It never happens that somebody can see me without books. I could write letters and letters about my interests and I could speak my whole life about books which I have read – and about books which I want to write."[59] In the novel fragment *Notizen zu einem Roman in Ich-Form*, Kräftner observes her writing process and the physicality of writing: "While lighting a fire with old paper I suddenly felt the desire to write in blue on white paper. . . ."[60] She further notes, "I would prefer handmade paper and leather binding (I loathe the forced gesture of my colleagues, who smear their thoughts on bad paper and claim that they do not believe the 'old form' to be valid); I would prefer even more to type on white, rough paper. Both can't be done."[61] Later, she continues, "I would like to have a green folder, in which I place a piece of paper every day, and on the outside it should read: 'Regarding my novel.'"[62] This passage of Kräftner's recalls Bachmann's female narrator in *Malina*, who is also a writer in search of an ideal writing situation that never comes to pass. Writing tools, such as parchment and ink, become the ideal means for producing written words of beauty, "das schöne Buch" (the beautiful book) or a fairy tale "Die Geheimnisse der Prinzessin von Kagran" (The secrets of the Princess of Kagran). Both women struggle to write in a less than ideal writing situation. In a humorous prose fragment "Poesie und Polizei" (Poetry and police) from 1950, Kräftner ridicules the hypocrisy of the literary market and traces the process of creating a poem that will please poet, reader, and editor. Showing a newspaper editor the line of her poem "Der Mond war grün wie eine Melone" (The moon was as green as a melon), the editor argues, "Never, the moon is never green. It is white or red or yellow, but never green."[63] Substituting the adjective "green" for "red," she wonders whether the journal would approve, stating, "I took care not to question my own opinion, and strove for objectivity. But what is it anyway? Did it represent in this case the reader or the editor?"[64] She concludes that a "poet will never be conscious of what he unleashes."[65] In an undated poem, Kräftner perceives the moon to be, however, neither green nor red: "Whenever the black disc moon/ fills itself with yellow into a thin curve, / its blood is poisoned with magic drugs."[66] Perhaps Kräftner's choice of imagery strikes a compromise between the wishes of the poet and the editor by describing the moon as black and yellow.

Kräftner's feelings of boredom and her critical attitude regarding the general Viennese literary scene surrounding writers Hans Weigel, Gerhard Rühm, Milo Dor, and Jeannie Ebner in Café Raimund are made evident in a long letter in which she describes her indifference, symptomatic of her depression: "Jeannie is powdering her nose and says in a low voice across the table to me: 'dead boring.' Weigel is proud and sad at the same time (proud because so many have come, sad because he's getting old). And me? I'm not interested anymore in music, not in literature, not in painting, – I am flirting with Kurt Moldovan."[67] Her frustrations as a writer are described in a poem: "She wrote always the same crooked line/ bent 'i' with an inaccurate hand/into the brown and purple fall-timeless-land/."[68] She also has mixed feelings about her dissertation, a project she refers to as "this dumb doctoral thesis."[69] While fantasizing about joining Redl in Vancouver, she is concerned about having to give up her identity as a writer and fears the domestic role of the traditional 1950s housewife, voicing her concerns in a letter: "I can't cook and even if I learn to, I'll never do it well. . . . Will I find work? . . . Will I find time to write with all this work? Will you encourage me to write?"[70] She is overwhelmed by her writing projects and commitments, as she writes in a letter to Redl:

There is an overwhelming pressure in my head; I feel it all the way into my eyebrows. I'm supposed to work! I'm supposed to write my dissertation in order to join you; I'm supposed to write a story for an almanac; I'm supposed to write a novel for a small book series; I'm supposed to write a novel so that I can finally find peace from the ideas that are related to it. – For a normal person that is definitely not too much, but I am more and more aware that I can't take so much anymore. . . . [71]

In another letter to Redl, she writes that she is unable to complete her novel and comments on her inability to cope with daily life and her many ambitions.[72] In a letter written that same year, 1951, five months before her death, Kräftner writes to Hirss, reminding him that her identity is that of a writer and lover, not that of a traditional housewife: "My heart, don't forget that I am not your wife (who writes about your apartment, laundry, meals), but your lover, who loves to write sentences like: 'When you are not there, I put a blue scarf around my neck and paint your image on my shadow-walls of the awake nights.'"[73] The signals of Kräftner's mental anguish that lead to her suicide, such as the image of the blue scarf of mourning around her neck, color the author's poetry, prose, diary entries, and letters.

In a memorial speech held in November of 1954, three years after Kräftner's suicide, Weigel comments that her death "was a mere gesture of fulfillment, just a step towards it, just a turning towards it. She had already been deeply in death; she had lived from it and toward it; . . . and if we don't understand Hertha Kräftner's death, it is our problem and not hers."[74] Critics, however, continue to make Kräftner's suicide their problem and seem to be unable to read her work outside the context of her tragic end.[75] Wolfgang Broer, for example, comments on Kräftner's physical appearance while pondering her death: "One tries to discover the riddle of her suicide in her eyes."[76] In the 1994 article "Das schnelle Leben der Hertha" (Hertha's fast life), Klaus Vollmann states that Kräftner, whose poetry makes evident her death wish, was likely plagued by a severe depression that on one hand paralyzed her and on the other hand provided her with an artistic drive. He supposes that she likely avoided psychotherapy for fear of losing her creativity, despite her familiarity with mental illness through her studies in psychology and her friendship with Frankl.[77]

Kühle Sterne lays out Kräftner's suicide as the key to her body of work by encouraging readers to note the relevance of the complexities associated with her multiple romantic partners, her bouts of depression and anxiety, and her final thoughts on death. Readers learn, for example, that Hirss attempted to take Kräftner to a clinic in Norway during a trip in which he prevented her suicide and that her friends were all well aware of her death wish. Kräftner's friend and fellow writer Ebner, who recalled that Kräftner suffered from severe bouts of depression, believed that her studies in psychology had given her the tools to fool her doctors into not diagnosing her depression. Ebner reveals that Kräftner's suicide was aggravated by an argument with Hirss, with whom she had long since wanted to break off her relationship; he apparently could not admit to himself that "Hertha's husband would also have to be her doctor."[78]

While scholarly responses to Kräftner's work often overemphasize the relevance of her suicide for contextualizing her work, Kräftner did reveal the certainty of her early death in her writing. In her narrative testament "Wenn ich mich getötet haben werde" (When I will have killed myself) from March 1951, Kräftner notes that people will speculate about her suicide and concludes that it is impossible to know the true cause of one's death.[79] In her novel fragment *Notizen zu einem Roman in Ich-Form*, she explains, "A man, whom I didn't love enough to keep me in this life, once said: 'To kill oneself?' – 'What for?' – 'That just leads to nothingness.' That's just it: it leads to nothingness. That's where I want to go. I couldn't have everything, so I don't want just something."[80] For Kräftner, this "nothing" that she had the power to experience in her death was the result of having to compromise between the "something" that Kräftner was able to experience during her lifetime and the "everything" that she longed to attain.

Kräftner's legacy as a postwar writer continues into the twenty-first century along with that of authors Aichinger, Bachmann, Ebner, and other Austrian women who wrote about their experiences as young women living in Vienna immediately after the war.[81] Kräftner became a published and respected writer soon after her move to Vienna in 1947. Hermann Hakel of the Austrian writers' PEN Club published her poems in his literary journal *Lynkeus* in 1948, and Hans Weigel included her in his legendary circle of writers and intellectuals at the Café Raimund in Vienna. In the 1950s, her poetry was published in the journals *Neue Wege*, *Die Zeit*, and Andreas Okopenko's *Publikationen Einer Wiener Gruppe Junger Autoren* (Publications of a Viennese group of young writers). The first edition of Kräftner's work, edited by Okopenko and Otto Breicha, *Warum hier? Warum heute?* in 1963, sold 65 copies and was republished in 1977. A book review by Peter Madler of the German 1963 edition in *Books Abroad from the University of Oklahoma* mentions that her poems were published in 1957 in an anthology entitled *Forgotten without Justification* and writes, "It seems as if [the title of the anthology] will become symbolic for the total literary production of this young Viennese poet."[82] Despite these earlier publications by Austrian and North American presses, Kräftner's work remained little known until her popularity was reestablished in Austria in the 1980s. In 1985, four of her poems ("Mit frühen Weidenkätzchen," "Litanei," "Die Frau des Henkers," and "Der Knabe") were translated into English ("With Early Pussy Willows," "Litany," "The Wife of the Hangman," and "The Boy") and published in the bilingual volume *Austrian Poetry Today* (*Österreichische Lyrik heute*).[83] In 1986, Günter Unger produced a recording featuring a selection of Kräftner's poems read by Traute Foresti, who interpreted the poems in honor of her husband, Weigel, who had promoted Kräftner as a young poet. As a tribute to the Burgenland author, the Hertha-Kräftner-Gesellschaft (Hertha Kräftner Society) was established in 1988 in the town hall of her hometown Mattersburg, under the direction of Unger, editor of the literary journal *Wortmühle* and art director of the Burgenland Austrian National Radio Station, ORF. In 2004 Unger gave the collection to the Austrian National Library, where it is now more widely accessible to scholars.[84]

Kräftner's suicide shattered the hopes of many within the

Austrian literary circle who saw the great potential of Kräftner's work and considered her a rising star in postwar Austria. Her work, however, continues to inspire contemporary artists and writers. The film *Das blaue Licht* (The blue light), co-written and directed by Stefan Wutschek and Herwig Art in 1983, sets Kräftner's writing against a backdrop of imagery taken from the mystical landscapes of the Burgenland and the ruins of postwar Vienna, in which Kräftner is portrayed as a young woman with utopian dreams of love that end in apocalyptic visions. In 1992, the dance troupe Konnex interpreted Kräftner's texts in their performance "heft narrt krähe – hertha kräftner – literatur und bewegung" (Notebook makes a fool of a crow – Hertha Kräftner – literature and movement), which portrays her work as both "melancholy and grotesque" and takes into consideration "tempo changes" and "unexpected changes in rhythm" of the texts.[85] In May 1996 in Eisenstadt, the dance trio Angela Schneider, Brigitte Antonius, and Roswitha Meyer performed *Wenn ich mich getötet haben werde* (When I will have killed myself), which, despite the title, interpreted Kräftner's life as one filled with joy and love.[86] That same month in Eisenstadt, the theater director Angelika Messner staged a scenic collage, also entitled *Wenn ich mich getötet haben werde*, portraying Kräftner "as a woman, as the fate of humanity," whose life was determined by the traumatic experience of her father's death.[87] Messner describes her performance as a collage of three female characters who slip into the role of the author: a dark-haired woman who loves death and hates life, a young woman who loves being in love, and a lonely woman who has been abandoned by everyone.[88] The piece portrays Kräftner's hopefulness as a child untouched by war and her despair and loneliness during and after the war.

Kräftner's life and work continue to fascinate readers today, perhaps because her short life is captured in and can be traced so intimately throughout her poetry and prose. Kräftner's writing weaves the sorrow, violence, and angst of the war and postwar experience with the surreal, intense imagery of German Romanticism and Expressionism, creating an expressive lyrical tapestry of poetry and prose. Kräftner, believing that an individual experience could reflect reality and in that sense convey history, once wrote, "Every image of the soul is also an image of the world. Even the most realistic image of the world is also an image of the soul."[89] Kräftner, her "soul" reflected in her poetry and prose, offers readers an "image of the world" that reflects the emotional and psychological reaction to her experiences of World War II and the postwar period on the Austrian home front.

Chapter Four

Speaking Her Mind, or Out of Her Mind?
The Older Woman in Postwar Austrian Novels by Ilse
Aichinger, Elisabeth Reichart, Eva Anna Welles, and
Johanna Nowak

> Old woman, you are becoming impudent!
> – Ilse Aichinger, *Unglaubwürdige Reisen*[1]

Just as Trahan's memoirs and Kräftner's poetry and prose reveal the deeply personal impact of World War II on the lives of Austrian women, narratives written in the 1980s and 1990s about women's experiences on the home front during the war reevaluate and rewrite this unique history through the lens of the present. Whether she is speaking her mind or is perceived as being out of her mind, the figure of the older woman in postwar Austrian fiction serves as an important conveyer of both memory and warning. Older women are witnesses to the political and social changes that brought about World War II and the Holocaust, cautioning younger generations of the horrors and tragedies of war brought on by decisions and actions made in the past, often by their own generation. The older woman's observations of war, shared with younger generations, give voice to women's experiences of war and the postwar period in Austria which are underrepresented in more popular accounts of twentieth-century Austrian history. When the older woman speaks her mind about the past and the present from her marginalized position in society, her statements, while at times considered wise, are also perceived by the younger generation as ignorant, senile, or mentally ill. The title of Eva Anna Welles' 1990 novel *Am Rande der Geschichte*, translated as "at the edge of history," aptly describes the locus and role of the older woman in society and history in a number of postwar Austrian novels. Not only does her role as an older woman place her "at the edge" of society because she is no longer considered by the society at large to be a fully active participant and because her perspective on life differs from those of the younger generations, but her experiences are often marginalized and therefore relegated to "the edge" of traditional accounts of history.

The older women or grandmothers portrayed in Austrian novels written between the end of World War II and the present represent different generations of women who experienced the war as either children or adults. For instance, the grandmother of the young protagonist Ellen in Aichinger's 1948 novel *Die größere Hoffnung* is an Austrian Jew who takes her life in the presence of her granddaughter. In Reichart's novels *Februarschatten* and *Nachtmär* and her narrative *Komm über den See*, and in Nowak's novel from 1994, *Gehorsam: Roman eines schuldhaften Lebens* (Obedient: Novel of a guilt-ridden life), experiences of older women who were girls and women during World War II are reflected upon in the context of the last two decades of the twentieth century. Welles' historical novel *Am Rande der Geschichte* examines the life of a woman who is marked by her experiences of living through two world wars in Austria. Reichart, Welles, and Nowak, because they did not personally experience the war, draw on the oral and written histories of women and men who lived through the war and on historical documents that provide authentic accounts of women's lives during the war. Whereas Reichart, who pursued graduate degrees in German literature and history, based *Komm über den See* on research about women resistance fighters in Austria during the Third Reich for her doctoral dissertation, Welles acknowledges her parents and friends for giving her historical accounts for her novel *Am Rande der Geschichte*.[2]

The role of the older woman "at the edge of history" reflects how the experiences and actions of women and their telling of history have traditionally been omitted in accounts of the past or, if recorded, have been forgotten in the present. By examining the role of the older woman in the context of World War II in Austria, this chapter also considers topics of gender roles, mother-daughter relationships, and aging. For instance, the portrayal of mother-daughter relationships in the novels, especially in *Februarschatten* and

Gehorsam, illustrates that the defiance of social norms and rebellion against maternal authority and expectations has the potential to inform, empower, and engage the younger generation.

Although the older women protagonists in the discussed narratives work through their experiences of World War II individually and with varying degrees of intensity, they possess similar characteristics. For instance, although some need to be prodded to confront their memories, most freely voice their opinions; they shun convention and traditional etiquette and, at times, risk their personal safety by uncovering the truths and injustices witnessed in personal, social, and political situations. They do not fear recrimination or consequences from a society in which they are no longer considered active participants or are made to no longer feel needed. The protagonists, who are older women during the postwar era, are burdened by twentieth-century history and feel compelled to work through this past in order to pass on the knowledge gleaned from their experiences to future generations. In their works, contemporary Austrian authors Aichinger, Nowak, Reichart, and Welles portray unconventional female protagonists who seek out truths about the past by taking action and risks, some of which have the potential for securing social justice and for healing trauma brought on by war.

The figure of the grandmother is central throughout Aichinger's body of work, from her novel, *Die größere Hoffnung*, in 1948 to poetry, personal essays, and short stories written through 2005.[3] In Aichinger's autobiographical story "Kleist, Moos, Fasane" (Kleist, moss, pheasants) from 1959, the grandmother's kitchen is fondly recalled as a tranquil refuge and gathering place in which Aichinger, as a child, was able to weather the storms of war. Aichinger recalls, "The powers of childhood held the world together. And my grandmother's kitchen lay right in the center."[4] Aichinger's beloved Austrian-Jewish grandmother and Aichinger's mother's younger sisters were deported to Minsk in May 1942 and murdered by the Nazis.[5] The trauma of losing her beloved grandmother surfaces in Aichinger's writing and figures most prominently in a central chapter of *Die größere Hoffnung* entitled "The Death of Grandmother."[6] In this chapter, the child protagonist, Ellen, is urged to help her Jewish grandmother take her life by swallowing poison in order to escape deportation and murder by the Nazis. For Ellen's grandmother, suicide is an act of defiance and resistance against Nazi oppression and terror. In her novel, Aichinger reconfigures the well-known fairy tale of "Little Red Riding Hood" as an allegory of resistance to war. In Aichinger's rewriting of the tale, World War II becomes the wolf who threatens to enter the grandmother's house and gobble her up, despite Ellen's attempts to rescue her: "The war had long, shaggy, dirty fur, almost like that of a wolf."[7] In the traditional German Brothers Grimm variant of the "Little Red Riding Hood" tale from 1812, a passing hunter saves the grandmother and granddaughter by cutting them out of the wolf's belly, and the three conspire to kill the wolf by filling the belly with rocks and drowning him. Yet in Aichinger's tale there is no happy ending – both the grandmother and Ellen die gruesome deaths in the war.[8] In general, fairy tales are a genre in which the impossible and magical can be hoped for and even attained. However, in Aichinger's novel, the fairy tale is juxtaposed with and undermined by the horrific realities of war. One could argue that the gruesome punishments, usually reserved for those who commit an injustice in German fairy tales, rise to the surface of Aichinger's tale and befall those who are good. Ellen attempts to prolong her grandmother's life by begging her to tell her more fairy tales: "While Ellen demanded a story, she demanded of her grandmother in the middle of a black, dangerous night the willingness to live."[9] However, because her grandmother does not have the strength or hope to tell Ellen a story beyond the phrase "once upon a time," Ellen instead encourages her resigned grandmother to live by narrating the fictitious tale of Ellen's mother, the grandmother's daughter. Ellen tells her grandmother that her mother has survived the war by escaping to the United States on a ship and has become a waitress in New York, and who, while knitting her daughter a red cap, hopes to later be joined in exile by her daughter. To the reader, it becomes clear that Ellen's mother has probably already been murdered by the Nazis and that Ellen is telling her grandmother a fairy tale about her mother's survival in order to give her grandmother the courage to live. Here again, any possible happy end for Ellen, her mother, or her grandmother is undermined by the realities of the war. Despite

Ellen's attempt to keep her grandmother from drinking the poison, the grandmother eventually demands it from Ellen and swallows it, fearing imminent arrest and deportation by the Nazis upon hearing heavy footsteps outside in the stairwell. Her agonizing death is in vain, however, as the passage ends with not the arrest of the grandmother by the Nazis but with the arrest of another victim: "In this night, a small, despairing deserter returned home at two o'clock and was arrested in the morning."[10] The war not only cruelly takes the life of Ellen's grandmother, but also leads to Ellen's vulnerability as a child alone in the war and to her eventual death.

Although Ellen's grandmother had represented for her granddaughter the safe childhood of pre-World War II Austria and is portrayed as one who defies the Nazis, references in the novel to grandparents in general represent an adult generation unable or unwilling to prevent World War II and the horrors of the Holocaust. Throughout the novel, grandparents are blamed for allowing the war and the persecution of their Austrian-Jewish grandchildren to take place. When one child, presumably Ellen, asks a group of children why they are in hiding and whether it is because they did "something bad," a child replies, "The grandparents. Our grandparents are to blame."[11] Later in the novel, a child states, "Our grandparents are despicable. Our great-grandparents won't act as our guarantors."[12] In Aichinger's novel, grandparents as a collective group come to represent an earlier, misguided generation that has created a society tolerant of National Socialism and the resulting war, under which future generations must suffer. By writing a novel in which one fictional grandmother argues for social conscience, for resistance, and for defiance, Aichinger memorializes her own grandmother's senseless and horrific murder by the Nazis.

For Aichinger, the act of writing is an essential tool for the emotional survival after her wartime experiences of loss. In a narrative passage from 1950, Aichinger writes of the life-affirming role of writing: "A person writes like she prays, instead of killing herself. Then it becomes life itself."[13] Writing her novel became a way to filter and to work through her experiences, such as her grandmother's deportation and her sister's exile to England.[14]

Aichinger's novel describes the devastation and loss brought on by war, especially for children, who are the most vulnerable victims of war. Without any family to fight for them, Ellen and a band of homeless children, hiding from the Nazis, roam the urban landscape (presumably Vienna) ravaged by war. At the conclusion of the novel, Ellen seems to run toward freedom as she rushes toward a bombed-out bridge, imagining that she might later rename the rebuilt bridge "The Greater Hope, Our Hope."[15] The novel ends with Ellen's death from an exploding grenade near the bridge, destroying the hope that she had expressed shortly before her death. In Aichinger's novel, Ellen's grandmother represents a key figure, a wise woman who foresaw Ellen's early death and the gruesome fate of her family. When Ellen was begging her grandmother to tell her a fairy tale to stave off her grandmother's certain death by suicide or at the hands of the Nazis, Ellen reminded her, "You always said, when darkness comes, the robbers come."[16] Her grandmother replied that she had unfortunately been "right about that," confirming that she had already predicted the terrible outcome of the war.[17]

In more recent Austrian narratives, such as those by Reichart, written almost forty years after *Die größere Hoffnung*, the older mother or grandmother becomes a carrier of the memory of World War II and the Holocaust in Austria. Reichart's novels, *Februarschatten* and *Nachtmär*, and her story *Komm über den See* depict older women who experienced World War II as children or young women and who must confront their traumatic past at the close of the twentieth century. Reichart portrays the older woman, with the exception of the reluctant protagonist Hilde in *Februarschatten*, as one who no longer feels compelled to conform to society and who can therefore speak her mind and reveal truths about the past.[18] Reichart's narratives, such as in *Komm über den See*, uncover painful truths about Austrian history through the use of thought-provoking language that calls into question the deeper and often conflicted meanings of commonly used terms such as "homeland" (*Heimat*) and "fatherland" (*Vaterland*).[19]

In *Februarschatten*, Reichart examines events that took place during the Third Reich in the town of Mauthausen in Upper Austria, the location of the concentration and forced-labor camp

Mauthausen, and explores how this history has impacted two generations of Austrian women more than forty years after the war.[20] The novel is haltingly narrated in fragmented, clipped sentences from the perspective of the recently widowed Hilde, who comes to terms with the sudden death of her husband and her childhood memories of loss and trauma during World War II in order to reestablish her identity and to confront her fractured relationship with her daughter Erika. It is the middle-aged Erika who prods her mother's memory in order to complete a novel about the events of the "Mühlviertel Rabbit Hunt" (*Mühlviertler Hasenjagd*) on February 2, 1945, during which National Socialist officers and civilians murdered most of the 500 Russian officers who fled the Mauthausen camp. Hilde, a child when these atrocities were committed, states that her means of survival while growing up and as an adult had always been to imperative "forget" these terrible events.[21] However, it becomes clear to Hilde that to salvage her self-worth, her mental health, and her relationship with her daughter, she has no choice but to confront the past by reclaiming her memories. She remarks that this process of confronting her past is painful: "Whether remembered or forgotten. The difference lies in the pain. The pain at remembering."[22]

Reichart's novel demonstrates that such an unearthing of memory requires both courage and patience and that this process does not guarantee that the pain and suffering associated with remembering will disappear; despite having unraveled the events of her past, Hilde is not rewarded with immediate healing or reconciliation with her daughter. Hilde's past affects the way she mistreats her daughter and underscores that this past reemerges in the present unless confronted. Although Hilde looks back on her own troubled childhood and unsatisfying life as a young wife and mother, she cannot accept or respect her daughter's choice to be a single, independent woman who is pursuing her goal of being a writer. Lonely and bitter, Hilde feels that society does not value her and that she is "excluded" from and has been "abandoned" by society.[23] Generational conflicts regarding perspectives about history, politics, gender roles, and social expectations threaten to drive the mother and daughter further apart. Hilde comments that her daughter "had always opposed her parents. Had believed that she needed to be ashamed of her parents. Had not seen how much her parents were ashamed of her."[24] Hilde, who is embarrassed that Erika has strayed from the prescribed traditional female role in which she was raised, criticizes Erika's career choice and ruminates: "Writing books. As if that were a lifestyle for a woman. She pretends that there were no unwritten laws for women. . . . She'll choke in her mountains of papers. Then it will be too late. For the right way. For the way of all women."[25] Hilde is irritated by Erika's persistent questions about her past and asks herself defiantly: "Why should I remember my childhood? I learned even as a child, the only way to survive is to forget."[26] When Hilde learns that Erika is writing about her and she asks why, Erika replies that she is doing it because she has disregarded her mother for too long.[27] With Erika's insistence on uncovering her mother's past, Hilde becomes a reluctant voice of history, the truth of which must be coaxed from her. In being forced to remember her childhood, Hilde realizes that one cannot repress past traumas because they are always part of one's memory: "All that is lived, experienced, just everything, is stored in our memory."[28] The retrieval of memory is portrayed as a means of reconstructing identity and finding a way into one's personal and national history.

In a montage of inner monologues and third-person narration of related but disjointed recollections, Hilde recalls her unhappy childhood, the poverty and hunger experienced during the war, her conflicted relationships with her parents and siblings, and especially the circumstances surrounding the death of her beloved brother Hannes, which is inextricably linked to the events of Mauthausen. Before revealing that Hannes was found hanging from a tree, Hilde realizes that her family never discussed the circumstances of his death. She tells her curious daughter, "I can't tell you anything more. I couldn't just ask him: why did you go to the tree? Somehow it's all very hazy. First there was a lot of noise about it. Then one wasn't allowed to talk about Hannes, or about his death."[29] After Hilde and Erika take a trip to Hilde's childhood town to confront the past more directly, Hilde experiences what can be described as a post-traumatic emotional reaction, after which she finally breaks her silences and tells the story of Hannes's murder. Reichart explores Hilde's complex feelings of guilt when recalling events during which she was a mere child. Hilde calls her emotional reaction the "beginning" of her guilt.[30] Hilde reveals to Erika that Hannes had gone against the National Socialist majority of his family and community by hiding an escaped Russian officer in his bedroom closet. Hannes had confided his act of resistance to Hilde and had asked her to help the injured Russian soldier by obtaining bandages and food from the military hospital. When she had replied that she would not leave the house and would rather like to forget the whole evening, he retorted that she would hardly be able to forget this night, reminding her, "Everyone who does nothing against this manhunt is guilty."[31] Hilde chooses not to help her brother save the prisoner. Even though Hilde had attempted to forget these events with the passing of time, as an older woman she must nonetheless confront the truth of her complicity in the atrocities committed by the villagers against the Russian prisoners. Not only do Hilde's resurfaced memories aid in reconstructing the events of the *Mühlviertler Hasenjagd* and reveal its impact on civilian life during and after the war, but they also demonstrate how the suppression of such memories negatively affect familial and social interactions for younger generations who struggle to come to terms with atrocities committed on the Austrian home front during World War II. Erika struggles to understand herself through her mother's history by healing their broken relationship in a confrontation with her mother's childhood experiences. Hilde, however, represents an older generation socialized as children under the Third Reich and who came of age in a traumatized postwar Austrian society hoping to forget past war traumas. Hilde, whose catchphrase had always been "to forget" the painful past, continues to thwart her daughter's efforts to unravel this past. Hilde questions Erika's refusal "to forget" and wonders, "Why then did she want to know everything? Why, though did she not accept my most important word?"[32] The novel concludes with the older Hilde overwhelmed by the confrontation with her past and yet empowered by the possibility of a new beginning for herself. When Erika asks her, "What will you do now?" Hilde replies, "I don't know yet."[33] Although Hilde has not yet made peace with her daughter, Erika has learned about her mother's troubled past and both have moved forward to a place of empowerment and possible future reconciliation. In *Februarschatten*, the older Hilde becomes a reluctant voice of Austrian history through a process of remembrance, thereby dispelling the shadows cast on her and the next generation.

With her story *Komm über den See,* Reichart continues to counteract the silence associated with Austria's complicity in the Third Reich through fiction focused on the underrepresented history of women during World War II, on the home front and in the resistance. As in her novels *Februarschatten* and *Nachtmär*, Reichart examines the situation of second- and third-generation Austrians living with the legacy of World War II. In this narrative, an older Austrian woman named Anna Zach, who was once a resistance fighter against the Nazis during the Third Reich, figures as the carrier of memory and truth that educates and empowers the younger protagonist, Ruth Berger. Ruth, a teacher who has just lost her job, moves to Gmunden where she takes on a substitute teaching position for the year. Due to her strong interest in the history of Austrian women resistance fighters during the Third Reich, she meets the older and withdrawn Zach. Through her encounter with Zach, Ruth uncovers her own mother's role in the Austrian resistance movement and the circumstances that led to her mother's early death when Ruth was a child. In confronting the events of World War II on the Austrian home front, Ruth establishes an identity for herself that is defined outside of what she perceives to be a conformist patriarchal society that wishes to undermine the achievements of women who risked their lives to combat National Socialism on the home front. Ruth's ex-husband ridiculed her continued interest in this history of Austrian women resistance fighters by berating her: "Your interest in these women is not normal!"[34] Despite this criticism, Ruth continues her personal research and soon realizes that the history of these women has been marginalized or even ignored.[35] She comments, "I barely found anything about the female resistance fighters, their lives only between the lines, nobody wrote about them, writing is also a question of gender, I will look for them."[36] The chapters that detail Ruth's journey to confront the past are linked by italicized passages of fictional transcripts of the recollections of female resistance fighters, prefaced by the capitalized heading "SHE" (*SIE*). Just as the capitalized pronoun "she" emphasizes that the women speakers are nameless and faceless, so does the placement of the accounts outside of or between chapters draw attention to their omission from traditional accounts of history. The narrator of one italicized passage speaks of the omission of her story from the traditional accounts of history: "Later we will not have existed."[37] Ruth remarks that the female resistance fighters did not document their experiences in writing, and she is therefore eager to capture their stories in an attempt to rewrite history to include this aspect of Austria's history during the Third Reich.

It is precisely Ruth's quest to uncover this history that compels her to reach out to the recluse Zach, who is treated as an outcast in her community of Gmunden. Zach, despite having been active in the Austrian resistance movement and tortured in a concentration camp, was never acknowledged after the war for her heroic actions against the Nazis. During the immediate postwar period, she was imprisoned by the American Allied forces for demanding, along with other desperate mothers, milk for her starving children, an action that once again, as it had during the Third Reich, pitted her against the mainstream majority.[38] The nameless, faceless, and voiceless women resistance fighters live in a shadow, much as memories and traumas reside in the shadows evoked in *Februarschatten*. As Ruth attempts to uncover Zach's story, she comes to view Zach as almost invisible, a mere "shadow on the wall."[39] However, through her encounter with Zach, Ruth uncovers the history of the women resistance fighters and also events related to her own childhood. Through her research and her conversations with Zach, Ruth discovers that her former childhood name, Brigitta, had been erased and changed by her parents in an attempt to forget the past, when her mother had also been arrested and tortured by Nazis for supporting the resistance movement. Ruth learns that her mother, while being tortured, possibly betrayed Zach, who had been her friend, because the Nazis had threatened to also arrest and torture her small daughter, Ruth. Despite Ruth's interest in learning her mother's history, she never fully uncovers the truth about her mother's work in the resistance movement or the circumstances of her early death; her mother's story remains a montage of Ruth's and Zach's fragmented memories.

Reichart's female characters, especially the second- and third-generation Austrian women, are portrayed as incomplete, fragmented, and unfulfilled due to their lack of knowledge about their nation's history, especially one that comprises the experiences of women, and in particular their personal histories, including the stories of their mothers and grandmothers. Reichart portrays the war generation, and the younger second and third generations, as children touched by war and the consequences of war – "prewar children, war children, postwar children."[40] Ruth calls herself a "child of ruins," who knows the ruins of war but not their origin, stating, "Not only my mother, all of Vienna was without memory. We children called ourselves children of ruins but didn't know where the ruins came from."[41] In *Nachtmär*, Reichart portrays those coming of age during the postwar as "Eichmann's children," a generation that must live with the guilt and shame of imagining what crimes their parents and grandparents may have committed through their collaborative actions or passive inaction during the Third Reich.[42] In *Komm über den See*, Ruth's friends Martha and Eva, also of the second generation after the war, suffer from mental illnesses stemming from their experiences as children of mothers who suffered during World War II. Martha's mother, like Ruth's mother, had been tortured in a concentration camp for her resistance against the Nazis, engaging in acts of sabotage during the war. After her mother's death, Martha's mental illness worsens until Ruth finds her catatonic in a home for the mentally ill. Ruth's college friend Eva introduced Ruth to "her" postwar Vienna, a city in which survivors lived "who could not deal with the fact that they alone had survived."[43] Eva, who cherished the quotation from Wolfgang Borchert – "That I didn't take my life, that horrified even me" – later hangs herself in her parents' attic, leaving Ruth friendless and grieving.[44] Reichart shows that Ruth, Martha, and Eva's feelings of alienation, isolation, and their consequent depression are symptomatic of failing to work through the traumas of one's personal and national histories. Their experiences of loss and trauma are illustrated by their fragmented manner of speaking about themselves; as Martha informs Ruth: "Have you not noticed that we have the same way of speaking about ourselves: broken pieces, scattered sentences, broken sentences, episodes – incomplete."[45] This notion of being "incomplete" heightens their feelings of isolation from their community and from their Austrian homeland. In both *Februarschatten* and *Komm über den See* Reichart considers the ambiguous term *Heimat* (homeland) and its associations with "feeling at home," with belonging, and with inclusiveness. She especially explores what this term means for those individuals whose opinions diverge from those of their community and homeland and who are therefore excluded, shunned, and even ignored. In *Komm über den See*, Ruth, for example, experiences a childhood in which, after her mother dies and she must move in with her aunts and change schools, she is labeled by her teacher as "asocial," therefore viewing herself as "exiled."[46] Zach also is shunned by her community and labeled a "criminal" by the school principal, who calls into question Zach's actions, informing Ruth: "everyone in Gmunden knows that Mrs. Zach was in jail – no, not just during National Socialism, he wasn't speaking about that, who would still speak about that? But even under the Americans, and she would, mind you, hopefully not insinuate anything about them."[47] For the principal, who symbolizes male authority and the opinion of the majority, Zach's actions against the general norm, during the Third Reich and the immediate postwar period, are considered criminal. By contrast, Ruth finds these acts by Zach heroic and feels that they should in fact be celebrated.[48] Ruth and Zach question their relationship to their Austrian *Heimat*, which neither welcomes their opinions nor includes them. Earlier in the novel, Ruth recalls inviting the now older Austrian women survivors and former resistance fighters Mali F. and Hermine J. to her classes to tell about their experiences during the Third Reich when they escaped on foot to Austria from one of the last transports to the concentration camp of Ravensbrück, located in northern Germany. Upon their return to Austria, they discover that an Austrian concentration camp had been built in Ebensee. Ruth wonders how these two survivors must have felt toward their homeland when an Austrian passerby comments that the survivors of this camp "had been freed instead of drowned in the lake,"[49] thereby aligning himself with the National Socialists and welcoming the death of anyone going against the "old order" of the homeland: "What happened at that moment with the word *Heimat*, were the lakes still blue, were the mountains there still white, is *Heimat* this landscape, is that enough?"⁵⁰ In an italicized passage, a fictional surviving resistance fighter wonders, "Is *Heimat* really a place for everyone, for the murderers as well as for their victims?"⁵¹

Komm über den See shows that the Austrian homeland excludes individuals who go against the authority of the majority, such as Zach, Mali, and Hermine, and that the younger generation, represented by Ruth, seeks recognition and justice for this generation of women that came before them. Although Ruth recognizes the powerlessness of the minority whose voice is stacked against the old and new orders of the majority, she becomes empowered to listen. She says of the generation of "children of war," which includes her friends Eva and Martha who suffered psychologically because they could not bear living with the untold past: "We were born too early, right into the middle of the crimes, without a chance to protect ourselves against them. And yet each one tried to protect herself from this truth, against which no blindness helps, ... The nightmare is in us, it is repeating itself in us, no repetition has been more senseless."⁵² The past returns as a nightmare to haunt the younger generation who has been socialized, like their mothers and grandmothers, to forget Austria's complicity in the Third Reich. Zach, who represents the generation of grandmothers, tells Ruth that the acts of being silent (*Schweigen*) and forgetting have become the "state ideology" of Austria. Zach recalls that in the summer of 1945 the Austrian press advocated that Austrians should "forget the last seven years" in an effort to prepare for the future.⁵³ Zach further tells Ruth that individuals who had spoken and acted out against Fascism in Austria during World War II do not "exist in the reality of this country" and exist only in "cemeteries of the nameless," "eat-in kitchens," and "homes for the elderly."⁵⁴ The cycle of being silent and being silenced repeats itself in the life of the older Zach. Her granddaughter Anna, who carries her name, is forbidden to see Zach again after her son divorces little Anna's mother. As a child, the granddaughter Anna once begged her grandmother Zach to tell her "fairy tales" of the resistance, the "stories of the mountains."⁵⁵ At the close of the twentieth century, even the younger Anna's knowledge of these historical events has been silenced. The novel concludes with Ruth's hope that despite Zach's hesitance to reveal her history and that of the other Austrian women resistance fighters, "one day perhaps Anna will tell her story."⁵⁶ Through the older protagonist Zach, Reichart's novel combats the silence regarding specific events in Austrian history and, in leaving the story only partially told, provides the impetus for readers to counter the act of forgetting and silence by revisiting Austria's history during the Third Reich through the critical lens of fiction.

The tension in *Februarschatten* between forgetting as a means of preserving one's sanity and remembering as a tool for working through regret, trauma, and mourning is also the main focal point of Reichart's novel *Nachtmär*. The title, the translation of which is both "a tale of the night" and a variant of "nightmare," reflects on the nightmarish history of Austria's involvement in the Holocaust, its complicity in the Third Reich, and consequences for future generations living with the aftershock of this traumatic past. *Nachtmär* is a montage of dreams, nightmares, and thought fragments that form an inner landscape of memories and multiple streams of consciousness.⁵⁷ In a central scene of this novel, the figure of the grandmother forces her grandson Ingram, who represents Austria's younger generation, to confront and to work through his repressed traumatic past. The nonlinear narration of the novel unfolds during the course of one evening from the ever-shifting perspective of Rudolf, Ingram, Paula, and Marlen, who have gathered to celebrate the eighth anniversary of receiving their doctoral degrees from the University of Vienna. The four friends, who grew up in the same small town and who live and work in Vienna at the close of the twentieth century, have grown apart over the years after betraying Esther, their American friend of Austrian-Jewish heritage. They had come to know Esther during their studies and learned that her Austrian-Jewish parents had fled Vienna to the United States during the Third Reich, where they led an unsuccessful life in exile. Esther tells her new friends that she discovered her Jewish heritage while applying for her passport only two years before moving to Vienna. Her parents, who were fond of their old homeland, had urged Esther to learn to know Vienna by studying there. The recent knowledge of her Austrian-Jewish heritage occupies her mind and "makes her crazy," as she tells her four friends during their first meeting:

> I could never imagine earlier that knowledge can be a burden. But since I know that I am Jewish, my first thought in the morning is: Actually I shouldn't exist, just as my parents shouldn't exist. This coincidence to have escaped an absolute law makes me crazy. On the other hand, at least now I have a monstrous history, something to hold on to: *Moses, the Bible, the Diaspora, pogroms, Auschwitz, and the Zionists. Somewhere between these memorial stones there will probably be room for me.*[58]

One of the four friends asks Esther why she returned to Vienna, "this horrific afterbirth locus of crimes, in the *midst of murderers and madmen.*"[59] Esther does not want to "gorge on the victims of her ancestors" or to gain anything from her suffering; she tells her new friends, "You didn't drive out my parents or cause my grandfather's heart attack."[60] Paula tells Esther that they don't know if they wouldn't have done it: "We have to live with this possibility, like you do with that of being driven out again, ..."[61]

Later in the novel the four friends drive Esther away because she becomes an uncomfortable and painful reminder for them of Austria's complicity in the Holocaust and of their role as Austrian citizens having to bear this past. Throughout the text it becomes clear to the reader how they betrayed her and why their actions and comments caused her to be driven away. While still writing her dissertation, Esther discovers that she is pregnant. Not wanting to appeal to the father of her child, Esther turns to her friends for help, but they reject her decision to bring a child into the world. When the four friends finally meet Esther under the large iconic Ferris wheel in the Viennese Prater Park, Rudolf lectures the group, commenting on "the fate of the Jews, especially in this second district" of Vienna, and states "that it is an old mistake of the Jews, only to always demand help and sacrifice from those who were standing on their side anyway."[62] After Rudolf's shocking statement, none of the friends dare to look in Esther's direction and hope Esther does not take it seriously. Esther disappears forever, and the four must live with the guilt of having betrayed her. At the conclusion of the novel, Paula searches for a grave at the "graveyard of the nameless," fearful of finding a gravestone bearing the date from their evening at the Prater Park. Not finding a gravestone, she remarks, "We didn't search for Esther, we didn't search for her even one day."⁶³ The betrayal is in fact doubled, or repeated, in Reichart's novel. Just as the four friends drive Esther away due to her otherness, her status as the daughter of an exiled Austrian-Jewish couple, so were Esther's parents, once Austrian citizens, betrayed by their community and Austrian homeland during the Third Reich. Not only do the four former friends see their identities bound to crimes committed by the previous war generation, in which the younger generation will always be "on the side of the perpetrators," but they always view Esther, despite her own resistance to this label, as a victim also.⁶⁴ Just as Bachmann's short story demonstrates the unresolved tension inherent in a postwar generation comprised of perpetrators and victims, so Reichart's novels explore how the second and third generations of Austrian citizens after World War II continue to face the challenge of confronting the country's complicity during the Third Reich and the task of engaging in a process of remembrance that will heal past traumas. The protagonists of Reichart's novel revisit yet resist the past, searching for what may have unraveled the formerly close bond of the friends, yet they are not able to fully recognize that their isolation has been caused by their betrayal of Esther and their attempt to disregard the past.

The fate of Esther and her exiled family is directly related to that of Ingram's grandmother. The grandmother struggles with her memories of World War II during which she failed to save her Jewish friend Neva, who had first hidden in the family's attic but then gave herself up to the Nazis because she couldn't bear living with the family any longer.⁶⁵ Despite her past experiences, Ingram's grandmother is an older woman "whom nothing more can distress."⁶⁶ Ingram, who had wanted to make creative films, works for a cutting-edge advertising agency, yet crosses the line of human decency when he films his dying grandmother, who lives with him in his apartment.⁶⁷ In the climactic central scene of the novel, Ingram's bedridden grandmother makes her way from her bed and, by blocking the front door, prevents him from leaving, thus forcing him to confront his past. In doing so, she forces Ingram to listen to her graphic description of his mother's suicide. Ingram is unable to look at his grandmother other than through the photographic lens of his film camera, "this cold, artificial eye," convincing himself that his agency will profit from this unusual footage.[68] Ingram's grandmother also reveals to him that she only pretended to be bedridden from the day World War II ended as a silent protest against the war, society, and her husband's unfaithfulness. Lying in bed had become her only form of control, which she then continued to exercise over her grandson. Ingram comes to realize that all of his imaginings of war, those of death and destruction, never included his grandmother's experiences: "During the war not only soldiers had fallen, but also photographs from her walls. His childhood was rich with such a history, it had prepared him for everything, except for the idea that she would move away from her place and block his doorway."[69] Reichart's description of the grandmother's "place" refers not only to her room in Ingram's apartment but also to the passive and unobtrusive space that the grandmother had occupied after the war. Before dying, she intends to prevent Ingram from escaping from the truth. She wants to reveal all the horrors so that he might know his own history and understand his own inability to maintain fulfilling and lasting relationships, as seen in his betrayal of Esther. Ingram's grandmother is a counterpart to Marlen's grandmother, whom Marlen is not allowed to question about the past. Marlen's sensation that her history is "cut off, over" contributes to her inability to write and express herself throughout the novel, despite the fact that she has wanted to be a writer since she was a little girl.[70] Reichart reveals that writing and that being true to oneself require a commitment to confront and work through the past. For Reichart, the figure of the grandmother is a revelatory protagonist who attempts to counter the identity crisis experienced by the younger generation of Austrians trying to come to grips with the history of World War II and the Holocaust. The protagonist Paula concludes, "Three generations later we are strangers to one another and depend on the memories of others."[71]

Reichart's novel *Nachtmär* and its theme of tension between the individual and society, past and present, can be read as a continuation of the author's previous works, *Februarschatten* and *Komm über den See*. In an interview, Reichart states that, in the course of writing, her work has moved from dealing with the past to the present and now to the future.[72] For Reichart, writing is a tool by which, on multiple levels, writer, reader, and protagonists engage in a process of confrontation with the past, remembrance, realization, and transformation. Through this process, Reichart's novels explore how language is able to either transmit or omit truths and how language plays into identity, both personal and national. As one of *Nachtmär*'s characters states, "It is difficult with language. It divides and binds."[73] In stripping everyday language of its clichés to expose essential truths, Reichart counteracts the trivialization or generalization that is sometimes associated with postwar fiction on the Holocaust and World War II. Reichart's novels are alternative narratives to the traditional representations of Austrian history since they address specifically the history of women during World War II. The older women and grandmother figures in Reichart's novels, *Februarschatten*'s Hilde, *Komm über den See*'s Zach, and *Nachtmär*'s grandmother, compel the younger generation to confront truths and to overcome the traumas of World War II in Austria. In doing so, the younger generation engages in a process of remembrance that allows for a possible reconciliation with the past and provides the impetus to experience a more fulfilled present.

Whereas the female protagonists of Aichinger's and Reichart's novels are directly impacted by the events of World War II and the Holocaust, the females in Welles' *Am Rande der Geschichte* and Nowak's *Gehorsam* are ordinary women "at the edge of history" who consider the social circumstances and events of war, especially of World War II, that contribute to their daily life experiences. Unlike the women portrayed in Aichinger's and Reichart's novels, the women in Welles' and Nowak's novels are not directly confronted by the Holocaust or by their involvement in or resistance to National Socialism or Austro-Fascism. *Am Rande der Geschichte* is a portrayal of women's daily lives in Austria during the first half of the twentieth century, with a focus on the economic instability in Austria and Europe that led up to World War I and II and the impact of these wars on civilian life on the Austrian home front. The novel recounts the fictional life of the Austrian working-class girl Friederike, also called Frieda or Friedl, from her birth in

1892 to her death four years after the end of World War II in 1949. Welles lays out Frieda's life in a circular fashion, from her birth to her death, against the backdrop of Austrian history, creating a historical novel that chronicles the life of a working-class woman during the first part of the twentieth century. The novel tracing Frieda's life is divided into sections prefaced by dates and short narratives in bold italics that cite historical facts and statistics, and show their significance for the lives of Austrian women. The prefaces provide the historical context for Frieda's experiences of daily life and illustrate how historical events affect those women living "at the edge of history." For example, the section prefaced by the dates 1920/1923 describes the hunger demonstrations of 1920 in Austria and the selection in 1922 of linguist Elisa Richter to become Austria's first female professor at the University of Vienna.[74] The first twelve pages of the book contain historical reproductions of photographs and prints, documenting the experiences of working-class Austrian citizens at the beginning of the twentieth century as they relate to Frieda's life story. This collection of images sets a tone of authenticity that validates the historical integrity of the fictional work. Images of ration coupons evoke Frieda's hunger during her childhood and the constant challenge to feed her own family during World War II. The engraving of a leather factory, related prints of industrial machines and equipment used in leather production, and a copy of a transcript for a business degree provide a visual context for Frieda's work and career ambitions. Photographs of groups of women standing in line with their children and of a woman carrying a heavy backpack underscore the harsh reality for women and children on the Austrian home front, whose lives revolved around daily survival, scavenging for food, trading on the black market, and seeking shelter from bombs.

In Welles' novel, the key figure of the older woman represents the voice of wisdom, resistance, and social consciousness. As a child, Frieda is strongly influenced by her grandmother, representing a strong contrast to Frieda's conformist parents, who voice the opinions of the majority without questioning the ethical and moral consequences of political authority and social mores. The novel moves through the significant stages of Frieda's life and shows how her identity as an older woman is shaped by the events and consequences of war, especially World War II. Frieda attempts to break out of her social milieu by pursuing an education and a career, yet her dreams are dashed by the limitations of her social role as a working-class woman and by the events of both World War I and II.

The novel's protagonist, Frieda, is a composite of women's experiences, gathered by Welles from the accounts of family and friends. The novel roots the course of Frieda's life in the social milieu into which she is born and in the wars she endures. The birth of Frieda is considered a burden for her family since they will have to care for her until she is old enough to work at the age of "ten or fourteen" and because her prospects of marrying into a secure financial situation are slim due to her frail health and the fact that her family has no money for a proper dowry.[75] Frieda's grandmother laments her granddaughter's birth because she expects that Frieda will experience a life that consists solely of work and of bearing children, most of whom she will "see into the grave."[76] The daily lives of the women in Frieda's family consist of doing household chores every day of the week, including "cleaning, sewing, washing up, scrubbing floors, washing and ironing clothes," lives in which they have no voice or power within the traditional Western European patriarchal family structure.[77] This powerlessness carries over into their role in society, in which some women, such as Frieda's mother, who cannot read or write, also have no voting rights. Because women's work is completed "mechanically," they resort to daydreams about a better future.[78] Within this society, Frieda is socialized to be obedient and well-behaved, although she wishes to be "strong" and "noncompliant" like her grandmother.[79] As a child, Frieda admires her grandmother for her critique of social injustice:

> Grandmother was critical. She knew a lot of people and always found out about the latest news. She liked to rail against the rich and the existing social injustices. She was of the opinion that people should not put up with everything, even though she probably did not know what she

actually wanted. With this attitude, she conveyed to the child that people did not have to put up with situations. There were ways and means to change things when a person had power. She did not know how to get this power, but it seemed at least remotely possible to obtain it.[80]

Frieda's grandmother, who transcends her social circumstances with her hardheaded attitude, represents the independent and assertive woman Frieda wishes to be. However, Frieda never succeeds in becoming like her grandmother due to the limitations of her social circumstances as a working-class woman. Although Frieda spends her childhood believing "One day, I will do as I please," she is unable to achieve her desired level of education and therefore cannot pursue a career in the leather factory, leaving her financially unable to break away from her loveless marriage and from her social class.[81] Her mother reminds her of a woman's role in society by asking Frieda, "why else are women there, if not to marry and have children?"[82] During the course of World War I, Frieda loses her mother, her father, and her grandmother to poor health and lack of affordable or available health care. After being dismissed from her job as an office worker in the leather factory because of her marriage to Hans, Frieda is resigned to running the family household. Once pregnant with her son and upset at the prospect of raising him in poverty due to Hans's meager income, Frieda convinces herself that she must obediently accept the situation, as she has done so many times before in her life.[83] The figure of the grandmother returns in Frieda's mind as a reminder of her earlier ambitions:

> Her thoughts circled indefinitely. All those years, her husband had lived on her substance, had hollowed her out. She had never defended herself against this since she had been brought up to keep her mouth shut and to be subordinate. In her mind she heard her grandmother ask what she wanted to do besides marrying. Now, she knew exactly what she would rather have done.[84]

Frieda perceives her life, during which her aspirations for independence and fulfillment have been thwarted by war and social circumstance, as a circle in which all "the unpleasant things in her life repeat themselves."[85]

In the prefaces that contextualize Frieda's life, Welles documents the Anschluss, the pogroms against Jews, and war's effect on women's daily lives. In a preface entitled "1941/1942," Welles describes an older woman who courageously spoke out against Fascism: "In April 1941 the senior citizen Theresia Rager was arrested by the Gestapo in St. Pölten because she had disseminated a satirical poem criticizing Hitler and Austria's role in World War II: We don't want war/ We don't need to win/ We want our free Austria/ And we are looking forward to Hitler's corpse!"[86] In contrast to the brave actions and accomplishments of famous Austrian women, Frieda's daily activities make up a simple and undocumented life, lived out "at the edge of history." Frieda's fictional life plays out against the backdrop of historical events and issues related to daily survival during World War II and the postwar period, such as hunger, scavenging for food, bartering goods for food on the black market, the bombings of Vienna, and the fear of being raped by Russian soldiers.

As mentioned in the two previous chapters on the works of Kräftner and Trahan, Austrian women writers often incorporate the fear of being raped or being raped by allied Russian soldiers at the end of the war into their narratives about World War II. In Welles' novel, Russian soldiers are lodged in Frieda's home, raising her fear of their rumored assaults on girls and women: "She had heard about rapes, and she froze inwardly each time one of the men came near her. Rapes occurred in front of husbands and children, and age or looks or pregnancy were not reasons that it didn't happen."[87] Due to her fear, Frieda keeps her distance from the rowdy Russians living in her home. Yet, disproving these rumors, the Russians, instead of mistreating her, share their meager food rations with her and her family.[88] Although she is keenly aware of the presence of the Russian Allied soldiers, Frieda's knowledge of the Holocaust and the murder of Jews and other victimized groups by the Nazis is limited to the disappearance of her former Jewish boss and factory owner, Grätzer, and her doctor,

Grünzweig: "Friedl had heard that many Jews were leaving the country, also that the Grätzers and Dr. Grünzweig had left overnight for an unknown destination."[89] In the long postwar years of hunger and suffering, Frieda does not get the proper medical care for a leg infection; she does not want to go to any other doctor than her family doctor, Grünzweig, whom, she believes, because he was an Austrian Jew, "has probably been gassed."[90] Dr. Grünzweig's disappearance ultimately affects Frieda's life, showing that the loss of some of Austria's citizens at the hands of the Nazis was a loss for all Austrians.

Looking back on her life, shortly before her premature death at the age of 57 from the complications of her leg infection, Frieda realizes that she has lived an unfulfilled life, one in which she has not been able to fully realize her potential. She regrets having led a traditional life as a wife and mother instead of pursuing a career at the leather factory: "She should have worked harder than any man, should have renounced everything, especially the husband and the child, then, maybe, it would all have been different."[91] An earlier scene, however, shows Frieda's conflicted thoughts regarding her future. After the Anschluss in 1938, described earlier in the novel, Frieda realized that working for a Jewish factory owner instead of marrying Hans may have also affected her life negatively since she would have either lost her job or been arrested for working with a Jew. The novel shows that despite Frieda's desire to achieve personal fulfillment, her social status, her gender, and the impact of two World Wars force her to focus chiefly on daily survival. The older woman who Frieda has become is shaped by her desire to emulate her grandmother in her will to overcome the narrow nineteenth- and early twentieth-century traditional gender roles for women and the events of war, especially World War II and its consequences for children and women on the home front. Frieda's ordinary life "at the edge of history" and her adulthood, overshadowed by deeply rooted social traditions and the events of World War II, are in sharp contrast to the achievements of the historically documented women writers, doctors, and activists cited in the prefaces to the chapters.[92] Despite the marked contrast, Frieda's daily life shows how even the actions of one individual are bound up with the public and national history of Austria. Welles shows how an ordinary life is significant because it is both the ordinary and extraordinary citizens who make up the sum of a community and a nation.

Just as *Am Rande der Geschichte* traces how Frieda's obedience limits her personal growth and prevents her from escaping the confines of her social milieu, Nowak's novel *Gehorsam* demonstrates how a life of obedience is socialized and passed on from one generation to the next, from grandmother to grandchild, causing its older female narrator to question her life and to doubt her self-worth. In Nowak's *Gehorsam*, an older woman, bedridden in a nursing home room shared with three other patients, reflects on her life before, during, and after World War II in a monologue interspersed with an inner dialogue carried on with the photograph of her dead mother, a figure who represents the beginning of the chain of socialization in the family hierarchy. The narrator demands reassurance and recognition from the mother concerning her set of values regarding the role of women in society and questions the life of her own daughter, a woman who represents the second generation after the war, whose life choices and perspective on her gender diverge sharply from that of her mother. The older narrator reflects on her controlled childhood, her strained relationship to her mother and daughters, and her daily life of suffering during World War II and the postwar period in Austria. The narrator feels compelled to recall her history and to review why certain situations developed in her life: "I can't stop to report. Something keeps driving me. Drives me. . . ."[93] From the lens of her present perspective, the older narrator observes, but does not accept, how her daughter's resistance to her mother's values of sacrificial motherhood and subservience to the nation-state, inculcated during the Third Reich, have led to her daughter's independence and self-fulfillment. The older narrator recalls her mother, who raised her to be a diligent, docile housewife whose identity would be validated by her husband, children, and community. To be good or obedient, thus the title *Gehorsam*, was a woman's creed and destiny.[94] The narrator is unwilling to appreciate her daughter Renate's refusal of these traditional values because she believes that approving these values would devalue her own life.

Nowak's novel emphasizes that women's socialization was

accomplished through both Catholicism and the National Socialist party but also that it is passed from mother to daughter, a relationship in which the narrator's own role as grandmother represents the most distant part of that chain. Throughout the novel, the protagonist describes the Catholic Church as complicit in its negative socialization of girls and women, casting them as sinful daughters of Eve, encouraging them to take on their role as mothers, and teaching them subservience to men and therefore also to church, state, and family.[95] The older narrator recalls her bouts of depression – "nervous problems," as she calls them – which prevented her from fulfilling her duties as a wife and mother and which ultimately led to her divorce.[96] The narrator's experiences of womanhood, spanning the early twentieth century through World War II and the postwar period, are underscored by defining statements that reinforced women's socialization during the first half of the twentieth century, as documented in citations taken from church sermons, school textbooks, propaganda, household manuals, and common adages. Like Welles' historical prefaces, Nowak's historical material, such as propaganda repeated in speeches and sermons, authenticates the experiences of women chronicled in this fictional account. The narrator's mother's pastor socialized girls and women to their familial duties through his sermons by making statements such as "To be a woman means self-sacrifice" and "To keep a marriage together is the moral duty of the woman, the failure of the marriage her failure; the commandment of the insoluble marriage is God's present to women."[97] The narrator's mother always told her, "Men have to achieve something, women have to be themselves, for women are love."[98] The narrator feels validated in her roles as a mother and dutiful wife on the home front by a saying from propaganda disseminated during the Third Reich: "The firm goal of all female education is to become a mother."[99] The narrator further learns from a visiting Nazi party official, who cites excerpts from Hitler's speeches, that a woman's goal should be to raise children for the Reich: "They tell me often that I want to drive women away from their careers. No, I just want to create the best conditions to enable her to start a family and have children because our people (*Volk*) need this above everything."[100] The narrator, who recalls her life as a wife and mother, observes how she raised her children to be compliant and submissive, just as much of the generation before her had done and just as the National Socialist party encouraged her to do. When the narrator was a young mother, her mother had reminded her to "stay firm when a child refuses to follow orders," and her husband Alfons had warned her, "When parents don't pay attention, even an infant learns remarkably fast to manipulate them."[101]

It is precisely this learned obedience that the narrator's daughter Renate comes to resist. The narrator recalls that she and her husband had discouraged Renate from pursuing her ambitions to become a writer, believing that "writing is harmful for girls."[102] Having entered into a loveless marriage after becoming pregnant, Renate eventually "rebels against her fate" of being subservient to the social norms imposed by her parents and divorces her husband.[103] After becoming a teacher and a successful writer and also marrying a fellow writer, Renate assures her mother that her life "circumstances have changed" and that she is "no longer the same as before."[104] Since pursuing her ambitions and breaking free of the values of her upbringing, Renate claims, "I have my life in control."[105] While the narrator recalls her own life as one in which she continually sought validation from her mother, husband, church, and state, Renate criticizes her mother's complacency, her apolitical stance, and her uncritical view of society. Renate's resistance to her mother and grandmother's value system, formed during the early twentieth century and encouraged by National Socialism, lead her to experience success and happiness at last, even though the narrator continues to voice criticism of her daughter's defiance.

After Renate's divorce, she decides to pursue her wish to become a teacher despite her mother's reservations. When Renate also takes up writing again, working on her stories in the mornings before going to teach, the mother is skeptical about what she tells her about her success as a writer: "Even before she went to school, she sat at her desk and scribbled on one piece of paper after the other, crumpled them again and again, and threw them away. 'I am writing stories. Many have been published and have appeared in newspapers and books.'"[106] Even at the end of her life, the narrator views herself in opposition to her daughter Renate and relates more to her obedient daughter Gaby. The narrator summarizes how her daughters' different strategies have contributed to their happiness or failure in society: "The clumsy Renate rebelled against her fate; Gaby, the competent one, the superior one, subjugated herself."[107] Despite her observations, the narrator still believes that her daughters should be controlled just as she was controlled, and she rants that neither has held to her "child's duty, determined by God," to always be obedient to her mother.[108] In her final rant at the conclusion of the novel, the narrator demands to know why she has been deserted by her daughters, when all she did as a mother was follow the rules and teachings of her church: "I obediently followed His rules and commandments, did that what He said was right."[109]

For the narrator, socialized to conform to a traditional social and political value system, any deviation is considered unacceptable, irrational, dangerous, and a sign of mental illness. As an exuberant and independently minded child, Renate is told by her parents, "Watch out; otherwise, you'll end up in the insane asylum like your Uncle Anton."[110] When Renate is caught talking with her pet bird because she feels misunderstood by her mother and sister, the narrator describes her daughter as "crazy,"[111] later wondering, "Had she finally gone mad?"[112] Throughout the novel nonconformity is equated with madness, yet the narrator does not realize that her own struggle with depression, anxiety, and madness is directly related to her socialized roles as obedient daughter, subservient wife, and controlling mother. Renate's success and youthful disobedience and consequent personal and professional success are shown in marked contrast to her mother's symptoms of senility, nightmares, and hallucinations and to her physical and mental deterioration in the nursing home. Like Welles' novel, Nowak's narrative unmasks the socialized subservient role of girls and women as a hindrance to personal development and fulfillment, critical thinking, and social and political resistance. The portrait of an ordinary life lived "at the edge of history" becomes representative for a generation of obedient citizens who were socialized to conform and obey political directives like those imposed under the Third Reich. In the novels of Reichart, Welles, and Nowak, the daughters who do break from tradition and a life of conformity, Erika in *Februarschatten*, Ruth in *Komm über den See*, and Renate in *Gehorsam*, achieve a level of self-fulfillment which their mothers never dreamed possible. The figure of the older woman, either the aging mother or the grandmother, is a key to compelling a younger generation to confront the past and to move forward, away from the "edge of history" and to a more central and active role in society.

The key figure of the older woman and grandmother in texts of postwar Austrian literature gives voice to the underrepresented history of women's everyday lives during World War II and the Holocaust. The older female protagonists in the novels of Aichinger, Reichart, Welles, and Nowak engage the younger generation in acts of remembrance, describing their daily life experiences as girls and women and their observations of war on the home front and insisting that their voices be remembered as part of a larger history. While at times perceived as "out of their mind," these older women protagonists speak their mind, or, as in the case of Hilde, are encouraged to find their voice, in order to guide and empower younger generations of men and women by conveying the dangers of personal and political passivity and apathy and of the horrors of war and in order to instill in them the significance of individual and civil responsibility.

Chapter Five

"As old as I am, I am so little": The Kindertransport from Austria to Britain in Memoirs by Martha Blend, Lore Segal, Helen Hilsenrad, and Mona Golabek

> It's interesting how you wish you could go back, to see again where you were as a child. And then you stand there and it is of course not there anymore."
>
> – Lore Segal[1]

Whereas the past three chapters discussed the portrayal of the lives of girls and women on the Austrian home front during World War II and the postwar period, the next two chapters explore the experiences of Austrian-Jewish girls and women forced into exile by the threat of persecution, deportation, or murder during the Third Reich. This chapter focuses on themes unique to Austrian girls who, along with ten thousand other children, or *Kinder*, from Austria, Germany, and former Czechoslovakia, fled the onslaught of National Socialism by means of the children's transport, or Kindertransport, traveling by train and ship to England, as recalled in *A Child Alone* by Martha Blend (1995) and *Other People's Houses* by Lore Segal (1964). Additional narratives of the Kindertransport experience, Helen Hilsenrad's *Brown Was the Danube* (1966), and Mona Golabek's memoir *The Children of Willensden Lane: Beyond the Kindertransport: A Memoir of Music, Love, and Survival* (2002), add depth and perspective to Blend's and Segal's recollections. Mark Jonathan Harris and Deborah Oppenheimer's 2000 documentary film and accompanying volume about the Kindertransport experience, *Into the Arms of Strangers*, in which Segal shares additional recollections, lays bare the often unresolved issues of wartime trauma experienced by the Kindertransport survivors; as one adult notes of his continued preoccupation with his childhood memories: "As old as I am, I am so little."[2] For Segal, whose story is also featured in Käthe Kratz's 2003 documentary film about childhood in exile, *Vielleicht habe ich Glück gehabt* (Maybe I was lucky), the notion of childhood, to which one "wishes one could go back," "is of course not there anymore."[3] Blend's and Segal's memoirs attempt to re-cover the loss of their childhoods by writing it into the narratives of their present lives.

Looking back from the vantage point of adulthood, Blend and Segal reconstruct their childhoods in Vienna as the only children of assimilated Austrian Jews sent by their desperate parents to the safe haven of England, their coming of age during war in London, and their adulthood as survivors in exile. Blend's and Segal's memoirs examine how the events of exile and war shaped their adult identities, enabling them to reflect on their formative Austrian childhoods and their conflicted relationships to their first language of German, as well as their Austrian-Jewish heritage. It is of note that, even though Blend and Segal's first language was German, both authors wrote their memoirs in English, their recollections shaped by their coming of age in England, voicing their experiences in the language of their adopted homeland.[4]

A brief history of the Kindertransport as it relates specifically to Austrian-Jewish children provides a larger context for Blend's and Segal's accounts. Germany's annexation of Austria in March 1938 fueled rising hostilities toward the approximate 192,000 Austrian Jews, of whom 170,000 lived in the nation's capital, Vienna. Following the Anschluss of March 1938, Austrian Jews, who had already experienced rising anti-Semitism caused by Austro-Fascist politics, were publicly terrorized, attacked, and humiliated by fellow citizens who followed the ideologies of National Socialism.

The German anti-Jewish laws, which had been set in place over the past five years in Germany since Hitler's rise to Chancellor in 1933, were quickly taken over in Austria's new regime as part of the Third Reich with the goal of purging Jews from all areas of society – the arts, education, employment, politics, housing, and the enjoyment of public spaces. In August 1938, SS lieutenant-colonel Adolf Eichmann was charged with organizing a mass emigration of Jews from Austria, which within eighteen months forced 150,000 Jews to flee their homeland to any country that was willing and able to take in these now mostly destitute and emotionally devastated refugees. In addition to robbing Austrian Jews of their professions, property, and homes, human and civil rights, and citizenship, the Nazis allowed Jews to take only very limited amounts of their possessions and savings with them, thereby forcing them to leave impoverished and homeless. In the greater German Reich, the terrors of the pogrom on *"Kristallnacht,"* November 9-10, 1938, led to the arrest and deportation of approximately 30,000 Jewish men to concentration camps, from which only a few were able to return home after being ransomed by their traumatized families.

Although the world was shocked to read reports of what was happening to Jews in the German Reich, only a few countries offered to take in the fleeing refugees. Britain, for example, was the only country that relaxed immigration controls for unaccompanied children who would not present a threat to British jobs and consume public funds. Anglo-Jewish leaders met with Prime Minister Chamberlain and urged him to allow children to enter the country; after this meeting, the House of Commons debated and approved the plan. Six days after the British meeting of Jewish and non-Jewish charitable organizations, such as the Central British Fund, the Quakers, and the Save the Children Fund, the British government produced its rescue plan. The British government sped up the immigration process by issuing travel documents on the basis of group lists instead of on individual applications, but it relied on the refugee agencies to cover the costs of the rescue operation. The age limit for unaccompanied children was seventeen, and the refugees were to stay only temporarily so as to not financially burden the state.[5] By contrast, in the United States, a federal bill in early 1939 to admit twenty thousand children refugees, since quotas for immigration from Austria and Germany into the United States had already been filled, died in committee. The powerful anti-immigration lobby had "depicted the entry of unaccompanied children as the 'thin end of the wedge,'"[6] and the United States Congress claimed that accepting children without their parents was "contrary to the laws of God."[7]

Through the financial aid and sacrifice of countless volunteers and multiple British national and international agencies and organizations, approximately ten thousand children between the ages of three months and seventeen years from Austria, Germany, and Czechoslovakia were safely brought by the Kindertransport to Britain. The first children's transport left on December 1, 1938, by train from Berlin, then by sea from the Hook of Holland to the ports of Harwich or Southampton. In Austria, the first train, on which Segal traveled, left on December 10 from the Vienna train station. Jewish children whose lives were in danger in Eastern Europe were also transported from Prague, from a camp at Zbaszyn, and from Danzig.[8]

Segal, just ten years old, recalls that the evening of her departure was filled with "grief," "panic," and "fury."[9] Her mother, Franzi Groszmann, describes her own emotional reaction to sending her only child away: "the hurt is unbelievable. That cannot be described."[10] Further, Groszmann recalls: "People have asked me, 'What did you feel?' Nothing. This was such a shock. When we came home, we didn't talk to each other. My parents, my husband and I, we did not talk, we didn't look at each other."[11] In her memoir Segal associates all her feelings of loss and guilt with a knackwurst sausage her anguished mother had run out to buy for her journey. Unable to eat it out of grief, Segal finds it impossible to dispose of it after it began to spoil: "My mind during that first breakfast was on my sausage. I had to do away with the sausage without doing away with it. It was difficult to focus on the problem; I kept forgetting to think about it, yet, all the time, the place where the sausage lay on the floor against the wall, under the bed, remained the center of my guilt, a sore spot in my mind."[12] Memoirs and recollections by *Kinder* make evident this shared guilt carried into adulthood.[13]

Once children arrived at the British ports, they were taken to Dovercourt, where a holiday camp had been established from which volunteers willing to take on the role of foster parents could select and pick up the children. The length of time children stayed at the camp before finding a more permanent home varied greatly.[14] The conditions of the camp were chaotic and funding for the care of children who had not been chosen by foster families was a constant issue. Blend's and Segal's memoirs recall their fears of what would happen to them after their arrival in England, the initial cold and damp conditions of the refugee camp, and the constant anxiety regarding the fate of their families at home. Segal could not recall specific days or the exact length of her time at the camp since "there seems to be only a certain amount of room" in her memory.[15] While the youngest children were typically the first to be welcomed into the homes of foster families, older children and teenagers were often not taken by families and had to live in hostels. Some *Kinder* were taken in to become servants or were forced to hand their working wages over to their foster families.[16] Many children had to care for younger siblings, and others, like Segal, were charged with finding sponsors and employment for their parents and other family members desperately seeking refuge from the tightening grip of Nazi persecution in their homeland. At the end of 1939, lack of funds and the beginning of war put an end to the humanitarian rescue mission of the Kindertransport. Those Jews who had not had the opportunity or found the funding to flee the Third Reich were faced with certain persecution, deportation, or murder in concentration and death camps. Most children saved by the Kindertransport ships would never see their parents or families again and were forced to live their lives overshadowed by their feelings of grief, guilt, and loss. Whereas Segal was able to organize sponsorship for her parents and bring them to England, Blend's parents were deported and murdered by the Nazis.

The majority of the children who came to Britain by the Kindertransport did not view themselves as a group of individuals with a shared history until the *Kind* Bertha Leverton organized the first reunion in 1989, which aroused public interest in the experiences of those who had survived the Holocaust through the Kindertransport and also encouraged *Kinder* to write memoirs of their experiences. Common experiences of *Kinder*, some of which are addressed in Blend's and Segal's memoirs, include suffering from a premature loss of childhood innocence and a lack of feeling of belonging in which "all attachments were precarious," as well as the desire to "do something good with their lives."[17] This wish to "do good" often includes an "investment in children and grandchildren" to make up for the loss of their own families who had been torn apart and murdered by the perpetrators of the Third Reich.[18] Differences among the experiences of *Kinder* include the "extent to which they informed their children of what they had endured," for while some did not want to burden their children with their painful past, others wished to share their stories "to ensure that the hatred and generosity would never be forgotten and that lessons would be learned."[19] Blend's and Segal's memoirs represent the recollections of *Kinder* whose experiences are part of Austria's larger history – one that, for many, took place beyond its national and geographic borders. Blend and Segal address themes common to the recollections of the *Kinder* as mentioned above. Their works also consider how national and religious identities relate to language, how game playing can be a way of coping with war trauma and how the act of writing is an act of remembrance that allows for identity construction and healing.

Blend's and Segal's stories of survival reveal differences in their coping strategies and demonstrate the way their escape to Britain has shaped their adult identities. Blend, who was nine years old when she left for England with the Kindertransport, was able to live with one permanent foster family and learned, after the war ended, that her parents had been deported and murdered by the Nazis.[20] Segal lived with five different foster families and was able to bring her parents to Britain on domestic service visas a year after her own arrival. Blend remained in England, where she married, raised a family, and continued to pursue her interests in literature and writing. Segal and surviving family members emigrated from Britain to the Dominican Republic in 1948, then to New York in 1958, where Segal married, raised a family, and taught creative writing and English and published numerous literary works. Blend's and Segal's stories of survival and emigration reveal shared experiences and common themes that are grounded in their Austrian-Jewish heritage and in their experiences as Austrian-Jewish girls in exile, coming of age during the war and the postwar period.

In retracing the events of their childhoods, both Blend and Segal seek to define their adult identities through their experiences of exile. Segal and Blend portray their lives chronologically, recalling their charmed childhoods with their parents in Vienna in the early 1930s; their traumatic departures from their loved ones by the Kindertransport from Vienna, by train across Europe and then by ship to London; their at times conflicted relationships to their foster families; their coming-of-age experiences; the bombings in London toward the end of the war; their educational and career paths; discovering after the war the horrors of the Holocaust and facing their own losses and grief; and their adult lives as mothers, wives, and professionals.

Though chronologically structured, the memoirs are nonetheless fragmented, revealing gaps of memory that constantly break, subvert, and reconstruct the life narratives. The memoirs read like collages of memories, in which recollections often overlap and events refer to previous ones in a spiraling fashion. Segal, for example, embeds the memory of her exiled cousin Paul, whose life would have otherwise remained unchronicled, into various parts of her memoir. The memory gaps of their childhoods are filled with historical descriptions that provide a context for their personal experiences, poetic reflections, recollections by family members who survived the Holocaust, and narrations from letters and diaries. The gaps also serve to make room for speculation about what might have been or what may have been felt at the time, and more often than not what should have been, such as the survival of loved ones, and what should not have been, such as the war, the Holocaust, and exile.

In order to gain control over these unknown events, Blend and Segal attempt to create linear narratives of their lives that are nonetheless fragmented, in part even imagined, in order to bring together scattered memories.[21] In their recollections, the authors use phrases that reveal their uncertainty or partial memories of certain events. Segal, for example, writes, "I remember only," signaling the incomplete nature of her childhood memories.[22] Segal learns more about her childhood and earlier life from her mother: "My mother tells me a story that I seem to have chosen to forget,. . . ."[23] This shows her reliance on the memories of family and friends to complete a portrait of herself and her childhood. In her memoir, Segal frequently describes snapshots of herself, fixed images that validate who she is as an adult. For example, describing herself as a young woman in exile traveling from England to the Dominican Republic by ship, she writes: "This is me, lying in a deck chair."[24] Segal, in the second part of her memoir, tells of her meager existence in the Dominican Republic, as well as that of her cousin Paul, whose experiences she chronicles through letters, conversations, and her own memories. In documenting Paul's life, she secures the story of both the survival of her extended family and her ties to a larger history of Austrian Jews in exile. She writes, "I have questioned Paul about this period in his life when I did not know him, and in a letter he described himself for me – using the third person – as a young man."[25] In her attempt to provide a rich history of her own life and the lives of surviving family members, Segal's memories are refashioned by way of poetic reflections and fictitious dialogues, demonstrating how a memoir can often take on characteristics attributed to the genre of fiction.

Like Segal, Blend reflects on her past in her memoir by using phrases that reveal the disjointed nature of her recollections of childhood. Blend views her childhood and youth from the vantage point of adulthood, prefacing her memories with phrases such as "Looking back on this scene, I realise now that," "Not till many years later did I discover," "I can merely conjecture," and "I had then no idea, but I found out later."[26] Blend writes that both her fond and traumatic childhood memories were buried until she wrote her memoir – almost fifty years after her exile to Britain. Blend views herself as an archaeologist, digging up memories like shards of pottery. Of her recollections of her Viennese childhood she writes, "I didn't know how to talk about them, so they remained buried in my mind."[27] For most of her life, Blend relied on adults to remember the events of her childhood, but in her memoirs she writes, "There is no one I can ask about it;" "it remains one of the many insoluble puzzles of my childhood."[28] Blend refers to her life story as a "drama" which unfolds in her memoir, in which she plays the main role of narrator.[29] Reassessing her childhood vexations about school work in England, she writes, "Compared with what young Jewish people on the Continent were going through, this now seems a very minor frustration, but I did not think so at the time."[30] After the war ended in 1945, Blend recalls reading literature about the war, skipping over pages detailing crimes committed during the Holocaust. She writes, "That part of my life was so dead to me, along with the characters in that now-distant drama, that I shut such information out of my conscious mind as far as possible."[31] By casting herself in a "drama," Blend creates an emotional distance from her traumatic childhood in order to recount her painful past. Through her memoir, in which she asserts herself as an individual with her own past, her story resists losing itself in the shared history of millions.[32]

The act of writing for both Blend and Segal is a means of recollecting and establishing identity and, as such, is a mechanism for coping with the loneliness and grief of childhood exile. Segal recalls that during her first weeks in Britain after her arrival on the Kindertransport she "wanted to be writing."[33] While living with her first foster family, she begins to write her autobiography, the intent of which she describes is "to let the English know, as I had promised my father, what had happened to us under Hitler." Yet she continues, "But when I came to write it down, I felt a certain flatness. The events needed to be picked up, deepened, darkened."[34] Segal continues this critical self-reflection on her writing about her personal experiences in exile through her memoir. Having gained perspective on the historical events of World War II and the Holocaust and having reflected on her childhood experiences in discussion with other Holocaust survivors and *Kinder*, Segal is able to give her work the depth she felt it was lacking when she began writing as a child.

Like Segal, Blend discovers her penchant for the English language and for writing during her childhood in exile. For Blend, writing becomes a tool with which to actively work against the alienation and isolation she feels. She recalls that one of the activities of her classmates' secret society "was to write a story a week for the entertainment of the other members."[35] She further observes, "This I relished and so began my lifelong love affair with the English language.... Its poetry and other literature have given me pleasure and provided some compensation for the loneliness of my life."[36] Yet Blend realizes as an adult that in reciting an English poem as a child she was "being forced to retreat" from her true origins and identity.[37] Writing allows for self-expression and the possibility of gaining acceptance among her peers and experiencing success and recognition.[38] She calls her life "a story" to which there is no happy ending, especially concerning the fate of her parents.[39]

Like writing, another coping device for Blend and Segal is the activity of playing games. Games fostered interaction and cooperation with peers, and the invention of new games mirrored the adult world around them. The experiences acquired through childhood game playing enable Blend and Segal to cope with their feelings of loneliness and vulnerability as children in exile. Games give Blend and Segal the power to control their environment, enjoy small successes, and form friendships. When Blend and her mother are detained in a cell by the Nazis after looking for her father who had been imprisoned without reason, they play a game known today as Memory, cut from a piece of cardboard. They draw pictures on the cards, two of each kind, such as two apples, two pears, and a set labeled "Mutti und Papa" (Mom and Dad).[40] Of this game, Blend recalls, "when these appeared together I regarded it as an omen that we too would soon be together again and for a moment I clapped my hands with joy. On second thought, though, it was hard to keep back the tears and stifle the fear that, unlike in the fairy tales, such a happy ending did not seem very likely."[41] Reuniting the cards "Mutti and Papa" signifies the hope that her father will join his family again after being released from jail. Though her parents are reunited after this incident, this recollection starkly contrasts with the fact that Blend's parents are ultimately separated from their daughter, first when she is sent to safety with the Kindertransport to England and then permanently when they are deported and murdered.

In another example of game playing, during the bombings of London, Blend recalls playing bouncing ball games against the wall of the air raid shelter. Her childhood joys are interrupted by her feelings of guilt when she imagines "the anxieties for those left behind."[42] She also recalls her enjoyment in pretending to battle the Nazi enemies while playing the game Battleship: "To sink enemy ships even in fantasy gave some feeling of control of events."[43]

Segal's game experiences, like Blend's, allow her to control her environment, in which she feels vulnerable and lonely. She recalls playing with another young refugee the game of mother and child: "I'll be the mother. You be the child. You have to cry and I'll make you feel better."[44] The role reversal gives her some power over her helplessness and allows her to identify with her mother's loss. Another game Segal invents is one in which she and another foster child have to guess in how many days they will receive a letter from their parents in Vienna: "First you guess and then I guess my letter, and the one who guesses too early has lost."⁴⁵ When Helene learns that her parents have been deported, she says to Segal, "I'm not playing anymore. . . I won't get any more letters."⁴⁶ Whereas playing games provides Blend and Segal with some semblance of power over events that are out of their control, games also become a way for them to cope with their grief over being separated from their parents and homeland and their fear of war, both in Austria and in England.

Another shared theme in the memoirs of Blend and Segal reveals their conflicted relationships to language. Their native tongue of German co-exists in tension with the English language of their new homeland of England, a country into which they were forcibly sent in exile. Blend prays for her parents' safety in German, "adding a short Hebrew prayer asking for God's protection" that her father taught her.⁴⁷ Yet she recalls her strong urge to assimilate, to learn English and lose her accent: "I cannot remember precisely when I shed my German accent, but it was some months after I arrived in England. To this day, when I tell people that I was born in Austria, they say: 'Oh, but you haven't got an accent.'"⁴⁸ While feeling "outwardly indistinguishable" from her English classmates by having mastered English like a native speaker, she realizes that "inside was another matter."⁴⁹ Segal, like Blend, finds that after a year in England, German is "uncomfortable" in her mouth.⁵⁰ To please her various foster parents, Segal is eventually perceived as English. She is proud to overhear adults saying about her, "That child is getting as chilly as the rest of the English" and "How nicely she carries around the tea . . . . Almost like an English girl."⁵¹ Later, she relates to a French refugee her strong identification with England: "I didn't have the opportunity to form prejudices. I came here when I was a child of ten so I'm about fifty per cent English myself."⁵² Yet, despite her integration into the English culture, she still feels a sense of alienation and isolation. Moving from one foster family to another, Segal is once reprimanded for "un-English" behavior: "You don't do that when you live in other people's houses."⁵³ The expression "other people's houses," which lends Segal's memoir its title, underscores her feelings of alienation and exclusion, further compounding the emotional consequences of her forced exile. It is not until Segal's arrival in New York City in the early 1950s that she feels at home in a culture and community that seems to embrace people of diverse backgrounds. The longing for their Austrian homeland and for the German variant spoken in Austria is made evident in Segal's and Blend's clear distinctions between Germans and Austrians. Both authors avoid referring to their native tongue as German in their memoirs – both view their mother tongue as an Austrian-German variant.[54] This distinction is made to clearly distinguish their heritage from that of Germans, who were considered guilty of war crimes. This complex issue of viewing solely Germans and not Austrians as criminals and Nazis is based on the immediate postwar belief held by many Austrians and on statements made by Austria's immediate postwar government that theirs was a country victimized by Germany.[55] Segal, for example, pits her warm relationship to her Austrian heritage and early childhood against Germany's role in National Socialism by writing that her grandmother spoke "pure Austrian," which emphasizes her Austrian heritage rather than her relationship to the German language and its association with Germany.[56] Later, as a young adult, Segal asks her cousin Paul whether all Germans are Nazis, to which he replies: "All Germans have the tendency, and yes, there are exceptions."[57] In addressing Paul's reaction to her question, Segal underscores the complexities inherent to the questions of national guilt. As a child, Segal finds it difficult to admit that Germany is similar to Austria. Of the train journey of the Kindertransport, she writes: "A big girl said we had left Austria during the night and were actually in Germany. I looked out, wanting to hate, but there was nothing out the window but cows and fields. I said maybe we were still in Austria. It was important to me, because I was collecting countries. Born in Austria, I had vacationed in Hungary and visited relatives in Czechoslovakia, which was three countries I had been in, and Germany would make it four."[58] Segal's description of her life as one in which she "collects countries" helps her cope with her multiple passages of exile – from Austria to England, then to Santo Domingo and, finally, to the United States. Her story of exile and survival is unique and differs from that of Blend, who remained in

England after the war and after learning of her parents' murders in the Holocaust.

Segal's parents, her father once a prominent bank director, had enjoyed the comforts of a large apartment and domestic help in Vienna. After their arrival in England, Segal's parents were themselves considered domestic help and were displaced many times, not just by their forced exile but also within England, where they were moved from family to family. The physical and emotional strain of exile and war and the loss of family and friends in the Holocaust, left Segal's father physically ill and psychologically broken. His health was further compromised by being twice imprisoned as a "German-speaking enemy" in England, which contributed to his premature death in England in 1944. Two years later, Segal's mother left England to join a farming colony for refugees in Sosua, the Dominican Republic, also known as DORSA, the Dominican Republic Settlement Association. In 1948, Segal joined her mother and grandmother in Sosua; her grandfather had died there in exile in 1946. It was in Sosua that Segal met her remaining family, such as her cousin Paul and his wife Ilse, who later died in exile along with her baby in childbirth. The family lived and worked in Cuidad Trujillo, now known as Santo Domingo. From Ciudad Trujillo, her grandmother, then a 75-year-old widow, moved to the United States with an American visa in 1949; Paul followed in 1950 and Segal and her mother in 1951. With these moves, the family settled permanently in the city of New York.

The permanence and stability of finally settling in the United States contrast with Segal's moves from country to country and from one foster family to another. She calls the chapter about this time in her life "New York: My Own House," referring to the city as a residence in which she has come into her identity as a writer, a wife, and a mother. Arriving in New York, approximately thirty years old, she feels that this will be her home and that she can shed her desire to be English. Looking at Riverside Drive, she tells Paul, "Why it's pretty. It's as pretty as the Thames Embankment," positively associating her experiences in England with those in the United States.[59] It is in New York that Segal confidently moves from her profession as a textile designer to her identity as a writer.

She notes that the vibrant city life, which seems to evoke for her associations with memories of her past experiences, allows her to feel at home: "New York is as full of my past as of my old textile designs walking about its streets; . . . It is, I think, the way our histories become charged thus upon the air, the streets, the very houses of New York, that makes the alien into a citizen."[60] Establishing a family of her own, after so many of her family members died in the Holocaust or in exile, allows Segal to belong and develop feelings of home; she writes of her marriage to her Jewish-American husband, David: "And so we made ourselves a home."[61] In establishing a place of her own with which she identifies, Segal consolidates the various cultural experiences of her past, the multiple languages she speaks, and the traumatic experiences she has endured. The home becomes symbolic of a unified, albeit multi-faceted and rich identity, in part formed by Segal's confrontation with her tumultuous past through writing.

Although Segal's and Blend's childhood experiences in exile reveal similar themes, Blend's adulthood differs in that it is overshadowed by the loss of her parents in the Holocaust. Blend, whose Jewish parents had come to Austria from Poland, decided to integrate into Viennese society by not living in the Jewish Quarter.[62] Her father's sister and her husband fled to Palestine when anti-Semitism made Austria dangerous. This aunt wrote to Blend from Palestine five years after her exile to Britain, awakening her memories of childhood, which she calls "my other life," stating of the letter: "Here was the proof that the distant world of my childhood really existed! It was a small breach in the dyke of my isolation."[63] Blend's aunt would also later reveal her father's fate in the Holocaust to her.

Blend's childhood in Austria shaped her identity although she felt some uncertainty regarding her heritage. Her mother had told her "You are Viennese," whereupon Blend wondered: "Certainly I was born there and spoke the German language, but did this make me Viennese?"[64] She writes of experiencing "contradictory impressions" throughout her childhood about her national and religious identity.[65] Blend also finds it difficult to describe her mother, Paula. She writes, "I still carry a physical image of her in my mind, backed up by a photograph taken in 1939."[66] In hindsight she wishes her mother had told her more about her own childhood: "I wish fervently that she had told me about herself, her upbringing, her ideas. Of course I was very young and she could not have anticipated her death so soon, but with hindsight, if I were in that position, I would pour out all I knew to my child and not leave so much tantalizingly revealed."[67]

Like Blend's parents, her foster parents were Polish; her foster father had also come from Poland and married his émigré Polish wife in London. Both were able to speak German to Blend after her arrival in Britain, which eased her transition into the English culture. She recalls that when the radio played a Viennese waltz on the English radio she resisted any identification with Austria of the Third Reich: "These [songs] touched hidden springs of emotion, but I could not abandon myself to this Viennese *Schwärmerei*, for how can you allow yourself to feel nostalgic about a country that has so utterly rejected you?"[68] During her school years, Blend was torn regarding her identity. Children called her "the refugee" and "the evacuee" and, hearing her maiden name, Immerdauer, decided that she was a German spy.[69] Shedding her German accent, she never talks about her Austrian past or her real parents with her English school friends: "For me the past was like a cupboard on which I firmly turned the key."[70] Five years after her arrival in Britain, Blend realizes that she has become someone else: "On the surface, it was as though I had shed my Austrian language and personality as a snake sheds its skin and had grown a protective English covering."[71] Of her identity as a young college student she writes: "The 'I' who entered Queen Mary College was the sum of many horrific experiences and confusing sets of values, as well as the recipient of much that was kind, positive and enlightening."[72] As a young married woman she is ill at ease about her identity as a once-exiled child. She calls herself a "closet refugee" and writes that she had repressed her past "mainly because the subject had become taboo" for her.[73] Writing almost fifty years later, Blend is able to reassess the events of her past and make them part of her adult identity. Writing her memoir is a way of reclaiming her past as part of her present identity and of liberating her from a past history she had once felt was taboo.

For both Blend and Segal, identities are bound not only to the

Austrian national identity but also to the secular Jewish religious identity. Raised as assimilated Jews in Austria, both Segal and Blend come to question their religious identity as young girls in England. Upon her arrival in England as a child, adults asked Segal if she was an orthodox Jew. She replied, "yes," in order to please the adults present; yet later she asked her father in a letter for the definition of the word "orthodox."[74] Segal's mother advised her that she could decide whether to be Christian or Jewish once she left Austria, leaving her conflicted about her religious identity.[75] Blend writes that, although her parents were raised in orthodox Jewish homes, they themselves "adapted their religion to the exigencies of modern life" by integrating into secular Jewish Viennese life.[76] Blend, however, comments that her mother "drew the line at cooking pork or bacon" and that she celebrated major festivals such as Passover. Once in England, Blend's foster parents, who are Jewish, urge her to celebrate Jewish festivals. Torn between her Christian and Jewish friends, she realizes that her "strong sense of identification with the Jewish tradition" provides for a continuation of her upbringing in Austria.[77] At her grammar school the Jewish students are separated from the Christian students, leaving Blend to feel isolated from the majority of her classmates: "to adolescent minds the message that came across was that to be Jewish was to be second-class."[78] As a young adult Blend joins a Zionist Club in London, where she is able to be proud of her Jewish heritage. She writes: "It was exhilarating to hear about some achievements by Jewish people," adding, "Here at last was something positive, something to be proud of."[79] As an adult Blend, however, is cautious about making her religious values public due to her awareness of right-wing extremism in Europe and fear for the safety of her children.

As adults, both Blend and Segal define their identities through their experiences as survivors of the Kindertransport. At the urging of their husbands, both women return to Vienna – Blend in 1968 and Segal in 1973. However, neither Blend nor Segal feels at home in the city of her birth. In 1988 Blend and Segal are able to meet with other *Kinder* at Kindertransport reunions in New York and London, respectively, during which their feelings of childhood isolation and trauma are validated and acknowledged by survivors who have dealt with similar experiences. In her memoir Blend states that her unique experiences of being a child refugee led her to teach race relations as part of an English curriculum for twenty-five years and that she joined the Council of Christians and Jews to forge mutual tolerance between faith groups. At the conclusion of her memoir, Blend urges her readers to remain vigilant about and active in combating xenophobia, warning readers, "The lesson that needs to be learned from this period, which is now passing into history, is to tackle extremism before it gets too powerful, by all the civilized means at our disposal. . . . There is no room for complacency."[80] The impetus for Blend's memoir is to inform readers about the past, to encourage political awareness and community service, and to uphold the values of humanity and tolerance.

Segal also concludes her memoir with observations about how her life has shaped her political awareness. During the Cold War in the late 1960s, she identifies herself as an American Jew whose heritage as an exiled Austrian Jew causes her to reflect on the tenuous state of peace and security: "I keep looking around me: The war is still cold, and overseas no one of my people, this moment, is ill; every day there are hours when I can write, and we have our friends. My husband is Jewish too, but he was born in America and accepts without alarm this normal season of our lives; but I, now that I have children and am about the age my mother was when Hitler came, walk gingerly and in astonishment upon this island of my comforts, knowing that it is surrounded on all sides by calamity."[81] Segal's and Blend's memoirs are historical documents in a poetic voice, impacting readers and urging them to bring peace through individual actions to a future that is as uncertain as it ever was.

Other memoirs by Austrian women written in the postwar period relate experiences of exile, parent-child relationships, and loss shared with Segal and Blend. Helen Hilsenrad's 1966 memoir *Brown Was the Danube* details her experiences as a young Polish Jewish woman with Austrian citizenship, as a wife and mother in Vienna, and of her exile to the United States. Much of the memoir describes the author's young daughters escaping from Nazi persecution to England on two separate Kindertransport voyages. Hilsenrad describes her daughters' experiences from what she imagines to be their perspective in Vienna in 1938:

> The poor children had now begun to realize how serious our situation had become. First, they had been abruptly ejected from their schools; then they had been turned out of their beloved park; their parents had become tense and thin and altogether different, and now even food was no longer to be taken for granted. Yes, for Ingrid and Gerda the times were clearly spelled out now. They had been singled out, were despised, deprived, and belonged to two haunted-looking people. So it was with Jewish families.[82]

Once safe in England, the sisters are taken in by two non-Jewish families, acts of humanity that Hilsenrad interprets as "showing Jews that they still had friends on the face of the earth."[83] She describes how at home in Vienna "everything seemed empty and desolate" and how she and her husband, Jim, "ached to hear the voices of the children." Yet despite this, she says, "But we felt reassured even in our loss, because they were safe. Let anything happen to us now! They were entrusted to good and noble people, with whom they would be happy."[84] While the children are safely in England, the parents are able to secure passports to the United States. Their departure from Vienna, first by train, then by ship, is marked with both despair at leaving "millions of innocent humans" "to the mercy of Hitler" and with hope: "There was hope to be reunited with Ingrid and Gerda. There was hope of preserving our identities, of starting a new life, however difficult, in America, a place of genuine liberty."[85] The parents' survival in exile is overshadowed by their "inferiority complexes" since they "were now impoverished refugees, living off the charity of relatives."[86] Hilsenrad writes, "Here, in peace and relative security, as Jim and I began to untangle our emotions and catalogue them, we found the complexes implanted; we could not shed them."[87] In New York she is burdened by the contradictions plaguing her, knowing that her daughters are safe and feeling jealousy toward the foster mothers and "indeed of anyone who was forming serious relationships with them in England."⁸⁸ She questions these "contradictions": "But were they any less than human? Were they not, in fact, the forces of reason and love at odds with each other? . . . . The longer they were away, the more they had eluded me. . . . To offset my preoccupation with the children, I threw myself vigorously into my daily life, reasoning that each step forward that we made somehow brought the day of reunion closer."⁸⁹ Thus, the author and her husband take English lessons, and with these lessons and with Jim's new job, "the awful pain, the defeat which had marked him that last year in Vienna, vanished by degrees."⁹⁰ The loss of her children while they are in exile propels Hilsenrad's personal narrative to a climactic conclusion during which, finally, the parents and daughters are joyfully reunited. Hilsenrad recalls, "The five years of separation in which we had lived in terror of losing our children were over. They were here now, ours again. November 30, 1943, was, without a doubt, the happiest day of my life."⁹¹ Hilsenrad's memoir ends here, marking her children's return as a definitive memory that provides her life narrative with linearity and closure.

Hilsenrad's epilogue contrasts sharply with her conclusion, in which she recalls the joyous reunion with her children. The epilogue is a narrative of loss and mourning for those who were murdered in the Holocaust, as related to the author by two relatives who survived. In stark contrast to Hilsenrad's own survival and the reunion with her children is the "story" of her sister-in-law Sala, who died of typhoid fever in the Lwow ghetto, where she hallucinated that her "long absent son [Addie], was standing by her bed. Delirious, she imagined their reunion, clawing at the air to embrace him." Hilsenrad, understanding Sala's longing, writes, "Poor, yet lucky Sala! You didn't live long enough to know the fate of our beloved Addie."⁹² Hilsenrad knows that Addie was transported "to the slaughterhouse in Belzec" in December 1942. Thus, though Hilsenrad feels pity for her sister-in-law in desperate delirium, she understands that for a mother perhaps such delirium is better than the truth. Hilsenrad's narrative is held together by her descriptions of the parent-child symbiosis, a mark of love and humanity, one that gave her hope and was contrasted with inhumanity and hopelessness for millions of children and their parents.

Another memoir, written by the daughter of an Austrian *Kind* who survived the war in England as a child, provides a further perspective regarding Blend's and Segal's recollections. Becoming a voice for her mother, who made the journey on the Kindertransport from Vienna to England, Mona Golabek, along with co-author Lee Cohen, tells the story of her mother, Lisa Jura, who was fourteen years old when she escaped from Vienna. The 2002 memoir – as this "true story" is called in its title, *The Children of Willesden Lane: Beyond the Kindertransport: A Memoir of Music, Love, and Survival* – is a daughter's tribute to her mother. Golabek says of her mother's stories of her past as a child refugee in England, "Her stories were my folklore, . . ." The author bases her narrative on the factual information passed on to her by her mother as well as her own research into these events: "Most of the names you read on these pages are the real names of Lisa Jura's friends and family. . . . The facts and conversations that follow reflect my mother's recollections, although I realize that some of her stories were clouded by time. In the places where there were gaps in her memory, my present-day research has filled them in. The spirit of the story is all hers."[93] It is this "filling in" of the gaps of memory that is often taken over by the second and even third generation of war survivors. As the subtitle of the memoir indicates, music becomes the element that ties Lisa Jura to her Austrian heritage and to her family left behind in Vienna when she is sent to Britain by the Kindertransport. The memoir's beginning is set in pre-World War II Vienna, with its urban topography marked by iconic structures such as the Prater Ferris Wheel and its landscape of rolling hills and the Danube. Golabek traces her mother's family's persecution as the Nazis take over all walks of life and destroy her father's business as one of Vienna's most famous tailors. Just as Jura's father, Abraham, tells his family of the *Kristallnacht* – "You need to know what I saw!" – Golabek takes on the role of bearing witness to crimes against Austrian Jews.[94] Like many Austrian-Jewish citizens following the annexation of Austria, Jura's father was persecuted by the Nazis, forced to strip naked and to scrub the dirty pavement. Following *Kristallnacht* in November 1939, Jura's parents attempt to save their family. Because they were initially only able to acquire one passage on the Kindertransport, the parents send Jura, the youngest of the three sisters, to Britain. Because one daughter is eighteen, above the seventeen-year age limit for the Kindertransport *Kinder*, the parents must make the heart-wrenching decision to choose between their two youngest daughters. A musical prodigy at age fourteen, Jura is viewed as the stronger of the two and her parents feel she would have her music to guide her.[95] In fact, as she rides with other *Kinder* in the train, the number 158 around her neck, she tells another *Kind* that, once in London, she will play "the music my mother taught me, ... The great music of Vienna."[96] Jura spends the next six years living in a hostel on Willensden Lane in London with other displaced children. She receives a prestigious scholarship from the London Royal Academy of Music with which she keeps her promise to her mother to "hold on to [her] music."[97] Throughout the memoir, music recalls the bond with her mother and family and allows her to survive emotionally during the war years. Her younger sister Sonia also manages to escape Vienna on the last Kindertransport train and lives with a foster family in the British countryside, able to visit her sister in London for the first time in 1943. Letters from Jura's family in Austria stopped arriving during this time, and only occasional letters from exiled Austrian relatives arrived from "other places," such as Mexico.[98] By the end of the war, news from the Red Cross and other organizations reveal the tragic details of the Holocaust, and confirm the murders of most of the families of the *Kinder*. The memoir's epilogue explains that Jura's parents were arrested by the Gestapo on April 14, 1942, and were deported to Lodz, from which they were sent to Auschwitz to be murdered. After the war ends in May 1945, Jura's younger sister Sonia moves to London where the two sisters reunite with their older sister Rosie, who escaped from Austria to France, where she managed to hide from the Nazis with her husband and baby daughter. The three sisters immigrate to the United States beginning in 1949 and now live with their families in Los Angeles. The memoir recalls the culture of prewar Austria as experienced in exile, in culinary traditions brought to London, such as the baking of Sachertorten and Apfelstrudel, and in Jura's fantasies of playing piano for "Viennese royalty."[99] Music becomes a means for Jura to explore and work through her emotional turmoil of anger, grief, and loss.

Those emotions surge while giving a piano concert toward the end of her stay in London:

> She began her story with the pianissimo that recalled the quiet despair of the agonizing separation from her family these past six years. The music deepened into thunderous chords retelling the years spent defiantly warding off the Nazi attacks. . . . She relived her own joys and tragedies, her terrible journey to London, and her passage to adulthood. She mourned her lost parents in the tragic tolling of the bells of the Rachmaninoff prelude; then, from its majestic progression of chords, she built a hymn of gratitude – to her parents' love, to their wise devotion, and to every mother and father who had the courage to save their child by saying good-bye.[100]

By tracing her mother's life and coming of age in the memoir, Golabek assigns meaning to her mother's gift of music and legacy as a *Kind*. The legacy of her mother's musical talents and survival become that which guides Golabek and her sister to also become concert pianists and to identify with their role as the second generation of *Kinder* survivors. For Golabek, piano lessons with her mother were also "lessons in life," one in which the act of playing piano memorializes and reaffirms the lives of those family members murdered in war.[101]

Just as Golabek was compelled to tell the story of her mother's life, so filmmaker Melissa Hacker was brought to write, direct, and produce the 1995 documentary film *My Knees Were Jumping*, which traces the experiences of her mother, Ruth Morley, who survived the war by being sent from Vienna to England by the Kindertransport. Hacker's impetus for the piece was her search for her own memories of childhood, so inextricably linked to her mother's: "I was born in New York in 1961 but my earliest childhood memories are located in another time and place, the Europe of my mother's childhood: Austria in the Nazi years. Somehow my mother's childhood memories became my own."[102] Just as the author Golabek writes to identify with her mother's memories, so do filmmakers Deborah Oppenheimer and Hacker make their film documentaries to validate and honor the memories of their mothers. In their documentary film *Into the Arms of Strangers*, Mark Jonathan Harris and Oppenheimer examine the history and legacy of those *Kinder* sent to Britain by the Kindertransport through personal interviews, historical documents, and film footage. Oppenheimer, in the book which accompanies the film, writes of her mother, who never shared her childhood trauma with her children for fear of burdening them with her "vast and deep" grief, which her daughter had "absorbed": "There is a terrific irony to my search. If my mother had told her stories, I would have never felt the need for this quest. Now there's so much I want to talk to her about."[103] Harris and Oppenheimer examine the motivations for surviving *Kinder* to reunite for the fifty-year reunion of the Kindertransport and to take part in interviews for the documentary film, citing the survivors' desire "to reclaim their past, to celebrate their successes, and to communicate their stories to grandchildren and future generations."[104] The need of the *Kinder*, late in their lives, to revisit their past allowed them to "make sense of their refugee experience and to integrate their past and present in an effort to construct a meaningful narrative of their lives."[105] Additionally, giving testimony allowed many of the *Kinder* to "see themselves and their histories in a new perspective."[106]

Whether writing as an act of remembrance in the form of a memoir or by giving testimony in the context of a documentary film, the *Kinder* who escaped Austria and survived in exile tell a story that contributes to Austria's multifaceted history beyond its national borders. One *Kind* writes of his role as a "repository of memory" and concludes: "with the years, the memories have not faded; they have grown stronger. We child survivors are but a small fragment of the first generation, finally finding a voice. . . ."[107] By telling the little-known history of exiled Austrian Jews, the Austrian *Kinder* Blend and Segal; the mother of *Kinder*, Hilsenrad; and the daughters of *Kinder*, Hacker, Golabek, and Oppenheimer provide an additional dimension to Austria's history during World War II, one that took place outside of Austria's geographic and national borders yet is firmly rooted in Austria's history and culture.

Chapter Six

"A Lost World": Imagination and Identity in the Memoirs of Exiled Austrian Jewish Women in Shanghai during World War II

History is not something to be read about in books. It is our reality, our life.

– Vivian Jeanette Kaplan[1]

Like those children able to escape Nazi persecution through the Kindertransport to England, other Austrian-Jewish survivors were able to flee with their families by train and ship to China. The unique experiences of the approximately 17,000 Shanghailanders, German-speaking Jewish refugees surviving in Shanghai during World War II, is documented selectively in history books, in a limited number of published memoirs, in unpublished autobiographies housed in archives, and in documentary films, such as *The Port of Last Resort* (1998) and *Shanghai Ghetto* (2002).[2] *The Port of Last Resort,* by directors Joan Grossman and Paul Rosdy, for instance, underscores the fragmented and disjointed history of this community by portraying the "remnants of this exile" found "in rare home movies, newsreels, secret documents, relief reports, and private and published writings by refugees."[3] The documentary also cites the experiences of German-speaking survivors, such as the couple Illo and Ernest Heppner, who survived the war in Shanghai and who documented their experiences in memoirs.[4] Oral histories are presented chronologically and thematically within a visual collage of home movie clips, photograph stills, and historical documents, such as passports, maps, and newspaper clippings. As does the film, memoirs and novels about the Austrian Jewish experience in Shanghai reveal a similar fragmented representation of history, symbolic of the dispersal of refugees around the world, in which authors reconstruct their scattered memories within the larger representation of history.⁵ In the more recent *Shanghai Ghetto*, directors Dana Janklowicz-Mann and Amir Mann explore the lives of Jewish refugees in Shanghai through interviews with survivors and historians, letters, stock footage, still photos, and footage shot in Shanghai in 2000 at the site of the Jewish ghetto, unchanged since World War II.⁶

The imagined lives of Europeans exiled in Shanghai in the 1930s are also portrayed in a small number of feature films, such as Josef von Sternberg's *Shanghai Express* (1932), starring Marlene Dietrich; Orson Welles' *The Lady from Shanghai* (1948); and James Ivory's *The White Countess* (2005), as well as in postwar novels, such as Vicki Baum's *Shanghai '37* from 1940.⁷ Franziska Tausig, in her memoir from 1987, *Shanghai Passage: Emigration ins Ghetto* (Shanghai Passage: Emigration to the Ghetto), describes this community of refugees in Shanghai as "a lost world," "like that of the old Austro-Hungarian or Jewish cities and towns in Eastern Europe," a world that is only "kept alive" through "the stories of people who experienced and created it."⁸ For Tausig and other authors whose memoirs capture their experiences of surviving World War II in Shanghai, the testimonies recreate this unique exile community and underscore its relevance for a broader, more inclusive Austrian history that embraces those Austrian citizens living outside of the geographic and national borders of Austria.⁹

A brief overview of this exile community provides a context for the lives of Austrian women who lived in this community and who share their perspective on this history in memoirs. Between 1938 and 1941, approximately 18,000 Jews, mostly from Central Europe, and including 17,000 Austrians and Germans, fled Nazi persecution to Shanghai.¹⁰ Even though Japan banned Jewish immigration after August 1939, German-speaking Jews managed to reach China over the next few years.¹¹ The largest wave of immigration came immediately following the Anschluss, after which Austrian and German Jews fled in large numbers. Due to the fact that most consulates in Germany refused to give out visas after 1938 and because the quota numbers of countries to which refugees were fleeing were limited – most waited one or two years before getting out – word spread of the opportunity to escape to

Shanghai, the one place on earth where no passports or visas were needed.¹² One of the reasons visas were not needed and passports were not checked in Shanghai is that the Japanese, who had invaded China in 1937, controlled Shanghai's harbor, the world's seventh largest port at the time. The Japanese gave Jews entry despite their "diplomatic ties" to Germany and Italy, which would have led them to reject Jews, because they believed in "racial equality" and, more importantly, because they needed the foreign capital from the United States, which they did not want to alienate.¹³ The United States, by contrast, made it virtually impossible for Jews to enter, as President Hoover, during the Depression, had "revived the stringent adherence to the 'public charge' provision," which meant that in order to be allowed to enter the United States, refugees needed to complete a great deal of paperwork and were additionally required to show records of military service, two certified copies of birth certificates, and two copies of all other available records.¹⁴ Many American consulates required the complete dossier, which was impossible to provide for those who had returned from labor camps or had been forced out of their homes into ghettos.¹⁵ For most of the Austrian Jewish refugees then, escape to China meant giving up their savings for safe passage on an 8000-mile, four-week cruise leaving, typically, from Italy, traveling by way of Egypt, Yemen, and India, docking finally in Shanghai.¹⁶

There were already two established Jewish communities in Shanghai before the refugees arrived. The first group consisted of the Baghdadi Jews, or Sephardim, who had come to Shanghai in the late nineteenth century and were, as British subjects, able to trade with Britain, and the second of Russian Jews, the Ashkenazim, who had fled the Bolshevik Revolution in 1917.¹⁷ Two prominent families, the Sasoons and Kadoories, aided the German-speaking Jewish refugees with housing and education. In the late 1930s, Shanghai had approximately four and a half million inhabitants, 50,000 of whom were Europeans, 5,000 of whom were non-Jewish Austrians and Germans, most of whom lived in the International Settlement or the French Concession.¹⁸ The arrival of 17,000 German-speaking Jewish refugees from Central Europe and a further 1,000 from Poland and other Eastern European countries added to the international flavor of the city by infusing it with European cultural and culinary traditions, as evidenced in the ensuing boom of bars, cafés, restaurants, cabarets, and a multitude of diverse businesses and trades. The influx of refugees, however, also strained the resources and aid provided by prominent Jewish families who had formed an aid organization in 1938 called the Committee for Assistance of European Jewish Refugees in Shanghai. To meet the growing demand for aid, they required further funding from the Joint Distribution Committee in New York. By 1939, half of the refugee population was dependent on financial aid for food and housing; for most, as is made evident in memoirs, their exile in Shanghai represented years of great poverty, disease, and desperation.[19]

Common experiences shared by the German-speaking community in Shanghai bound together this desperate group of refugees. Their Jewish faith and traditions, maintaining relationships with family and friends, and the building of community through education, employment, and the arts forged bonds between individuals and families of varied educational and class backgrounds. Due to the unique experiences of persecution, exile, and war, the identities of both female and male refugees were redefined beyond country of origin and socio-economic background. Instead of being divided by having been born in either Austria or Germany, the refugees' common German-speaking Jewish heritage and European customs allowed them to sympathize and identify with one another. Experiences shared by the refugees included the will to survive, the rediscovery of humanity in themselves and in others, and the goal after the war for a few to return home and for most to reach a new homeland, such as Australia, Canada, Israel, or the United States. Memoirs by Austrian and German women exiles reveal additional shared experiences, such as issues regarding physical and mental health, maintaining households with limited means, caring for ailing family members, and employment outside of the home in order to survive.

Two Austrian memoirs in particular, Franziska Tausig's *Shanghai Passage: Emigration ins Ghetto*, first published in 1987 and republished in 2007, and Vivian Jeanette Kaplan's 2002 memoir of her mother Gerda Kosiner, *Ten Green Bottles: The True Story of One*

Family's Journey from War-Torn Austria to the Ghettos of Shanghai, trace the daily lives of Austrian-Jewish women refugees in China. Tausig wrote her memoir more than forty years following her return to Austria from exile in China as a testimony to those who lived in the "lost world" of Shanghai. Kaplan wrote her memoir "in the creative non-fiction genre," in the voice of her mother, Gerda "Nini" Kosiner, née Karpel. Kosiner had fled Vienna to Shanghai, where she married and gave birth to her daughter, Vivian Kaplan. When Kaplan was two years old, her parents immigrated to Canada and settled in Toronto.[20] Kaplan validates the authenticity of the memoir by stating, "the events are as true and accurate as I can make them" and by calling it a "personal account, filled with vignettes told to me throughout my lifetime."[21] She adds, "I am so intimately aware of the facts of this life that it seems almost as if I had experienced it myself."[22] Kaplan, who was born in Shanghai, writes that her mother tongue and cultural heritage are German, "or more precisely, Viennese."[23] She attributes the writing of the memoir to her mother, "who struggled to retrieve memories, distant and painful," to aid in her "understanding of her most guarded emotions."[24] Kaplan, like many second-generation survivors, writes the memoir in an effort to reconstruct her mother's story, which is integral to her own identity.

Other German-language memoirs, supplemental documents, historical novels, and documentary films provide an intertextual context for Tausig and Kaplan's portrayal of Austrian-Jewish women's life in Shanghai. One such memoir that underscores the experiences of German-speaking women in exile in Shanghai, Ursula Bacon's 2002 *Shanghai Diary: A Young Girl's Journey from Hitler's Hate to War-Torn China*, details the life of a German Jewish woman surviving in exile. Although she is of German heritage, not Austrian, Bacon's experiences in Shanghai intersect with and expand upon those of the Austrian-Jewish women Tausig and Kosiner, Kaplan's mother, at many points. Like other victims of war who were unable to voice their traumatic experiences until decades later, Bacon wrote her memoir more than sixty years following her escape from Nazi Germany. She explains, "There must be a reason why it took me so long to write this story. Perhaps I thought no one would want to read it, but I changed my mind."²⁵ She goes on to clarify her authorial intent by implicating the reader: "I am not writing a book, I'm telling a story. I'm glad you're listening. Once I started the process, I couldn't stop. My subconscious mind, the storehouse of my being, prodded me with pictures and events of the past. It's all here. I remember."²⁶ At the conclusion of her memoir she notes, "I didn't exactly let go of the past, though, but at least I stored it for safekeeping far away at the very edge of my memory. One day I would come for it, take it out of storage, examine it, talk about it. And when I'd done that, then I'd toss it into the winds. The past made me what I was and what I would become."²⁷ For Bacon, the process of storytelling becomes an affirming means of coping with war trauma.²⁸

Tausig, Kosiner through her daughter Kaplan, and Bacon work through the trauma of persecution, exile, and war in their memoirs while describing firsthand their escape from the Third Reich and their new lives as refugees in Shanghai. Although each memoir is narrated in an individual voice telling a unique story of escape from Nazi persecution and exile, the authors describe common themes, such as bonds to their Austrian or German homeland, the sustained anguish of being forced to leave behind everything and everyone they had known and cherished, and their daily lives as women refugees in Shanghai.

Kosiner, her story told by her daughter Kaplan, identifies with her Austrian homeland; her name Gerda and her nickname "Nini" connect her "firmly" to her Austrian heritage.²⁹ For Kosiner and her family, Austria represents freedom, family, home, and national pride. Kosiner recalls that her father was "a patriotic Austrian" who often reminded his wife and three children of "their duty to the beloved country" and urged them to cherish their "native land."³⁰ After her father's sudden death when Kosiner was only six years old, she knew that he had left his family his "most precious gift," their "Austrian homeland."³¹ Kosiner's narrative is not only tied to her Austrian homeland but also firmly rooted in her Austrian-Jewish identity. Interwoven in her depiction of her life as typically Austrian are descriptions of her family's daily life as integrated Jews of Vienna. She cites, for example, their family traditions connected with Jewish rites, their visits to the synagogue on High Holy Days, and Yiddish lullabies sung by her mother. For

Kosiner, being Austrian and Jewish are not antithetical but represent a symbiotic Austrian-Jewish identity, positing a counter-narrative that resists the Austro-Fascist narrative in which Austrian Jews were not considered Austrian but rather a foreign and dangerous "other" that needed to be expelled and destroyed. Kosiner anticipates her family's escape to China by juxtaposing her home in urban Vienna with other cities and continents learned about in school, the "exotic," "mysterious and dangerous," "dark and ominous" "primitive foreign lands" of Asia to which she will be exiled.[32] She recalls thinking: "In my real world, in Vienna, we feel secure and safe in a very predictable place where all the people are the same."[33] Kosiner's recollections of her childhood before the Anschluss romanticize Vienna; she gushes, "How proud we are to be Austrians, in the cultural centre of the world."[34] Despite the looming threat of Hitler and rising anti-Semitism, Kosiner explains her youthful optimism at the time: "In the end, what are we but Viennese? For me, there is no other way of life and this, I believe, will always be my homeland, so there is no choice but to live every day to the limit and to revel in all that a youthful spirit can attain."[35] When, at age twenty, Kosiner meets her future husband, the Polish Jew Leopold, or "Poldi," who has fled Poland to Vienna, she foreshadows her own displacement, describing the fate of Poldi's parents, who planned to follow him to Austria: "They will be displaced, with no landed status, strangers to a foreign place and new language."[36] After Poldi's parents arrive in Vienna, Kosiner is invited to a Passover Seder in a kosher home, which is significant for the shaping of her Jewish identity. She recalls, "It is especially significant to me because our family has lost touch with religious traditions. Mama and Papa were secular, modern and assimilated, considering themselves Austrians first, Jews second, a sentiment that is currently popular in Vienna and the way that I have felt myself."[37] Despite their families' different expressions of their Jewish faith, Kosiner and Poldi are drawn to one another.

Recalling life in Vienna and contemplating the impending forced exile, Kosiner's story is couched in the narrative of the "wandering Jew": she states, "the ancient Jews, my people, my ancestors, penniless and destitute, were driven on by willpower and faith."[38] Within this narrative, her life unfolds, takes shape, and gains meaning in the context of a larger narrative and history of Jewish persecution, pogroms, and exile. Following the Anschluss, Kosiner, once having considered herself an Austrian citizen, remarks, "The majority of Austrian citizens greet the news with jubilation," and concedes to feeling a devastating loss of identity, stating, "We are only Jews now, nothing more; our identities as Austrians have evaporated."[39] The Anschluss is followed by the horrors of *Kristallnacht,* during which countless Jews are arrested, savagely beaten or murdered, and synagogues and Jewish businesses are destroyed. Kosiner co-opts readers through the cries of a victim who pleads with her friends: "Listen to me, I saw it with my own eyes. Listen to me!"[40] Realizing that their lives were in grave danger, Kosiner made arrangements for her family to escape persecution in 1939 via ship passage from Trieste, Italy, to Shanghai aboard the *Conte Biancamano.* After narrowly escaping arrest in Austria, her family's passage to China is peaceful but, as Kosiner describes, is overshadowed by the reality of their forced exile. She recalls the voyage as "the most peace and normalcy we have had for some time. . . . We are stateless refugees aboard a ship to a strange land."[41] She associates her plight with that of other refugees she had "seen so often trudging into Vienna"[42] and mourns the loss of her homeland, once having been "confident that the Austrian homeland would always protect" her.[43] Like many refugees about to arrive in Shanghai, Kosiner's journey by ship would offer her short-lived comfort and the hope for a "safe haven ahead."[44]

Like Kosiner, Tausig roots her three-part memoir of forced exile in her Austrian identity. In the first part, Tausig traces her childhood memories of Austria-Hungary and her coming of age and early years of marriage in Vienna. Tausig was born in 1895 to parents who were assimilated Austrian Jews living in Vienna. Tausig's mother periodically returned to her hometown of Temesvar, part of Hungary until 1918, where family members who were doctors assisted her with the births of her children. It is during a holiday in Temesvar that Tausig, eighteen years old, meets her future husband, a lawyer. They marry one month before the outbreak of World War I and have to cut short their honeymoon to Belgium and England. After their hastened return to Temesvar, and after only two days in their apartment, Tausig's husband is forced to leave for war with his Austro-Hungarian army cadre. A soldier for four years, Tausig's husband is badly wounded during the last year of war. Tausig travels from one hospital to the next to be by his side during his treatments, especially for his hearing impairment. When her husband's home falls to Romania in 1918, he is no longer able to practice his law profession since Hungarian and Romanian language, laws, and cultures differed. Tausig describes this first loss of homeland as one after which they had to build up their lives again: "His homeland didn't exist anymore. The part of Hungary had fallen to Romania, a country, whose language and laws were totally foreign to him. So he couldn't practice his career anymore. My father had a big business and hired him as an employee.... We had to start all over again. My husband had a new career. In 1922 I had a son, a true Viennese. We lived a working and successful life in Vienna for twenty years."[45] Tausig ties her husband's experience of loss of homeland during the fall of the Austro-Hungarian Empire to their expulsion from their homeland Austria under Nazi domination. This narrative of the earlier loss of homeland sets the tone for their later forced exile under the Nazi regime. Tausig's strong bond to her Austrian homeland, which becomes more marked during her exile, nonetheless does not deter her from taking action to save her son and family from persecution by fleeing Austria.

The second part of her memoir, "1938 und seine Folgen" (1938 and its consequences), underscores Tausig's feelings of renewed forced homelessness following the Anschluss and the consequent persecution of Jews, of which she writes, "After twenty years we were once again uprooted with stump and stem."[46] Tausig inscribes herself into the narrative of twentieth-century forced migrations during and following the two world wars as well as the geo-political battles for the expansion of nation states. She does not reveal her Jewish faith until the second part of her memoir, in which she notes that her son was expelled from his secondary school in Vienna not because of bad behavior or poor grades but rather because his "religious affiliation was considered unacceptable in the eyes of the new rulers."[47] Tausig manages to secure a last-minute passage for her son on a Kindertransport to

England; tragically, it would be the last time Tausig's husband would see his son. The Nazis forcibly removed her father's business and savings, and Tausig had to work in order to support her husband and extended family. For a short while before their flight to China, Tausig supported her family by keeping house for Jewish families who had been forced to let go their Aryan housekeepers. The Nazis arrested Tausig's husband, but she managed to free him by using a false travel document "proving" that they were planning to leave Austria. After the Nazis took their apartment and its belongings, Tausig was able to purchase two tickets on the steamship *Usaramo* to Shanghai with the money they had earned from selling the rest of their belongings together with her parents' last savings. The two tickets were only available because their previous owners had committed suicide a day earlier. It is at this juncture in her recollections that Tausig marks the farewell from her parents as their last meeting; she would discover after the war ended that her parents were deported to the gas chambers of Theresienstadt and her siblings murdered in Yugoslavia. Tausig and her husband fled to Hamburg by train, where they were invited to spend the night in the safety of a stranger's apartment. Tausig, who dubs the stranger the "star of Bethlehem," memorializes the woman's deed in her memoir: "It would be worth setting up a memorial for her. A pot of hot tea, when you are freezing, a bed, in which you can sleep in, your clothes that dry next to the stove; that can give you the courage to survive. She was much older than us and probably is not alive anymore, and I want to lay a wreath for her here."[48] For those forced to flee their homeland by ship, the passage was spent writing letters, knitting, taking English courses, and gossiping, all the while avoiding thoughts of home.[49] The Tausigs' son's letter to them from England, sent to the ship, mourned "the lost homeland, the longing for the lost home."[50] Her husband's depression and related health issues worsened; he wore sunglasses all the time, from behind which he wept for the loss of his only son.

Bacon's family's flight to China is as harrowing as those of Kosiner's and Tausig's families. While still living in Germany, Bacon's father begged of her to "try to forget this day, this night," during which he was arrested and tortured by the Nazis.[51] Bacon's memoir defies her father's wish that she suppress these traumatic events by recalling the experience in the voice of an eleven year old: "I don't want to remember getting my father out of the Gestapo prison. I'm petrified that just thinking about it could bring it all back. But we made it; we did!"[52] As an adult, Bacon chose to recount her father's arrest and release in detail, more than sixty years after she, as a child, wished never again to recall this event. In order to free Bacon's father from the Gestapo by proving that the family would leave Germany, Bacon's uncle Erich hastily bought the family tickets aboard the German ship *Gneisenau*, which, seven days after the purchase, they were to board in Genoa, Italy. En route to the ship by train, at the Brenner Pass, she and her mother individually were forced to endure traumatic body searches by a female Nazi officer – something she never revealed to her parents but only to her readers, also sixty years after the fact. Bacon's own ship voyage was marked by the gift of three blank diaries, the later contents of which she refers to in order to write her memoir. Her family escaped from Germany to Genoa and on to Shanghai with 456 other Jewish refugees.[53]

Other refugees, like Illo Heppner, interviewed in the documentary film *Shanghai Ghetto*, came to Shanghai not by ship like Kosiner, Tausig, and Bacon but by rail through Siberia – a grueling trip that lasted more than four weeks.[54] For most refugees, arrival in Shanghai proved a stark contrast to their previous experiences of living in Europe and to their ship voyages, during which they enjoyed modest comforts, plentiful food, clean water, and warm beds; a former refugee interviewed for *Shanghai Ghetto* described the arrival in China as "a shock of a lifetime; it was a whole other world."[55] This "shock" was both the culture shock coming from a Western European culture to a non-Western, developing Eastern culture and also a reaction to the stark poverty and destitution most Jewish refugees would experience while in China. Tausig, for example, in the third part of her memoir, entitled "Die Jahre in Shanghai" (The years in Shanghai), describes her exile as nine "bitter years in Shanghai."[56] She writes, "They were like a goblet filled to the rim with a horrific fate that I had to drink to the last drop."[57] For most refugees, the years of exile would be fraught with financial, personal, and emotional hardship.

After being met at the dock, refugees were taken by truck to refugee shelters or *Heime* (homes) created by the Committee for Assistance. The *Heime* were located in the bombed-out section of the Hongkew Ghetto, called a "ghetto" because impoverished Chinese citizens and stateless refugees were forced to share these densely populated slums controlled and occupied by the Japanese. By the end of 1939, about 2,500 people lived in *Heime*, "sleeping anywhere from six to 150 to a room. And an additional 4,500 individuals ate in soup kitchens set up in the *Heime* but lived elsewhere in rented rooms."[58] The six refugee camps were the "last resort" for those refugees who, for the most part, had no funds whatsoever. Former refugee Farb, interviewed in the documentary film *The Port of Last Resort*, describes the common reaction to this situation of "difficulties," such as the "dread of spreading diseases," his feelings of "despair," and his "complete breakdown."[59] Multiple families shared cramped quarters and had no privacy. Typically, there was one washbasin for eight to ten people, and the toilet facilities were buckets that were emptied and collected by Chinese workers each morning. The food was "monotonous," consisting mostly of soups and bread, and the water smelled of the chemicals used to purify it. After 1940 serving dinner was dropped, and after the bombing of Pearl Harbor only one meal, a vegetable meat stew and hot tea, was served each day.[60] Many refugees, once they had found work and had saved a little money, moved in with other families in and outside of Hongkew, sharing one apartment or house with multiple families. Again, flushable toilets were very rare, and hot water for tea, cooking food, or personal hygiene had to be bought from a vendor in the street. The cooking of bought or scavenged food was done on little clay stoves. Dysentery and stomach ailments were very common and often fatal. Memoirs emphasize that family members and friends had to collaborate and compromise in order to survive.

Survival depended largely on finding employment, which was therefore significant for an individual's physical and mental well-being during exile. For those professionals who had held established careers in Europe, it was often impossible to practice in Shanghai. Professions practiced by male refugees included those of artisans, bakers, butchers, plumbers, teachers, lawyers, physicians, artists, barbers, engineers, and clerks.[61] Of the many physicians who came to Shanghai as refugees, only twenty percent were able to practice professionally.

In their memoirs, women write of having gained life and work experience as well as independence while refugees. Whereas many women had previously not worked outside the home, to support their families they now washed clothing, knit shawls, or made hats.[62] Most girls and women had to work outside of the home in order to survive.

Kosiner, for example, worked at first as a hostess in a "posh nightclub;" her German and English skills enabled her to gain this position among the well-heeled European residents of Shanghai.[63] Kosiner writes of her sense of pride at being able to work to help her family survive: "I smile. Against innumerable odds, I have earned a reasonable day's wage and carved a safe corner for myself in this unbelievable spot on the globe."[64] Later, Kosiner and her husband, Poldi, managed a bar together. Kosiner's family worked wherever they were able to find employment. Her sister Stella, for example, worked in a gift shop, whereas her other sister taught needlework in a convent. Other young girls and women, like Illo Heppner, worked as nannies for children living in the foreign community.[65] In his research on the Jewish refugees of Shanghai, James Ross describes the limited opportunities for refugees to find employment. About women refugees in particular, he states, "There were even fewer opportunities for women. Some women found jobs in workshops or did piecework at home. Housework rarely paid more than $6 a month, whereas nurses, cooks, and dressmakers could make as much as the equivalent of $8 a month."[66] Such a salary could hardly sustain a family; for example, during this period of time in Shanghai, one loaf of bread cost $2.50 and one egg more than $1.[67]

In a further example of employment opportunities for women refugees, Tausig was immediately hired to bake Austrian cakes and tarts at a local hotel. In order to be employed, however, she first had to bake a perfect and quintessentially Austrian *Apfelstrudel* (apple strudel). She writes that she never again baked such a perfect *Apfelstrudel* and that, years later, the hotel's Chinese cook could bake an even better one.[68] Following a series of jobs baking and cooking Austrian dishes for Austrian clientele, she and her husband were hired to run a bakery and pastry shop, dubbed by patrons as the "Demel of Shanghai" and frequented by Viennese immigrants who considered the shop a "piece of their homeland."[69]

Some women refugees, faced with the abject poverty of exile, were forced into prostitution. Kaplan's memoir of her mother Kosiner's experiences, illustrates the grim reality of prostitution for young women in Shanghai. Referring to the experiences of Kosiner's mother's acquaintance Herta, who had "descended into prostitution," Kaplan illustrates how women and female refugees are victimized in situations of war.[70] She explains, "Poverty, hunger, and fear have forced many to make a living in this way."[71] She also writes about the young Chinese prostitutes who are victimized by the Japanese occupiers: "Like the ammunition and machinery, they will be used up and discarded as a necessary sacrifice to the war. These are some of the many casualties that will never appear in the lists of wounded or dead."[72] Kosiner is nonetheless understanding of Herta's situation: "I can understand Herta's choice, although I am concerned about her path. I am aware of the violent beatings that prostitutes are known to endure and the exposure to venereal diseases that have already debilitated and killed many. Still, I understand."[73] She realizes that survival depends on circumstance as well: "Herta has no family, and that has made the difference between her and me. Without the support of a husband or any relatives, she has had to rely only on herself, and who can blame her for that? For us it is different, we have one another. . . . We have escaped as a unit."[74] Later, during the bombing of Hongkew, Herta is described as helping the wounded, a sign for the narrator that she "still feels part of the community," despite having to rely only on herself.[75]

Tausig, in her memoir, focuses less on the prostitution of women refugees than on the fate of the Chinese girls who are forced into the sex trade in order to support their families. Tausig describes their circumstance as a "horrible tragedy" and the victimized girls as the "unhappiest creatures on this earth."[76] Tausig recalls befriending a prostitute whom she names "Nefertiti" after the beautiful Egyptian queen. The young girl of approximately seventeen was prostituted daily in the market square in order to support her impoverished family. Tausig notes that Nefertiti was the only person to visit and console her after her husband's death. She ends the portrait of the young woman by recounting the story of Nefertiti's death by drowning herself in the ocean, having scrubbed herself clean with soap and wearing a crown of tuberoses in her hair. Tausig explains her fantastical memory of Nefertiti as one of many memories that after many years seem surreal:

> Those are comparisons that one typically evaluates as exaggerated. But the longer our life takes, the more unreal it appears to us. The smaller the piece of our life-bread becomes, the tinier life becomes and the number of memories grows. Many of us live just from our memories. And they don't become dull from wear. On the contrary, the more one wears them out, the more glittery and sparkling they become.[77]

Tausig's creative recollection of her friendship with Nefertiti reveals the emotional response to the kinship she shared with this young girl who, like Tausig, had become a victim of terrible circumstances in war. In their memoirs, both Kaplan and Tausig confront the vulnerability of girls and women in war; their own ordeals of survival are pitted against even grimmer tales of prostitution and victimization.

For girls and young women exiled in Shanghai, education, like employment opportunities, were limited. Education gave children and young adults a sense of continuity and gave refugees hope for survival. Schools for refugee children ended at age 14, although there were professional and business schools that offered further instruction. Many adults took English classes since they needed this language skill to work and trade in Shanghai. Refugee children who could not afford tuition were educated at some of the local schools funded by the Kadoorie family. Select *Heime* offered vocational training for several hundred youths – such instruction enabled these refugees, who had grown up in Shanghai, to continue their education and embark on careers in their next countries of exile.[78] A workshop at the Kinchow camp, for example, enabled approximately 60 girls to make knitted goods, which were sold in local shops.[79] The historian Ross notes that, at the Shanghai Jewish Youth Association School, girls learned to cook in a modern kitchen.[80] Bacon received, along with fifteen other Jewish girls, free tuition at the French convent Order of Sacre Coeur, where she learned French, English, and the catechism; she writes that she became a "Jewish girl with Lutheran ancestors and Catholic manners."[81]

Beyond their education and employment, women often had to take on the additional role of caretaker for all family members. Some girls and young women exiled to China with their parents often found their roles reversed when parents were unable to work due to illness or depression. Illo Heppner wrote, for example, that her mother had been "afraid to go out" and that much later she realized that her mother had been clinically depressed.[82] When Heppner's mother died of dysentery, she had to run the household and take care of her now despondent father.[83] In her memoir she explains her transformation: "Overnight, I became a homemaker, not only having to deal with my grief and loss but also learning how to make meals from whatever was available."[84]

Like Heppner's mother, Kosiner's mother also succumbed to disease, a tragic turn of events that changed Kosiner from a hopeful to a desolate young woman. She describes her mother's death as the loss of her identification with her Austrian homeland and a break with her happy childhood memories:

> Mama's death has a profound effect on me. I am desperately lonely despite all the others who are still here, even Poldi. Mama meant home to me, my Viennese youth and nostalgic longings. As long as she was alive, there existed a bit, just the smallest remnant of the old way of life, a tie to the Sunday teas, the aunties and uncles and especially the connection to Papa. Although I knew that those memories were gone forever, I find this a cruel finality that is hard to bear. The loss of Mama now, so far from home, destroys my courage and strength.[85]

Like Kosiner, Bacon also recalls having to care for her parents as a young woman. She recalls, "I had a feeling I would have to do a lot of taking care of my parents,"[86] and she "wondered what a kid" could do to help support her family.[87] Throughout her memoir, Bacon takes on the voice of her teenage self by commenting on generational conflicts and typical experiences of coming of age, saying things such as, "Grownups! I don't always understand them" and "Grownups: they can be most irritating at times."[88] Shanghai is the place where Bacon comes of age, develops her talents through education and employment, builds friendships, and meets her husband. She learns of sexuality by going to work with her father, who painted and decorated nightclubs and bordellos in his newly established business, the China Art Painting and Decorating Company.[89] Her childhood imagination becomes a mental refuge where she recovers from her life as an exile and escapes from the despair around her: "Not a night passed without my calling up the pictures I carried with me in my mind."[90] She further recalls her ability to surpress her plight and detach herself from her current life in order to survive her ordeal:

> Ever since my very first day in Shanghai, I never lost the odd sensation of living a dream-like experience – that I was just a casual visitor, a sort of uninvolved observer to my life in China. My past lay in Europe, my future in America, and the present was merely the passage that led from yesterday to tomorrow. I kept myself somewhat detached from my surroundings – not looking for roots in China soil. I had places to go – faraway places. That feeling never left me.[91]

Bacon assesses her atypical coming of age in exile: "We didn't know how to behave like carefree teenagers. The demands life made on us robbed us of those young and carefree years, and we acted just like all the adults around us — worried, fearful, and concerned with daily events and a veiled, uncertain future. … We grew up with grownups; we grew up old, and whether we liked it or not, we learned from them."[92] She laments the loss of her childhood during war: "My childhood had ended abruptly. I skipped a whole set of classes, and graduated into adulthood – almost overnight."[93] In one example of an event that robbed her of "those young and carefree years,"[94] Bacon reports that a Japanese soldier attempted to rape her in the Ghetto one night. She writes that, having taken Jujitsu classes, she struck him in the throat and killed him, returned home, and did not tell anyone what had happened to her. Recalling what she felt at the time, she writes of the traumatic attack: "Maybe I would be able to sort it out later... Maybe I would not remember ... maybe ... never?"[95] Sixty years later, she nonetheless writes of the attack in her memoir. For Bacon, the act of writing a memoir draws upon memories yet leaves the trauma "unsorted." In order to protect herself, she chooses to never again revisit these events: "Finally, it became a dark memory that moved into the deep recesses of my soul. May it rest in peace."[96]

Beside being threatened by physical violence, women and men exiled in Shanghai experienced physical, often fatal illness and disease, mental illness caused by stress, grief, and prolonged suffering, and limited resources with which to cope with these health problems. Especially for girls and women, issues of reproductive and sexual health played an important role in their overall well-being and survival. Married women and women in relationships had to consider the consequences of reproduction. Illo Heppner, for example, comments on the situation facing many young women in exile in Shanghai: "But now I found myself with a new problem: birth control. That was *the* major concern for a married [woman]. Not only was the survival rate of babies very low, but also the odds of raising a healthy child were dismal under our living conditions. Looking back at the birth control options that were available to us, we were very lucky."[97] Many women who had no access to birth control and got pregnant under these dire circumstances of disease and abject poverty felt their only option was to have an abortion.[98] Kosiner gave birth to her daughter, Kaplan, only to have her almost die of typhoid fever, from which she was cured with the then experimental drug penicillin. For Kosiner, the birth of her daughter signified "salvation . . . from dark thoughts and melancholy" brought on by the news of the

Holocaust and its six million Jewish victims, including most of her family.[99]

Cultural and religious life enabled refugees to identify with their former urban lives as well as to distract themselves from mourning their murdered families and friends; their loss of homeland, residence, and personal possessions; their lack of suitable employment; their fear of disease; and their hunger. Shanghai boasted German and Yiddish theater productions, ballet productions, and cabaret evenings as well as poetry published in German and Yiddish in the local newspapers *Die Gelbe Post* and the *Shanghai Jewish Chronicle*.[100] The Hongkew Ghetto alone offered 52 Jewish newspapers, a tribute to its rich cultural life.[101] One cabaret revue was called *Morgen ist's besser* (It'll be better tomorrow), its title signaling the hope for a brighter future for most refugees.[102] An operetta at the Jewish Club included a piece about a dentist and his wife who have a difficult time adjusting to the life in Shanghai and who dream of landing on Mars where they can be free.[103] Other gathering places for refugees, such as the dozens of Austrian- and German-style cafés, emulated such institutions in their homeland. While most Chinese had escaped the ruined area of Hongkew for the French Concession, some Jewish refugees with financial means rebuilt the ruins in a European style, featuring European-style restaurants, clubs, offices, and cafés. Later calling it "Little Vienna," refugees compared the area around Broadway Avenue to the vibrant urban centers of Vienna and Berlin. Kaplan describes this recreated neighborhood of traditional Austrian and German daily life:

> There is a little bakery, then a patisserie, with sweet smells caressing our nostrils once again. There is a tailor, a hairdresser, a restaurant serving authentic home cooking like sauerbraten and goulash. In the midst of this chaos we have tried to rebuild the Vienna that we knew. . . . A row of pretty shops has appeared, one by one. Chusan Road has become a little oasis of home in the very midst of the Chinese squalor. Food shops with Viennese and Bavarian sausages hang in the windows in chains of tempting fat links. . . . If this

is to be our home, not for months, but now as it seems, interminable years, we are determined to live as the educated human beings that we are.[104]

In Shanghai, despite having recreated a sense of home for themselves, Austrian and German Jews also had to deal with anti-Semitic pamphlets handed out by German Nazis living in Shanghai and working for the German consulate. One such booklet read: "A warning – The Chosen People have invaded Shanghai. Be prepared to resist an economic invasion."[105] After 1941, however, the refugees not only had to endure Nazi propaganda, their situation once again led to forced relocation and persecution. After the December 1941 attack on Pearl Harbor, the United States entered World War II. The British and Americans, as well as the Baghdadi Jews who were British subjects, were now considered "alien enemies" by the Japanese forces and were made prisoners in camps on the outskirts of Shanghai. In 1943, due to the Japanese occupation, German-speaking Jewish refugees were again subjected to restrictions of freedom and, for many, the loss of their possessions and livelihood. On February 18, 1943, the Japanese issued a proclamation requiring stateless refugees to move to the Hongkew Ghetto, another forced displacement like that which many Jews had already experienced in Europe. Colonel Meisinger, known also as "the Butcher of Warsaw," was said to have negotiated with the Japanese to murder all the Jews in Shanghai. Instead, the Japanese decided that all German Jews would be treated as "de-nationalized" and would be placed under strict surveillance in the Hongkew Ghetto.[106] The Japanese never used the word "Jew" and instead called the European refugees "stateless refugees."[107] Once again, the Jewish refugees were forced out of their homes; those who had businesses and residences outside of Hongkew had to sell them for next to nothing and leave their homes. Kosiner and her husband, for example, lost their business and were forced to move into Hongkew where approximately 18,000 other refugees were to be relocated.[108] The tyrant who oversaw the ghetto was the infamous Japanese Ghoya, who called himself "King of the Jews" and whose cruelty is mentioned in most memoirs written by Shanghailanders. Tausig, who encountered

Ghoya at least once when she needed to leave the ghetto for work, states that the German-speaking refugees named him "the dwarf with the iron fist."[109] Illo Heppner refers to him as the "Japanese psychopath," who "alternated physical abuse with occasional favors" when dealing with refugees who wished to temporarily leave Hongkew on business.[110] On July 17, 1945, however, American forces attacked Shanghai and bombed Hongkew Ghetto since the Japanese had a communications transmitter and a munitions dump in this area. Bacon writes of the bombing's death toll in her memoir: "Forty refugees had been killed. The number of dead Chinese was estimated at four thousand."[111] This attack by United States forces signaled the end of the war and the defeat of the Nazis. After World War II ended, refugees discovered the fate of their relatives, most of whom had been murdered in death camps, a realization Bacon describes as "beyond the capacity of words to express."[112]

For the German-speaking Jewish refugees, therefore, leaving behind the hardships endured in Shanghai was bittersweet; whereas many of their families and friends in Europe had been brutally murdered, they themselves had survived. In memoirs, authors create a narrative in which their lives gain renewed purpose through their own survival because they give testimony to the Holocaust and remember their friends and family members who were among its six million Jewish victims. Refugee Walter Manes writes in his collected papers of his bittersweet farewell from Shanghai:

> As hard as life was there for us, climatically, living conditions, and health hazards, we were grateful that we were able to survive. We were looking forward for the New Land that would be the home in our future. I am grateful to the Jewish Organizations for their efforts they made to get us out of the Far East and a chance for a new life. Thank you, thank you, thank you! I wish that our parents would have had the chance to join us on this trip and not be sent to Auschwitz to their deaths.[113]

For Manes and other refugees who have written of their exile in Shanghai, memoirs give testimony to their ordeal, bear witness to the Holocaust, memorialize murdered family and friends, and express their hope of a "new life" after the war.

When reflecting on their exile experience in memoirs written fifty to sixty years after the end of World War II, refugees also recontextualize the perspective of their own suffering during exile in Shanghai in light of the horrific murders of the six million Jewish victims of the Holocaust. Bacon, for example, writes: "Suddenly, our misery of the Shanghai ghetto paled in comparison to the horrors of Hitler's death camps. Shanghai turned out to have been the paradise for survivors. I am eternally grateful. I survived, and lived to tell about it."[114] She also writes, "Hitler's concentration camps were beyond comprehension. . . ."[115] She wonders about their place and role in this greater history of World War II: "And here we were. We were alive. Why?"[116] In order to answer her query, she assigns meaning to her suffering by leading a well-lived life and later writing about her successful future following her exile to China. She recalls that, after countless tears shed after learning about the Holocaust, she felt an "all-embracing, overwhelming and nourishing surge of power, . . . that life force that could not be denied. And life went on. It would be a life of purpose; a life of love."[117] Bacon identifies herself as a survivor and storyteller; her survival takes on additional meaning for her because her memoir bears witness for those who were murdered in the Holocaust.

For Kaplan and her mother, Kosiner, their Jewish faith binds them to the Jewish Holocaust victims. Kaplan writes of their bond: "Our lives are connected as always with the events unfolding in Europe. Our estrangement from the continent of our births has not released us from the destiny of our people. We are bound together through the faith that has been both our heritage and the cause of persistent persecution. Despite the trials our people remain cemented together by our deeply rooted respect for Jewish life."[118] In Kaplan's memoir of her mother's experiences, the persecution of Jews is an inevitable horror from which only a few are spared who "must carry on": "Some ancient words come suddenly into my mind: 'In every generation an enemy will arise to destroy us.' So it is written in the Passover *Haggadah* that we recite every year. 'And in every generation the Lord will reach out His hand to save a portion of his people to carry on.'"[119] Kosiner and her husband, Poldi, learn the horrific details of the Holocaust from newspapers and radio broadcasts and become aware of the "unspeakable atrocities, the torture and deprivation, the gas chambers and mass graves."[120] Kosiner, overwhelmed with grief and despair, vows never to tell anyone about her suffering in Shanghai: "Already we have seen refugees attempting to bury the nightmares so deeply that they will never have to be faced. We are no different. We have vowed to ourselves not to tell our children we may nurture one day, nor anyone in the outside world, what we have suffered. … Forget it all."[121] Kaplan's memoir, written from her mother, Kosiner's, perspective, contradicts this wish to "forget it all;" instead, Kaplan crafts her mother's memoir from her later recollections of events. In her memoir, Tausig, like Kosiner, places her forced exile within the common Jewish narrative telling how Jews are destined to wander the earth. She writes, "It probably had to have been many centuries ago that our people wandered around. We had forgotten that we were born with a walking staff. Maybe because we didn't want to see the truth we always stuck our head in the sand."[122] Their renewed exile, this time from Shanghai to their homeland or to other countries willing to take in stateless refugees, such as Australia, Canada, Palestine, New Zealand, and the United States, reinforced for many Jewish refugees the narrative of the plight of the wandering Jew.

The majority of German-speaking refugees left Shanghai on liberation ships between 1945 and 1949. Bacon, who left in 1947, writes of making preparations to leave for the United States, a Western nation she idealized and one that had not experienced the physical devastation of World War II on its soil: "But I knew one thing with absolute certainty: the day I would put my foot down on American soil, I would be coming home in every sense of the word."[123] Of the moment when, recently married, she and her husband, Wolf, boarded the *SS Gordon* on August 8, 1947, she writes, "The years fell away, and I saw myself – I saw that young girl and her parents walk off the *Gneisenau*'s gangplank eight years and three months ago."[124] She notes that although nothing had changed about Shanghai since her arrival, she had come of age; she realizes, "Only I had changed. I had grown up. And as I looked at the city that had sheltered us from the horrors of Hitler's war against the Jews and against the world, a huge wave of gratitude engulfed me. Tears washed my eyes and cleared my vision."[125] The ship voyage to the United States and her new life in Denver, where she raised two children and pursued her interests in writing, marked the beginning of a "life of purpose" for her; she concludes, "Finally, I was free to follow my star."[126]

Unlike Bacon and her family, who forever turned their backs on Germany and immigrated to the United States, Tausig chose to return to her Austrian homeland that had forced her into exile during the Third Reich. Two years after World War II had ended, Tausig boarded the U.S. ship *Marine Falcon* to sail to Naples so that she could return to Vienna to finally be reunited with her son, who had returned, together with his young wife, from his exile in England. After a nine-week journey by ship, Tausig and other refugees were transported by cattle car on a one-week journey to Vienna. Her memoir ends with the reunion with her son, Otto, who greets his mother bashfully: "Excuse me, Madam . . . are you perhaps my Mama?"[127] Tausig defines this moment as the end of her exile and the start of a "new period of her life in her homeland."[128] In the 2007 edition of her memoir, Otto attributes his mother's postwar trauma to the facts that she was unable to save her husband in Shanghai, she was powerless to stop her parents' deportation and murder in Treblinka, and she was never able to explain her sister's disappearance during the Holocaust. He reflects on his mother's intense involvement in his life after exile: "Only I was still there, the only one, in whose fate she could still intervene."[129] It is of note that while Tausig's memoir does not describe her life in Austria after her return from China, Ruth Beckerman documents that Austrian Jews returning home were not always made to feel welcome.[130]

Kosiner, pregnant with her second child, and her husband, Poldi, and their two-year-old daughter, Vivian Kaplan, left Shanghai in 1949 on the American ship *SS General Meicks*, bound for San Francisco, where they then traveled by train to their new home in Toronto. Kosiner hoped that Canada would be a new home where "the next generation . . . might live peacefully in a hospitable homeland where they can feel accepted."[131] Except for Kosiner's mother, buried in Shanghai, and Poldi's parents, who were murdered in the Holocaust, their families joined them in Canada, where they began a new life. Kaplan portrays her parents' survival as a counternarrative to that of the victims murdered in the Holocaust. When her baby brother is born aboard ship to the United States, she writes in the memoir, "The child is a boy, healthy and strong, whose voice proclaims his right to exist in an unjust world that does not welcome him easily, a Jewish child to replace one of the many thousands that were killed. His screams are defiant, protesting the cold space into which he has been thrust, demanding to be heard, echoing the cries of so many other innocents that did not survive."[132] Kaplan concludes her mother's memoir by weaving her family's survival and exile into the narrative of the Exodus: "There were so many, so very many who did not live to witness this day. We have survived our own Exodus, making our way across a great part of the world to arrive at a new beginning in peace."[133] For Kaplan, writing her mother's memoir allows her to reconstruct the history of her Austrian Jewish heritage and to bear witness to the Holocaust by memorializing murdered family members and recounting the story of her family's survival.

Whereas memoirs represent authentic perspectives of Austrian and German-speaking women's exile experience in China, more recent historical novels rewrite history to ensure that the experiences of women in exile are included. One such example of fiction depicting the lives of Austrian Jewish women exiles in Shanghai is Lois Ruby's 2006 young adult novel, *Shanghai Shadows*. Ruby takes events from the real-life experiences of exiled refugees in Shanghai to create a narrative overview of the time period from the first-person perspective of a young Austrian-Jewish girl, Ilse Shpann.[134] Ilse initially perceives China as barbaric, "a place where people didn't even use knives and forks," and yet, at the same time, a "huge, bustling, exotic" place of possible adventure.[135] Despite coming of age in China, Ilse identifies with her childhood firmly rooted in Austrian culture. Through Ilse's prewar recollections of a Western European and refined Austria, in which she casts herself as a "law-respecting" "Viennese lady," China is seen as an uncivilized counterculture.¹³⁶ Nonetheless, the fictional Ilse allows herself just enough acculturation to continue to live in Shanghai; Ilse befriends the Chinese street boy and thief Liu, who encourages her survival through street smarts and petty theft. Such friendships between Chinese citizens and Europeans, however, were actually rare, as evidenced in memoirs by European refugees, due to cultural differences and language, class, and gender barriers. Ilse, despite enjoying her newly found freedom and developing her skills as a resistance fighter, "grieves" and longs for her former self as she was in prewar Austria: "the good girl" and "the before-the-war girl."¹³⁷ Such self-descriptions seem to be an attempt to remind young readers that crime is only appropriate when the stakes are ethical or moral. Names of historical figures and locations that also play significant roles in memoirs of life in Shanghai, such as the charitable Iraqi Jewish family Kadoorie, the sadistic Japanese guard Ghoya, and the infamous torture chambers of the Japanese, add a framework of historical authenticity to the novel. A selected bibliography at the close of the novel provides both a mark of historical accuracy and an encouragement for young readers to further study the historical time period and events in China. Ruby addresses common subjects and themes from historical sources and memoirs, such as poverty, hunger, disease, and the changing roles of women during war. The poverty of Hongkew Ghetto is described in great detail, as are Ilse's pangs of hunger and the near starvation of many of the poorer refugees. Ruby's novel presents a moral imperative to learn from war and to engage in personal and civic responsibility. These traits, along with the empowerment of youth and the will to alter destiny by overcoming extraordinary obstacles, are emphasized in Ruby's novel and are posited as the reason that the fictional characters, such as Ilse and her brother Erich, are able to survive and to escape to a better life. Erich, who has joined the fictional resistance group *REACT* to fight the Japanese in Shanghai, leads Ilse to question her own personal actions and ethical values. The question Ilse asks of herself, "What would you die for?" clearly implicates the intended young reader.¹³⁸ Later, Ilse joins the group and discovers that "REACT was right on the money."¹³⁹ She explains, "I began to feel I was truly part of something important, that even a girl like me could make a difference." She concludes that resisting the Japanese was "something worth dying for."[140] The novel maintains an energetic and hopeful tone and register; unlike those of actual memoirs about coming of age in Shanghai, it assumes a contemporary readership and speaks to it. Humorous comments from Ilse, such as "Mother will kill me if I drown in this filthy water," remind readers of the guaranteed happy ending of this fictional historical portrait.[141] Such pluck and high energy as Ilse displays in Ruby's novel is, however, rarely articulated in memoirs of refugees who survived the Holocaust in Shanghai; instead, an individual's energy was devoted to daily life, such as scavenging for food, finding clean drinking water, maintaining physical health, and surviving emotionally and psychologically. Although most topics of personal hygiene are only alluded to as "imagine the worst" and psychological trauma is appropriately muted for a young audience, Ruby does touch upon gender-specific experiences affecting women refugees in Shanghai.[142] The mother of Ilse's friend Tanya, for example, is forced to prostitute herself to Japanese soldiers in order to survive. To protect her reputation, Tanya's mother pretends to teach Japanese students. Tanya responds to Ilse's question about her mother's activities: "Teaches? I guess you could say that. One student, every Friday at two o'clock. But not the same one every week."[143] Tanya's flippant account of her mother's dire situation is in stark contrast to the more sympathetic reaction to the real-life experiences of women refugees forced into prostitution as described in the memoirs of Austrian and German refugees.

In addition to novels such as Ruby's that attempt to capture the everyday life of the German-speaking Jewish community in Shanghai, the history of this group of exiles is also referred to peripherally in the works of other postwar Austrian authors, such as Ilse Aichinger and Ingrid Jacoby. In Aichinger's personal essay from 2004, "Erlebnisgarantie für Wiener in Shanghai" (Guaranteed experience for Viennese in Shanghai), the misery and uncertainty of the Austrian-Jewish exile experience in China is juxtaposed with the "guaranteed experience" for present-day tourists traveling to China, as promised by a travel guide. Aichinger recalls a family friend, Dr. David Weisselberg, who was unable to escape to Shanghai as planned; instead, she says that he was "the only one of our friends who hoped to flee there" and that he "became even less of a Shanghai citizen than he ever managed to become a real Viennese citizen."[144] Aichinger underscores that, as an Austrian Jew in the Third Reich, Weisselberg was not considered an Austrian citizen and that in Shanghai he would have been a stateless refugee and not a Chinese citizen.[145] Weisselberg's failed attempt to escape Nazi persecution by ship is contrasted to another of Aichinger's personal experiences, when her twin sister was able to escape from Vienna on one of the last Kinderstransport ships to England in 1939. Nonetheless, whereas Aichinger's personal essay on this topic reflects the positive aspect of her mother and sister's survival, it also memorializes her maternal grandmother and her mother's younger siblings who were murdered in Minsk.[146] In Aichinger's essays, the individual stories of Austrian-Jewish survivors are inextricably linked to those stories of individuals who were murdered under National Socialism.

In a further reference to the Austrian-Jewish refugee experience in China, Jacoby's 1998 memoir, *My Darling Diary: A Wartime Journal – Vienna 1937-39, Falmouth 1939-44,* includes Jacoby's family's lodger, Otto Seifert from Vienna, who was deported to Dachau and, once released, escaped to China. Jacoby writes of her youthful flirtation with Seifert: "I kiss his photograph every evening and I have written a book about him called: *With Him to China.* It is five weeks now since he left. I know he loves me, even though he is in China."[147] She also writes of her friend who manages to escape to China with her family: "Lotte has gone to Shanghai with her parents! On the boat they met an Indian who gave her twenty pounds and his address. I always knew that something special would happen to Lotte."[148] References to the refugee experience in China show China as a "special" destination in Jacoby's childhood imagination. While the voice in which the memoir is written is intentionally that of a naive and hopeful child, it is clearly disconnected from the author's adult life. In light of Tausig's, Kosiner's (through her daughter, Kaplan), and Bacon's recollections, the everyday hardships experienced firsthand by Austrian-Jewish refugees in China are far harsher than Jacoby's fictional imaginings intended for young adult readers.

The memoirs and historical novels highlighting the lives of

Austrian-Jewish refugees in Shanghai not only revise Austrian history of World War II to include women's experiences but also expand the history to include the stories of those citizens, like those of the children who escaped by the Kindertransport to England, who lived out the war in exile, outside the borders of Austria.

Chapter Seven

Writing About War for Children Today: Vigilance, Personal Responsibility, and Forgiveness in Novels by Renate Welsh, Christine Nöstlinger, and Käthe Recheis

> The things we remember are our own story.
> – Lisl Weil, *To Sail a Ship of Treasures*[1]

Since World War II, numerous Austrian fictional texts and memoirs have described women's experiences of persecution, exile, and survival on the home front during the war and the postwar years. Narratives focusing on girls and young women include novels such as Aichinger's *Die größere Hoffnung*, short stories by Bachmann and Haushofer from the 1950s to the 1970s, and memoirs by authors such as Blend, Klüger, Segal, Trahan, and Kaplan. These novels and memoirs discuss childhood and coming of age from the perspective of adulthood and are written for a mature readership. By contrast, Welsh, Nöstlinger, and Recheis have written about childhood and adolescence during World War II and the postwar period in Austria for young readers. As adults these authors have reconstructed their own coming-of-age memories and rewritten the past from the perspective of childhood. Within a cultural and historical context, targeting a younger generation of readers, these narratives offer significant contributions to the larger body of Austrian postwar writing on war.

Even before World War II, Austria boasted a large number of authors of fiction for children and young adults. Many of these authors, for religious and political reasons, were forced to flee Austria before or shortly after the Anschluss. Between 1933 and 1938, approximately 140 Austrian authors, exiled from Austria, wrote children's books as their primary profession; others wrote them in addition to writing in other literary genres as a means of escaping reality.[2] Names of lesser known authors such as Friedrich Feld, Hertha Pauli, Bettina Ehrlich, and Mira Lobe join that of the Viennese journalist Felix Salten, whose animal story *Bambi* was made famous by Walt Disney's 1942 animated film.[3] Lobe's books, in particular, reflect her longing for a homeland and for peace and tolerance in the world.[4] Her work for young adults focuses on the experiences of children in exile and, like the work of Welsh, Nöstlinger, and Recheis, aims to counter intolerance and to prevent war.

Six novels for young adults by Welsh, Nöstlinger, and Recheis – Welsh's *Johanna* (1980) and *Dieda oder das fremde Kind* (Her, over there or the strange child, 2002); Nöstlinger's *Maikäfer, flieg!* (June bug, fly! 1973) and *Zwei Wochen im Mai* (Two weeks in May, 1981); and Recheis' *Geh Heim und Vergiss Alles* (Go home and forget everything, 1964) and *Lena: Unser Dorf und der Krieg* (Lena: Our village and the war, 1987) – consider the lives of children touched by war and reflect on individual responsibility and the lessons of war offered to future generations.[5] Themes of childhood and war in these narratives show how Welsh, Nöstlinger, and Recheis engage young readers so that they might reflect on social justice, vigilance, and personal responsibility.

The authors recreate postwar Austrian history, targeting young readers through an age-appropriate narrative style and language. Narrative techniques include short chapters and subchapters; a profusion of dialogue; simple sentence structures as well as lengthy sentences expressing associative, non-linear thoughts; and the inclusion of colloquial language and vocabulary from Austrian regional dialects.[6] Although the themes of the narratives center on war and the immediate postwar period on the Austrian home front, including experiences of fear, loss, trauma, mourning, hunger, and starvation, the war also provides a context in which to examine other topics relevant to young readers who are coming of age, such as education, illness, homesickness, friendship, and familial issues such as parent-child relationships, sibling rivalry, and finally, love and sexuality. Additionally, the narratives clearly target a specific readership. Not only do the publishers market to a particular age group by advertising that the novels by Welsh, Nöstlinger, and

Recheis are appropriate for teenagers, but the cover designs of the novels specifically target a young female audience. This is done despite the fact that fathers, grandfathers, brothers, and boyfriends are also featured in these novels and therefore the works might appeal to male readers. Nöstlinger's two novels provide a historical context that attracts readers while at the same time fulfilling an intentional didactic goal. Both are written in the first person, from the perspective of Nöstlinger as a child, about World War II and the postwar period on the Austrian home front. Both *Maikäfer, flieg!* and *Zwei Wochen im Mai* are intended to appeal to young readers eager to learn more about Austria's history during the war and postwar period. Both front covers show historical black and white photographs. *Maikäfer, flieg!* portrays an anxious young girl with a haunted gaze standing by a house as a war plane flies overhead while what seem to be tracer shells, or perhaps the overexposed images of June bugs, rush through the sky.[7] The cover of *Zwei Wochen im Mai* is composed of two photographs, one above the other, with the bottom one portraying a long line of people dressed in typical Austrian attire. One young girl, with a suspicious and annoyed gaze directed at the camera, leans against a wall, most likely waiting for food rations. The gazes of the other girls are also directed at the viewers, urging them to uncover the root of the girls' anxiety and sadness. Instead of a historical epilogue, as in Welsh's novel, Nöstlinger's *Zwei Wochen im Mai* closes with a four-page montage of advertisements and articles from the 1945 newspaper *Wiener Kurier*, portraying the postwar experience for Austrians. Food shortages lead to ads for books such as "Canning without sugar," a manual for the homemaker who must learn to can fruits during times of sugar shortage. Strangely, an ad on the next page makes the canning instruction booklet irrelevant, as it announces that 25,000 tons of raw sugar have arrived from Cuba, bought by the United States to aid Austria, raising hope for those starving on the home front: "Additionally a ship with sugar is on its way on the high seas."[8] A short article points out the need for more educational facilities and schools following the war. Ads with images of movie stars announce that Michael Curtiz's *Casablanca* and Julij Reismann's *Die letzte Nacht* (The last night) are showing at the Apollo and Tabor theaters. The centrally placed advertisements for food and films underscore the desire of those on the home front, weary of the war and the postwar period, to find comfort in food and fantasy. The visual significance of the book covers and the historical context documented by epilogues and reproductions of contemporary war-related advertisements provide a framework for these narratives and validate their significance as historical references.

Historical events contextualize and frame historical novels as well as memoirs. Lisl Weil, in her 1984 memoir for children, *To Sail a Ship of Treasures*, notes, "The things we remember are our own story."[9] In her children's book about a girl who sails across the ocean to escape persecution, Weil concludes for her young readers that childhood experiences shape adult identity: "Good or sad, everything one remembers is important. Our memories help us make us the people we are. Each of us has different things to remember, different things to wonder about, different people to recall and love."[10] It is these memories that are recalled to paint a picture of the self, an attempt to shape a linear narrative of the self, one that calls for a filling in of the memory gaps, providing a historical context for events that seemed to have no significance in childhood but were nonetheless linked to larger historical events. It is the individual experience, relived in fragmented memories, that takes on a more cohesive form when viewed as a shared experience or as a life to which meaning has been assigned. Weil's story is one in which the persecuted figure as survivors.

Survival on the home front is the main focus of the youth novels by Welsh, Nöstlinger, and Recheis. The preface of Nöstlinger's *Maikäfer, flieg!* situates the story within the context of the shared experience of history. The preface tells readers that this story is twenty-five years old, having first been published in 1973. Nöstlinger's reference to the children's wartime song, "June bug, fly! Father is at war," continues with the stanza "Powder Land has burned."[11] The author confides to readers, "However, the June bugs were never at fault when Powder land burned, even twenty five years ago."[12] It is within this context of coming to terms with the past (*Vergangenheitsbewältigung*) and historical revision that Nöstlinger seeks out the truth of Austria's role in World War II –

and more importantly, the lasting consequences for children traumatized by war. The back cover of the second edition from 1996 confirms its authenticity: "The story told here is a Powder land story, and it really happened."[13]

In the opening passage of Nöstlinger's novel, the eight-year-old Christine says of her childhood: "It was war. War had existed for a long time. I could not remember at all that once war had not existed. I was used to war and the bombs too."[14] The story is rooted in typical events of World War II, such as the bombs dropping in and around Vienna, the losses on the home front and the front, and the Russian occupation. Central to the story is Christine's relationship with her family, especially with her father, who returns home wounded after five years on the Russian front. Depictions of everyday life during the war and postwar period, such as doing household chores, scavenging for food, and playing games, provide a framework for Christine's coming of age.

Certain childhood themes, such as game playing, enable Christine and others to reenact and work through difficult situations. Detailed descriptions of childhood games and their symbolic value are also pronounced in Blend's and Segal's memoirs of their childhoods in exile during the war. Games created by children allow them to control their environment and provide structure and organization for a daily routine overturned by war. One of the games Christine and her friends play is school with a class of ornamental garden gnomes they discover in the garden of a summer residence belonging to a family acquaintance and Nazi sympathizer, Mrs. von Braun. Because Christine's family home in Vienna has been destroyed by bombings, Christine's mother offers to care for Mrs. von Braun's villa in order to find refuge for her otherwise homeless family. Since the children miss the daily routine and social interactions of school, they create a school of their own: "The one with the whetstone was the stupid one in the class. Hildegard was the teacher. I imitated the voices of umpteen gnome students. My favorite role was the stupid one with the whetstone."[15] The theme of going to school as a forum for childhood social interaction and acculturation takes on an important role in stories of war from the perspective of a child. At one point, Christine's mother demands that she "unlearn" the swear word

"*Scheiße*" (shit), telling Christine's father, "The times will slowly return to normal, and she can't talk like that when school begins!"[16] Upon hearing this, Christine vows never to stop swearing, "never to go to school again, and to do everything possible so that times will never again be normal;" she decides "to never want normal times again."[17] While war is familiar, peace is an unknown factor for these children of war.

In another game called the Which-Uncle-Am-I-Thinking-About-Game (*An-welchen-Onkel-denke-ich-Spiel*), Christine and her sister take turns guessing of which "uncle," from the many portraits of older men hanging in the villa's music room, they are thinking: "The 'Which-Uncle-Am-I-Thinking-About-Game' was not an easy game. The uncles all looked very much the same. They all had light blue bug eyes and a beard and ears that stuck out and they were partially bald."[18] In another moment of play, the father entertains his daughters in the villa by making paper ships out of books found in the owner's library. Nöstlinger as an adult writer sees the irony in the game in which the father tears pages from a book of Hitler's speeches, the cover of which reveals a large black swastika.[19] This episode demonstrates that game playing is therapeutic for adults as well as children; the girls benefit from some play time, and Christine's father is able to act out and thereby deal with his disgust at the Fuehrer and the war.

Nöstlinger's novel voices the common Austrian fear of the Russian occupation during the postwar period yet demonstrates that the majority of Russian soldiers stationed in Austria were also deeply affected by the hardships of war. Christine tells her father that she heard that Russians "chop up women, then throw them into barrels and salt them."[20] Her sister agrees that "the Russians cut off women's breasts and shoot children and plunder houses and torch everything and everyone burns."[21] When the Russians occupy Mrs. von Braun's villa, in which Christine and her family are living, Christine learns that the Russian soldiers wish that they were at home in Russia rather than being forced to follow orders to remain in Austria. Christine befriends the cook Cohn, in whom she finds the possibility of coming to love the "other" – in this case the feared Russian – and who comes to embody the ideals of understanding, tolerance, and forgiveness in war. Christine remarks: "[Cohn] was the first ugly, stinking, crazy person I ever loved."[22] She explains further that she had "loved the cook because he was not the war. Nothing in him was war, not a thing. . . . He was an enemy and had a gentle, deep, sleepy voice. He was a victor and got kicked so hard that he flew right through the outdoor kitchen."[23] Later in the novel, when Christine's grandfather shields her from strangers whom he fears are Russian soldiers, she tells him what she has learned from her own experiences, that "the Russians rarely do bad things."[24] Nöstlinger demonstrates children's capacity for understanding and empathy in the face of the complexities brought on by war. When her friend Gerald cannot come to terms with his father's death, Christine recalls similar reactions among her friends: "I thought of Berger Schurli from our bombed house. Despite the death notice hanging outside, he didn't believe that his father was dead, even though I explained it to him many times. Nothing could be done. I said, 'It's possible! Maybe your father joined the resistance and is now fighting the last Nazis.' Gerald liked that."[25] Again, Christine's empathy mitigates the terrible realities of war.

As in novels such as Reichart's *Nachtmär*, Nowak's *Gehorsam*, and Welles' *Am Rande der Geschichte*, the figure of the grandmother plays an essential role in Nöstlinger's account of the narrator's childhood experience of war. In *Maikäfer, flieg!* the grandmother represents the voice of reason and truth, as painful and absurd as it may seem. Whereas the eight-year-old narrator views her grandmother as merely "wild," she understands that the neighbors believe her to be crazy and a danger to herself and to her community during the war.[26] Christine is torn between respecting her grandmother's critical observations about Hitler and the horrors of war and protecting her from nosy National Socialist neighbors. The narrator fears her grandmother's arrest by the Nazis, saying, "That Mrs. Brenner already said a couple of times that women like my grandmother should be reported to the Gestapo."[27] Christine also confides in Cohn that her grandmother has the potential to become mean and wild.[28] Later, she realizes that she has exaggerated, that in her stories "her grandmother became from day to day bigger and fatter and wilder."[29] Nöstlinger as an adult analyzes Christine's admiration for her grandmother and her own knack for manipulating reality into a good story to relieve her own anxieties and to please others. Christine says of her storytelling, "I told a lot of stories, told long stories, and even if I did not always stay with the truth, I did so only so that my mother would find them funny and friendly."[30] The grandmother and grandfather survive a bombing, yet Christine's grandmother is forever changed. She is traumatized and no longer demonstrates her earlier wild spirit against injustice. Instead, she is spiteful, irrational, now the deranged person others had thought her at the beginning of the war. Christine comments, "My grandmother did not really exist anymore. Of course, my grandmother was never so wild and big and wonderful as I had described her to Cohn, but my grandmother was never so small, so shaky and pitiful as that old one there, the one standing in the doll kitchen; that was not my grandmother."[31] By tracing the grandmother's state of mental health, Nöstlinger shows young readers that war not only destroys physically but also psychologically and emotionally. The conclusion of the novel describes the family's return to Vienna. When the mother urges Christine to look at everything once again in order to remember this episode in her life, Christine instead closes her eyes to the reality of war. The novel, based on personal experiences, represents Nöstlinger's ability to open her eyes again and to *see* her childhood and her experiences of war from the vantage point of adulthood.

In Nöstlinger's sequel, *Zwei Wochen im Mai*, she describes, from the perspective of a twelve year old, her life in postwar Austria during its reconstruction, three years following the end of World War II. She describes the occupation by the Allied Forces, especially her encounters with Russian and American soldiers, the food shortages and rations, the black market, the ruins in and around Vienna, the human losses, and daily survival. She reveals that she had imagined peace as a time of plentiful food and nice clothes, quite different from the reality of the postwar years. The author states in the preface that her story, published in 1981, is now more than thirty years old, yet it is still relevant today. Although everything in Austria has changed since then, the author finds the roots of today's culture in that time: "But everything began then, whatever still exists today."[32] She feels that although adults taught children how to behave in postwar Austria, she herself felt more comfortable within the context of war:

> I had known war well, I had known my way around in war. I had to first learn peace and I was not a good student of learning peace because what I was supposed to learn had nothing to do with what my "child's-war-belief" had imagined as "peace." And the adults were not honest teachers. Because even today they are often not honest, my old story is perhaps still suitable.[33]

Here Nöstlinger seeks to draw in a younger audience defiant of authority and intent on unmasking the social hypocrisy of older generations. The themes discussed in this novel center on parent-child relationships, especially that of the first-person narrator and her father. Christine's growing fondness for her friend Hansi and her sexual awakening also play an important role, especially since sex is portrayed in the world of adults as a form of escape from the harsh postwar realities. Christine dreams that one day she and Hansi will meet more intimately: "I saw myself with Hansi in the graveyard sitting in the grass between the fallen tombstones and learning Latin."[34] Later, the father catches Christine and Hansi as they engage in an embrace shared by adults: "First [his lips] were cold and tasted like chives."[35] Almost immediately, Christine's father urges Hansi's mother to send him to a foster family in Switzerland who will care for him since he has suffered from malnourishment. The narrator wonders what became of Hansi since her father claimed their separation was really for her "own protection;" she retorts, "But I don't believe it. Even today I don't believe him. He just couldn't stand it that I could love someone else as much as him. He just wouldn't stand for it."[36] Nöstlinger's narrative confirms the strong bond between father and daughter while at the same time acknowledging the genuine emotion felt for a first love.

In *Zwei Wochen im Mai*, Nöstlinger further explores the false morals of the war and postwar period. The first-person narrator questions the truth as proposed by adults: "And all this about honesty, that much I knew, was not followed by adults. Most of them stole after the war. They had cleaned out food supplies. They had taken things from apartments from which people had fled. And they had stolen the last buckets of coals from the cellars."[37] Her grandfather shares with her his wartime morality: "Only, you can never, under any circumstance, take something from somebody who has less than you do. You have to decide on a case by case basis if you can take something from someone."[38] Nöstlinger also portrays certain rituals from the preteen years, such as the eating of so-called boogers and scabs, in order to appeal to young readers. Hansi challenges the reader's tolerance for such childhood experiments by asking Christine, "Aren't you grossed out?"[39] It is the exploration of such childhood pleasures, as well as the clear demarcation between childhood and adulthood, that define this unique body of children's literature on childhood during war.

Like Nöstlinger's novels, Welsh's stories for young adults challenge and confront the traditional representation of Austrian history during World War II. Welsh, born in Vienna one year before the Anschluss, wrote *Johanna* in 1979 to describe the social and political life in rural Austria before the Anschluss amidst growing Austro-Fascist and National Socialist movements. *Johanna* primarily appeals to young female readers from its cover design to its content. The cover, for example, features an edited photograph of a young woman carrying a heavy basket of laundry to an outdoor well. Her figure is stooped and her eyes are directed toward the laundry to be washed. The image makes apparent to readers that this is not a story about carefree youth; rather, for the protagonist the story tells of the hard work of completing endless chores and for the reader the harsh – and dirty – realities of history. The title *Johanna* draws attention to the life of a young girl and her fate as a foster child who survives as a maid to farmers in rural, prewar Austria. Her relationship with the socialist Peter, who rebels against the growing Austro-Fascist movement in rural Austria, evolves into a happy union after an unplanned pregnancy. The private life of a young girl coming into her own is portrayed in the context of public prewar politics. Welsh's dedication, "For Johanna's grandchildren," speaks to third-generation postwar children, whose grandmothers came of age during the prewar period and World War II. The table of contents indicates that the narrative is grounded in historical events. The five sections of the novel are presented in linear progression from prewar events occurring in 1931 to the final part entitled "Beginning," which takes place in 1936. The subtitles of the sections, "Farewell," "Homesickness," "Sickness," and "Fear," clearly deal with grave issues.[40] The afterword by Johann Luger, a historical overview, provides a synopsis of the socio-cultural and political life in Austria from 1931 to 1935.[41] According to Luger, Austria's involvement in World War II is rooted in the fall of the Austro-Hungarian monarchy and the end of World War I. Luger points out that in 1931, the first year covered in the novel, Austria counted 302,000 unemployed, not to mention high numbers of graduating students who could not find employment. Farmers, he notes, were less affected by the economic crises of the war and postwar years. Luger thus glosses over Austria's involvement in Austro-Fascism and National Socialism and its willingness to accept the German annexation by portraying the relationship as a "way out of economic difficulties and mass unemployment."[42] He then continues to portray the National Socialists as enemies of a Social Democratic nation who through "waves of terror" in January, June, and July of 1934 murdered the Austrian Chancellor, Engelbert Dollfuß, initiating a steady decline of Social Democracy and the rise of the Nazi regime. Luger ends his historical portrait with a description of Hitler's troops marching into Austria on March 12, 1938, and Hitler announcing Austria's annexation a few days later. Luger omits the fact that Hitler's troops were greeted by cheering crowds of Austrian citizens in the Heldenplatz Square in Vienna, welcoming the Anschluss and the regime of National Socialism. The afterword reinforces "the historical lie" (*Geschichtslüge*) of the immediate postwar period that posits Austria as a victim of Germany and National Socialism. This perspective diminishes the effect of Welsh's intention to urge readers to be personally responsible for their actions and for history. Luger's emphasis on ideals of nationalism and patriotism as the causes of war and tragedy undermines the specificity in Welsh's narrative of personal actions and decision-making that lead to what is later described as history. Despite Luger's premise concerning Austria's role in National Socialism, Welsh's focus remains nonetheless on the consequences of political life on the individual lives of Austrian citizens. Within the socio-historical context of growing Austro-Facism and National Socialism, Welsh recounts the story of Johanna, a foster girl who is sold to a farming family when she is two months old and is later sent to another farm where she works, yet dreams of learning the trade of a seamstress. When the farmer Firstner resists Austro-Fascism by preaching about Socialism, he is sent to the concentration camp Wöllersdorf.[43] Johanna's boyfriend Peter, also a Socialist, tells her that those who resist Nazism do so only if part of a larger group "because each dictatorship needs the same kind of people, regardless of what dictatorship it is. And all of them can say nice words."[44] When Johanna goes shopping one day in the town of Gloggnitz, she notices that the shop of the Austrian Jew Löwy has been destroyed. The words "Jews, out" (*Juden, raus*) are prominently spray-painted on the walls, and Löwy has been attacked and wounded. Johanna views this as a tragic injustice not only because of its violence but also because the Löwys were the first to treat her as an equal despite her low socio-economic standing. This event highlights the anti-Semitism already prevalent in Austria before the Anschluss. Johanna recalls, "Almost all the people said that Jews were to blame for everything, for unemployment, for the high prices. Some claimed that Jews were ruling the world."[45] Johanna and the Socialist Peter do not share these hateful views; in fact, their child from Johanna's unplanned pregnancy signals a new hope for Austria, one not related to National Socialism and the Third Reich. Readers, for whom Johanna's story unfolds chronologically, are left to imagine her fate during the war and postwar period. Johanna ruminates about her future, "My child and I, we have to find our own place. Maybe with Peter, maybe without him."[46] When she meets Peter, who states that he intends to marry her and invites her to live with him at his parents' home, she insists that she will first contribute financially to her future by working until the baby is born. The concluding sentence of the novel indicates Johanna's newfound self-esteem and empowerment as an employed, soon-to-be-wife and mother. Her new employer, the owner of the inn where Johanna has been hired to work as a server, remarks on Johanna's proud posture:

"How you carry your stomach so in front of you."⁴⁷ Having overcome some of the obstacles of social class and gender and having come of age, Johanna's life-giving potential as a pregnant woman counters the death and destruction that will soon befall Austria in the 1930s, a nation firmly rooted in the growing rural movement of Austro-Fascism.

A second young adult novel by Welsh about a young girl's experiences on the Austrian home front during World War II, *Dieda, oder das fremde Kind*, details the experiences of the war for the fictional protagonist, the child Ursel. Following the shock of her mother's sudden death from what appears to have been a brain tumor, Ursel decides to call herself Dieda, or "her-over-there."⁴⁸ Her father sends her to the Austrian countryside to live out the war at his parents' home, where she is perceived as a "stubborn, headstrong, defiant" and even "dangerous" child.⁴⁹ Themes dealing with coming of age during World War II become the framework in which Ursel comes to terms with her mother's sudden death, her father's remarriage, her tense relationship to her grandparents, and her stepmother's pregnancy with Ursel's little sister, Theres. Other themes of war, such as hunger, starvation, illness, and death, are prominent in Ursel's childhood and youth. For example, like most Austrians on the home front, Ursel suffers from hunger during both the war and the postwar period. During the war she made up the German rhyme "*Mein Herz ist schwer, mein Bauch ist leer*" (My heart is heavy, my stomach is empty) in order to cope with her constant hunger pangs.⁵⁰ During the postwar period, she again compares hunger with sadness, stating that the sensations "feel similar."⁵¹

After the war ends, Ursel learns of the Russian soldiers who have marched into Vienna and pose a threat to girls and women, something she cannot fully comprehend. A woman urges her not to travel to Vienna to meet her father, warning, "The Russians are in Vienna! Be happy that we are here!"⁵² Toward the end of the novel, Welsh, like Nöstlinger, tempers the stereotype of the predatory Russian soldier. Ursel, having returned to school in Vienna, learns that some Russian soldiers did not attack women, who had feared the worst and smeared ash on their faces to dissuade the soldiers from sexual advances or rape.⁵³ During the immediate postwar period, Ursel meets American soldiers, with whom she practices her limited school English. Common English phrases, spoken with a German accent, such as "*Mai nähm is Dieda*" (my name is Dieda) and "*Gut Mohrning*" (good morning) surely endear the protagonist Ursel to young Austrian readers learning English in school.[54]

During the postwar period, Ursel is also confronted with the consequences of Austria's complicity in the crimes committed during the Third Reich. When Ursel observes a stooped, skeletal man standing in line at a bakery, an older friend becomes upset and informs her that he must be a former prisoner from the Mauthausen camp. When Ursel attempts to read the newspaper's headline detailing the prisoners' release from the camp, her grandfather, still a staunch supporter of National Socialism, calls the reports about the camp "lies" and tears the paper out of her hands.[55] Upon hearing the locals discussing the names of places such as "Ebensee, Mauthausen, or Hartheim," Ursel observes how "shadows fell over faces and fingers cramped up." She states that she no longer dares to ask about them for fear "of the shadow."[56] Signifying the specter of silence in Austria regarding the crimes committed at Mauthausen, the "shadows" – shadows to which Elisabeth Reichart also refers in her novel about Mauthausen, *Februarschatten* – are illuminated and even cast aside in historical fiction, whose authors counteract the silence by inscribing Mauthausen into their narratives.

Not only does Welsh's novel address Ursel's experiences in the war and postwar period, but it also examines how gender figures into a young girl's experiences of war. Gender plays a central role in Ursel's coming of age as she struggles to establish her self-worth in a society that regards girls as "bad luck." After the war, when Ursel has returned to her father and stepmother's home in Vienna, her stepmother gives birth to Ursel's sister. When a female neighbor comments, "The poor man, another daughter. Such a nice person, and he's had back luck again,"[57] Ursel counters, "A girl can bring luck too."[58] Despite her retort, Ursel nonetheless questions the worth of her gender: "Bad luck, Bad luck. I am the first bad luck, and now he has the second."[59] When Ursel later asks her father's friend Brigitta why "girls are worth less," Brigitta states,

"Girls are worth just as much. Some people just don't know it."⁶⁰ She adds, "People are stupid. . . . The stupidest people are women, because they go along with it" and urges Ursel to never let anyone make her feel "less worthy than others. . . ." ⁶¹ When Ursel finally meets her newborn sister Theres, she is empowered in her role as older sister and urges the baby to call her by her real name, Ursel, and not by her nickname, Dieda. In the novel, the dire events of the war and postwar period are a series of challenges that Ursel overcomes while coming of age and coming into her own.

Like Welsh's and Nöstlinger's narratives about young girls during war, Recheis's novels for young adults confront and unmask Austria's complicity in the crimes committed in Austria during the Third Reich. *Geh Heim und vergiß alles* and *Lena: Unser Dorf und der Krieg* are both based on Recheis's experiences as a child and teenager in Hörsching, near Linz in Upper Austria during the war and postwar period.⁶² Whereas *Lena* details her years in Hörsching from the Anschluss to the end of the war, *Geh heim und vergiß alles* describes her experiences as a volunteer nurse in the liberated concentration camp Waldlager Gunskirchen beginning May 1945, where her father, a local doctor, cared for freed Jewish prisoners and where he died of typhoid fever only one month after the liberation.⁶³ Recheis says that she writes about war for children and young adults because she intends to show them "how terrible it is" and because she believes young people should know what humans are capable of.⁶⁴ She describes the war as a sad time and recalls being terrified of bombing raids, yet despite this she managed to type and send to the front resistance letters written by priests against Hitler. She admits that writing *Lena* almost fifty years after the war ended was a difficult decision for her because she knew that her memories of this time would resurface through writing.⁶⁵ Having written more than sixty books for children and young adults that have been translated into more than twenty languages, as well as countless texts for school books, Recheis is committed to countering xenophobia and prejudices through writing and continues to be particularly engaged in writing about the fate of North and South American indigenous peoples.

Recheis notes that although she does not consider *Lena* to be autobiographical, it is "like a mosaic" of her own memories and also those of her family and friends.[66] For Recheis, going back forty years into the past to retrieve these memories was "arduous, often agonizing," and while some were like "photographic memories," others were harder to recall.[67] She confesses that at age twelve she was, like so many of her friends, persuaded by the propaganda of the Nazi ideology, a truth she had repressed after turning her back on National Socialism during the war but rediscovered in her childhood diary.

In *Lena*, Recheis details experiences unique to Austria during the Third Reich working through the contrasting political positions of the time through dialogues that engage young readers in a discussion and enable them to form their own responses to ethical and moral questions. Topics range from the personal, such as Lena's relationships to her brother Christoph, her parents, and her friends and neighbors, to general topics of war that affect Lena, such as food rations, bombings, death camps, prisoners of war, and the resistance movement. Events that affect Lena during the prewar period and the war range from the rise of Austro-Fascism and the Anschluss to the last day of World War II on May 9, 1945. In the epilogue of *Lena*, Recheis reminds her young readers that there were many resistance groups in Austria and Germany which worked against Hitler's regime and that she herself came from a Catholic family who taught her to realize the inhumanity of the National Socialist ideology.[68] The novel illustrates that children are more vulnerable than adults in war; not only have they not contributed to the decisions made by adults which lead to war, but they are more susceptible to propaganda and likely to join organizations such as the Hitler Youth without question. A chronological narrative structure from the perspective of a child allows for critical commentary on the actions taken and the crimes committed by followers of National Socialism but also shows the growing awareness that Lena shares with members of her family and community regarding the inhumanity of the regime. Recheis shows the ambivalence that many citizens faced regarding the Anschluss. When Lena's mother and her aunt take apart the red-white-red Austrian flag and sew on a swastika to make the Nazi flag to hang outside of their house, her aunt saves the white stripe in a drawer in the hope that she will be able to recreate the Austrian flag one day.

When all the villagers are encouraged by the Nazi regime to vote in favor of the Anschluss, the pastor criticizes those who support the regime for their cowardice; he warns the boy Willi, "today none of us were heroes, and in all of Austria there were very few. This is not an election with which we can change things anymore.... Do you want them to lock up your father?"[69] Later in the novel, shortly before the war ends, the pastor wonders if Austrian citizens should have shown more courage to prevent the Anschluss and whether their inaction demonstrated their complicity with the regime.[70] Lena shares the pastor's concern and questions her role in the war. She blames herself: "I said to myself that we had always been against it and never wanted it, but it didn't matter. I began to feel partly to blame for it."[71] Lena's view of Austria's role in the Third Reich is ambivalent; on the one hand, Lena acknowledges her complicity in the events of the war, but on the other hand, she describes Austria as a victim of German occupation.

In *Lena*, Recheis portrays Austria as a nation that is unique in regional language and culture, different from Germany, and portrays the Anschluss as Germany's colonization of Austria. Lena remarks, "We kept being encouraged to become as capable as the Prussians! We had nothing against the Prussians, but we did have a lot against them being held up as an example. The Fuehrer, who was Austrian himself, didn't think much of his homeland. Even the name of Austria was forbidden."[72] In an interview, Recheis comments on the linguistic uniqueness that sets Austria apart from Germany, noting that an individual's language reflects a certain mentality. She cites, for example, the Austrian word for a cake, "*Guglhupf*," "something that sounds light, like something that rises." By contrast, the northern German word for this same cake, "*Napfkuchen*," makes her "think of something that has collapsed."[73] In commenting on the "collapsed" and heavy-handed German culture, Recheis seems to echo the popular postwar Austrian perspective that Germany was an aggressive force that had occupied Austria during the Third Reich. Yet, despite Recheis' claim that Germany occupied Austria, her novel *Lena* does acknowledge that many Austrians were caught up in Austro- and National Socialist rhetoric and propaganda. To further explain the unique qualities of Austrian culture, the novel concludes with a dictionary of National Socialist terms and Austrian words and expressions. References to Austrian culture and its dialects set this novel apart from other works about World War II written in standard high German.

Torn because of her family's growing resistance to Hitler, Lena is at first drawn to the goals of the Third Reich and writes in her diary about her "enthusiasm for the warplanes, the enthusiasm for the German Reich, which should win."[74] In her epilogue, Recheis comments on her own initial enthusiasm for the ideals of the Third Reich in order to explain to readers the powers of Nazi propaganda over children: "At the time of the blitzkrieg, as a twelve year old, I was like so many others seduced by an ideology that lured us young people with mendacious ideals."[75] The novel also illustrates Lena's ambivalence about the Third Reich: when Lena asks her brother Christoph if the English and French are now Austria's enemies, and therefore also hers, reminding him, "but we haven't done anything to them," he replies, "in war – everyone is an enemy."[76] Lena learns of Hitler's plans to murder those who are considered different – those with a mental illness, those with differing political opinions, and those who are Jewish. For example, Lena observes how mentally ill patients are brought to the Hartheim castle in a neighboring community and are reported to have died there of pneumonia. After this happens to a friend's father, Michel Mur, Lena discovers that people have been murdered at Hartheim. Lena's father, who is now clearly against the regime, counters the denial of such events by Mrs. Schieder, a follower of a Nazi party, at a church service for the murdered Mur by saying, "You know very well what is happening in the Hartheim castle. You just don't want to believe it."[77] Showing her naiveté regarding Hitler, Mrs. Schieder argues, "No, I will not believe it because it is not true. Because it is slander. The Fuehrer would never allow such a thing."[78] From the start, the novel deals with the Holocaust and its millions of victims. The novel begins by describing acquaintances of Lena's family, a Polish count and countess who live in a nearby villa, who escape to Poland shortly before the Anschluss but who, at the end of the novel, are reported to have been murdered in a death camp in Poland. Lena learns about death camps from her uncle, who witnessed prisoners being murdered in gas chambers in the nearby forced-labor camp at Mauthausen. To make young readers aware of these atrocities, Recheis describes the murder of children at the camps: "Uncle said he had seen children in the camp, not even as old as Christoph and Lena, sometimes even very small children."[79] To further emphasize the vulnerability of children in war, Recheis comments on events of the war related to children. For example, Lena questions the bombing of Cologne in 1942 by the English, in which mostly women and children were killed and decides not to acknowledge wartime honors: "I didn't want anything anymore to do with medals awarded to someone because he had killed other people."[80] Toward the end of the war, witnesses describe two young soldiers, hanged by the SS for deserting the losing German army and for attempting to return home, as "poor children."[81] Recheis underscores that, in war, soldiers themselves are often just children.

By reflecting on how war affects children, Recheis also raises ethical and moral questions regarding actions in war carried out by young soldiers and children on the home front. Christoph asks how soldiers like his friend Florian, who returns a broken young man from the Russian front, justify following orders if they go against their consciences. He raises Lena's consciousness by saying, "I think about what I would have done in his place. What would you have done?"[82] Lena, who discusses this issue with her mother, is not sure if she could muster up the courage to risk death for the sake of her conscience. Such dialogues throughout the novel encourage young readers to critically observe the complexities and consequences of making ethical decisions. Scenes of successful acts of resistance empower young readers and offer positive reinforcement for positive deeds. In one scene, for example, Lena, Christoph, and their friends Willi and Berni take part in a daring act of resistance by decorating the graves of unknown Russian prisoners of war with flowers. In another example, Lena's father is threatened by local Nazi officials for having "committed crimes against the Volk" by filling out prisoners' death certificates with the true cause of death, "hunger," although the starving of prisoners broke the laws set by the International Red Cross.[83] These acts of resistance by Lena and her family are put into perspective by their mother, who is torn between teaching her children to abide by nationally imposed laws that are often unethical and unjust and following such laws with a moral conscience. She tells them, "I have asked myself often whether it is good when we always tell you to keep your mouth shut, that you shouldn't do anything that is forbidden. We just want to survive these terrible times! I believe that we have the right to. Hitler won't stay in power forever."[84] The mother comments as much to her children as to the reader when she explains why such ethical and moral issues were difficult to navigate during the Nazi regime: "when everything is over, they will ask us why we permitted it. Because nobody who has not experienced it for himself will understand how helpless one is under such a government."[85] Lena and Christoph are faced with making ethical choices, of which their mother had spoken, and continue to resist the Nazi regime by reading forbidden leaflets, by listening to forbidden news on the radio, and by not divulging the identities of resistance fighters.

When the war is finally over, Lena comes to realize she will be unable to forget it.[86] Lena recalls for young readers that the Allied Forces occupied Austria for ten years following the war and that "children born now know about the war and dictatorship only from stories that we tell them. And perhaps they will never fully understand what peace and freedom meant for us then."[87] Recheis follows this last comment with the imperative to appreciate the value of peace and freedom in a didactic epilogue that emphasizes the dangers of dictatorships and the passivity and ignorance of citizens who let such a "murderous regime" take over. She cautions young readers not to condemn the Austrians who lived through World War II but rather to learn from the events leading up to war and to recognize that the mechanisms created by dictatorships can lead people to commit crimes and to be guilty of inhumanity.[88] Recheis recommends that readers reflect on their own intolerance and prejudices, noting, "Every instance of intolerance against people who are different from us carries with it the roots of imminent injustice."[89] Like Nöstlinger's and Welsh's novels, the intention of Recheis' novel is to educate young adults about Austrian twentieth-century history and to teach them to practice vigilance and tolerance and work toward peace.

Recheis' *Geh heim und vergiß alles* follows *Lena* chronologically, recounting the events of the months following the end of the war. However, whereas *Lena*'s fictional protagonist chronicles the prewar period and the war in Upper Austria, *Geh heim und vergiß alles* is written from the perspective of Recheis as a seventeen-year-old girl. Here Recheis recalls her experience as a volunteer nurse working with her father, who had set up an emergency medical clinic for former prisoners from one of the liberated reception camps (*Auffanglager*) of Mauthausen, near Hörsching, to which Eastern European Jews had been deported during the war by the retreating German army. In her preface to *Geh heim und vergiß alles*, Recheis points out that her parents, who were not National Socialists, taught her that "a person's freedom and dignity are threatened in every dictatorship."[90] During the war, a relative who lived in the town of Mauthausen told her family of the terrible things he had witnessed from outside of the forced-labor camp, although Recheis says that she and her family only learned about the death camps close to their home after the war.

The novel begins with the narrator Christine's ambivalent relationship to her memories of this traumatic time; her first sentence, "I have forgotten it. There is nothing anymore that reminds me of it," is soon disproved in the second paragraph by her realization that some evenings she does in fact remember events: "Sometimes I remember. And then I suddenly know: I have not forgotten it."[91] The narrator recalls scenes as if from a photographic memory, such as the grey camp barracks that occupy her recollections: "I see them exactly in front of me."[92] The novel recalls the months following the liberation of the camps in May 1945, the emergency clinic built by Christine's father, and his work to heal former prisoners with the aid of fellow doctors who are freed Eastern European Jewish prisoners, his daughter, and other volunteers. Christine narrates the events in the voice of a young woman who is coming of age, often insecure about her outward appearance, a woman who matures through her growing self-confidence in her ability to do her duties and in her compassion toward the infirm and dying victims of the camps. She realizes her vulnerability as a human being, as a young woman during the postwar period with limited access to the supplies necessary to help her father. After confronting the American commander in charge, who has previously refused her father medical aid and supplies, Christine receives what she demanded the next day. Later, she discovers why he was unwilling to help at first: he was an Austrian Jew, his wife and children had been murdered in concentration camps, and though he had been enlisted by the American army to oversee the postwar reconstruction in Upper Austria, he did not want to help his former homeland which had taken his family's life. When the commander initially refused to help her, he told her to "go home and forget everything."[93] Recheis' novel, the title of which is taken from the commander's words, disobeys his command "to forget everything" by instead remembering the events. The narration of events focuses on Christine's growing personal relationships to the victims, most of whom die of starvation, typhoid fever, mental illness, or despair despite her care, and others who survive physically though not emotionally. When she returns home from her work at the camp, she realizes that her relationship to her home and to her past have forever changed through her experiences: "When I reached for the light switch, I knew suddenly that everything, the peaceful garden and the peaceful house, had been a deception. The camp had followed me, it filled the room; it filled the entire house."[94] Confronted with dying patients of whom she has grown fond, Christine relates to their vulnerability and despair. She laments, "For the first time I felt close to the sick, suffering men; in a strange way I had become like them, as if I too were sick, plagued, abandoned, and helpless like them."[95] Her growing empathy for others and her awareness of the suffering around her transforms her from a naive child to a young woman.

Central to the novel is Christine's coming of age during the war and postwar period. When the former prisoner Imre, who was once an artist, draws a portrait of Christine, she questions her attractiveness to others: "Was I really pretty?"[96] Christine is aware of being a young woman whose dreams of living a carefree youth have been cut short by war and the postwar reality: "I was barely grown up, my clothes were too big for me, and I had to wear men's shoes. . . . But [Imre] kissed my hand, like one kisses a lady's hand."[97] After the camp receives supplies from the commander, Christine gains self-confidence because she was the one who secured the aid: "Everything which had happened earlier, before that night with the commander, seemed clear to me and sharply separated from my current life. I looked at my shoes. I didn't care that I had to wear men's shoes. I would never again be embarrassed or shy because of it."[98] She also experiences affection for the kindhearted man Penny, an American soldier, and learns that sharing her grief with another relieves her suffering and creates clarity in understanding the events. In the course of a conversation with Penny about mourning the dying prisoners, she realizes that she felt compelled to help her father at the camp despite his wishes because of her former passivity and ignorance while watching a dying prisoner in a ditch toward the end of the war.[99] Her vulnerability is most evident toward the end of the novel when both Christine and her father suffer from typhoid fever that they have caught at the camp. While bedridden and near death, she also has to work through her grief at her father's death. Christine understands her father's death as a logical consequence of the inhumanity of war: "My father was dead. He would not be dead if that commander had helped us earlier. His parents, his wife, his children, his entire family was murdered in a concentration camp."[100] Christine attributes her maturation to the loss of her father and to having witnessed the suffering of others throughout the war and postwar periods.

Recheis imparts to young readers the ideas of redemption, sacrifice, friendship, responsibility to others, and civic courage that accompany Christine's coming of age during the postwar months. The book ends with a conciliatory note: Penny, who is childless, will adopt the Polish orphan boy Jari, whom Christine has helped recover both physically and mentally in the camp. Penny's act shows readers how his love for Jari has the potential of saving them both from loneliness and despair. Both *Lena* and *Geh heim und vergiß alles* are deeply personal novels for Recheis, the writing of which was "a difficult decision" because she knew that the memories would "come alive" and because in writing them the "imagined reality" had "to become real."[101] The "imagined reality" of these novels, created through Recheis' recollections and the oral histories of her community, contributes to their authenticity as documents of a young woman's experiences during the 1930s and

1940s in Upper Austria. Welsh, Nöstlinger, and Recheis look to their own experiences as children of the war and the postwar period to explore coming of age during war from their adult perspectives. Themes of childhood and coming of age, such as game playing, body consciousness, and relationships to family members, distinguish these novels from those written for adults, which focus largely on how the trauma of war plays out in adulthood. Childhood and youth are portrayed by adult authors within a socio-historical context, in which events are recast and retold using analytical and critical thought processes.

By rewriting history to include their own experiences as children and young women of the war and postwar era in Austria, Welsh, Nöstlinger, and Recheis have written novels for children and young adults in an effort to educate and to contextualize their homeland's history leading up to, during, and in the years following World War II. The authors aim to motivate young readers to seek out peaceful solutions to conflict, to practice vigilance in the face of autocratic governments, and, foremost, to practice responsibility toward themselves and toward the local and global community.

Conclusion

> That I remember when the time comes.[1]
> – Petra Ganglbauer, *Der Himmel wartet* (*Heaven waits*, 2006)

> Everything I could say about what is written here, one can of course better discover by reading it.
> – Elfriede Jelinek, "Das flüchtige jetzt" (The fleeting now)[2]

In writing about war in fiction and memoirs, Austrian women and those of Austrian heritage write themselves into Austria's history of World War II and the postwar era. They do so with the intent of reshaping the history of the war and the postwar period, which has too often disregarded the experiences of girls and women on the home front, in the resistance movement, in concentration and death camps, in hiding, and in exile. By engaging in themes of war, writers invite readers to become part of the process of working individually and as a community through the horrific events of World War II and the Holocaust. Some authors who describe the history of the war and the postwar period to younger generations challenge readers to reflect on war and to value tolerance and justice.[3] In her memoirs, Trahan demonstrates that the war and the Holocaust are ever present in the minds of survivors and that this legacy continues to shape their present. Kräftner's poetry and prose, which conveys a palpable anguish in her suffering endured during the war, reminds readers how war takes its toll on survivors. For the postwar writers Aichinger, Reichart, Welles, and Nowak, the older woman figures as the voice of truth about the war, with which present-day readers must reckon. For Austrians forced into exile, such as Blend and Segal to Britain or Tausig and Kosiner to Shanghai, experiences as refugees are bound up with their heritage and former homeland; theirs is also a story of Austrians during the war and the postwar period.

The writers Nöstlinger, Recheis, and Welsh, who came of age during the war and postwar period, urge readers of younger generations to practice tolerance, justice, and peace. As the first decade of the twenty-first century draws to a close, it is evident that the discourse on World War II and the Holocaust is far from over, nor are authors finished writing about these topics. Despite significant and provoking dialogues in literary texts that engage the past by "coming to terms with the past" (*Vergangenheitsbewältigung*) or by a process Klüger calls "coming to terms with reality" (*Wirklichkeitsbewältigung*), Austrian-Jewish authors in particular, writing at the end of the twentieth century and beginning of the twenty-first century, continue to ponder Austria's role in the Third Reich and to examine how the Holocaust still informs the identities of generations of Austrians and Austrian Jews living in Austria or elsewhere in the world.[4]

Like second-generation Austrian-Jewish writer Beckermann, whose writings on Austrian Jewish identity are discussed in this volume's introduction, first-generation writers Aichinger and Klüger of Austrian-Jewish heritage revisit their past in personal essays and memoirs written at the start of the twenty-first century. Unlike Klüger, who has made her homes in Germany and the United States, Aichinger lives in Vienna and engages readers through journalistic writing, published as personal essays, in a remapping of Austrian history that includes the stories of Austrian Jews. Aichinger's recent writings, almost sixty years after the publication of *Die größere Hoffnung*, interweave the author's personal history with current events. The volume of personal essays written between November 2001 and December 2004, *Unglaubwürdige Reisen* (Unbelievable Journeys), is divided into two sections. The first set of essays were written over three years for the travel section of the newspaper *Standard*; the second part, written between 2003 and 2004, is entitled "*Schattenspiele*" (shadow games). Read together, these essays recontextualize Aichinger's life and writings. Her personal history, almost never discussed publicly or written about until recently, is interspersed throughout her essays on film, famous personalities, travel, and political events. Through fragmented memories, Aichinger reveals aspects of her childhood and her coming of age during World War II, showing that the murder of her family in the Holocaust has determined the course of her life until today, "even every happy turn of events."[5]

Like Aichinger, Klüger also continues to write about her experiences during the Holocaust and the postwar period well into the twenty-first century. Klüger, for example, examines anti-Semitism in the works of Austrian-Jewish authors in her essay "*Die Ödnis eines entlarvten Landes*" (The wasteland of an unmasked country), the title taken from Aichinger's novel *Die größere Hoffnung*.[6] For Klüger, Aichinger's novel portrays Austria as the "private hell" of a child who "clings to straws on the way to her death, where the mother is exiled, the father an enemy."[7] Austria "abandons or devours its own children."[8] Klüger's 1992 memoir *weiter leben – Eine Jugend* describes her own childhood as an Austrian Jew and her survival during the Holocaust. With her second memoir, from 2008, *Unterwegs verloren: Erinnerungen* (Lost along the way: Memories), she confronts the ever-present traumas that haunt her in the form of ghosts who "seek her out," coming from her "unsolved, unredeemed past."[9] She writes that these ghosts are responsible for both "trifles and enormities" and that, "like the living, they take what they can."[10] She concludes, referring to the title of her memoir, that "what goes missing on the way is always you alone, and the next place of arrival consists, as do earlier ones, of the now and the then; there is no new beginning, only continuations on a path that noticeably narrows."[11] Austrian postwar authors such as Klüger write to stave off their feelings of loss, to keep ghosts at bay, and to invite readers to walk along the narrowing path. Klüger's 2008 memoir, a reckoning of her personal and professional past, considers not only her losses but also the injustices and affronts she has suffered, due to what she perceives as persecution because of her gender or heritage, or both.[12] For Klüger, writing is reality; there is no such thing as a coincidence in literature. She argues that readers need literature because of its intentional and deliberate nature. Realism, as revealed in the authentic experiences she recounts, is "not a pale imitation of reality but rather the interpretation of it."[13] For readers then, such an interpretation of experience provides a way into history that can otherwise seem depersonalized by traditional modes of dissemination.

The atrocities of war, as described in the narratives by Austrian women included in this volume, are moderated by individual accounts of survival, by declarations of friendship, love, and loyalty, and by bold acts of resistance. Many authors write with strength drawn from acts of humanity they have witnessed and with the hope for a more peaceful future. Writers who themselves did not live through times of war but who have gathered memories from members of older generations have gleaned knowledge from a wealth of literature on World War II and the Holocaust and have thoughtfully reconstructed portraits of this time. Fictionalized historical events and creative nonfiction encourage readers to examine past events as they relate to the present. Both memoirs and fiction about World War II and the postwar era bear witness to the past and, as such, demonstrate how the past has shaped the present. The power and significance of these narratives lies in their affirmation of the principles that individual choices and actions do in fact affect the outcome of personal and public histories, that courage comes in many forms, such as in the unearthing of painful memories in writing a memoir, and that the possibility for a more cooperative and peaceful future lies within the grasp of each individual.

Notes

Acknowledgments and Preface

[1] Kirsten Krick-Aigner, "Girls Coming of Age During World War Two and the Postwar in Austria: Novels by Christine Nöstlinger and Renate Welsh," *PostScript*, no. 23 (Spring 2006): 102-126.

[2] Spaces in the poem are placed by Rich. Adrienne Rich, "Dark Fields of the Republic: Six Narratives," in *Women on War: An International Anthology of Writings from Antiquity to the Present*. ed. Daniela Gioseffi (New York: The Feminist Press at the City University of New York, 2003), 23-24.

[3] Yann Martel. *Life of Pi* (Edinburgh: Canongate), 2002, x.

[4] Most novels and memoirs I discuss are available in both English and German and, if no longer or currently in print, are widely available in public and private libraries.

[5] This diverse Austrian culture, a monarchy until 1918, once including parts of Hungary, the former Czechoslovakia, the former Yugoslavia, and Romania, is now a democratic nation, comparable in area to the state of Maine, with a population exceeding eight million. During the reign of National Socialism, Austria was annexed into the Third Reich in 1938. After World War II Austria was divided into four occupied zones by the Allied Forces: Lower Austria (Niederösterreich), the Burgenland, and the Mühlviertel were occupied by the Soviets; Upper Austria (Oberösterreich) and Salzburg by the Americans; Tyrol (Tirol) and Voralberg by the French; and Carinthia (Kärnten) and Styria (Steiermark) by the British. Walter Göhring, Robert Machacek, and Friederike Stadlmann, *Aufbruch aus dem Nichts: Entstehung und Geschichte der 2. Republik Österreich* (Vienna: Verlag des Österreichischen Gewerkschaftsbundes, 1980), 16.

The popular slogan in the newspaper *Kurier*, "Austria will be free. We will regain our homeland in its entirety," marked Austria's sovereignty after the departure of the Allied forces in April 1955. (Österreich wird frei. Wir bekommen unseren Heimatboden in seiner Gänze zurück.) *Kurier*, April, 1955, in ibid., 35.

[6] Modern-day Austria borders Germany, Hungary, Italy, Slovakia, Slovenia, Switzerland, the Czech Republic, and Liechtenstein, nations whose languages and cultures are bound to the diverse regions of Austria. The Austrian regional linguistic intricacies and idiosyncrasies are unique and are inherent to the language of its literature. Its people speak primarily German as well as some Italian, Czech, and Hungarian. During its reign as

one of the most powerful empires of the western world, citizens of the Austro-Hungarian Empire spoke a variety of languages, such as Hungarian, Romanian, Polish, Yiddish, German, and Italian.

[7] Sigrid Weigel states that in Bachmann's memory "literary enterprise and Germany were identical" and points out that Austria did not even acknowledge the young author until a year after she had already been heralded a literary star in Germany. Sigrid Weigel, *Ingeborg Bachmann. Hinterlassenschaften unter Wahrung des Briefgeheimnisses* (Vienna: Paul Zsolnay Verlag, 1999), 270 and 276. The works of Austria's internationally recognized literary figures, such as Aichinger, Bernhard, Handke, Marlen Haushofer, Elfriede Jelinek, Ruth Klüger, Christine Nöstlinger, Elisabeth Reichart, and Renate Welsh have, for the most part, been published by German publishing houses, such as Piper and Suhrkamp (Bachmann), Fischer (Aichinger), Beltz (Nöstlinger), Rowohlt (Welsh), and Friedrich Oetinger (Welsh). Austrian publishing houses, including Milena, Picus, Residenzverlag, Wiener Frauenverlag, and Zsolnay, have embraced the uniqueness of Austrian literature and have published, among others, works by the authors Graziella Hlawaty, Ildi Ivanji, Ruth Klüger, Elizabeth Welt Trahan, and Eva Anna Welles.

[8] Even though there was scholarly interest in Austrian exile studies well before 2002, the opening of the *Austrian Society for Exile Research* in 2002 formally acknowledged the scholarly field and enabled Austrian exile literature to "become a legitimate subject for academic research and debate." Charmian Brinson, Richard Dove, and Jennifer Taylor, eds., introduction to *"Immortal Austria"? Austrians in Exile in Britain*, vol. 8 of *The Yearbook of the Research Centre for German and Austrian Exile Studies* (Amsterdam: Rodopi, 2007), xiii.

[9] Archives include the Literaturhaus Wien in Vienna and the Literaturhaus in Salzburg, the Leo Baeck Institute in New York, the Wiener Library in London, and the Library of the United States Holocaust Memorial Museum in Washington, D.C.

Introduction

[1] Charlotte Shedd. *Thank You, America* (Riverside, CA: Ariadne, 1997), 288. Shedd kept a diary starting from the time she arrived in the U.S. on January 11, 1939.

[2] Shedd, 288.

[3] For example, I include limited information from Ruth Klüger's internationally celebrated memoirs and comment only briefly on the work of the Nobel Prize-winning author Elfriede Jelinek. The writings of these

prominent authors have already led to much scholarly work. Selected relevant scholarly texts on both Jelinek and Klüger, especially for English-speaking readers, are included both in the main text and in the endnotes of this volume.

[4] Italics by the author. Bernhold quotes S. Myer and E. Schultze, "Aspekte des Geschlechterverhältnisses untersucht am Beispiel der Auswirkungen des Zweiten Weltkrieges auf Familien," in *Lebenslauf und Familienentwicklung: Mikroanalysen des Wandels familialer Lebensformen*, ed. A. Herlth and K. P. Strohmeier (Opladen: Leske & Budrich, 1989), 231–56. Monika Bernhold, "Representations of the Beginning: Shaping Gender Identities in Writtten Life Stories of Women and Men," in *Austrian Women in the Nineteenth and Twentieth Centuries*, ed. David F. Good, Margarete Grandner, and Mary Jo Maynes (Providence: Berghahn Books, 1996), 199.

[5] Bernhold, 199.

[6] Ibid., 204.

[7] "Dort, wo Geschichte zu Literatur verarbeitet wird, überschneiden sich die beiden Bereiche." Ruth Klüger, *Dichter und Historiker: Fakten und Fiktionen* (Vienna: Picus, 2000), 17.

[8] "Und wir waren doch junge Menschen, die gerne Erklärungen gehabt hätten für den Erdrutsch, den sie gerade mit knapper Not überlebt hatten." Ibid., 36.

[9] "Und wenn man jetzt zurückblickt, so kann man nicht umhin zu fragen, ob das alles nicht eine Flucht vor der Geschichte war, nämlich einer Geschichte, die man am eigenen, fast verbrannten Fleisch erlebt hatte." Ibid., 36–37.

[10] "Für die Historiker wie für die Literaten ist die Geschichte, das Geschehen, Rohmaterial, dem sie eine Interpretation, eine Form angedeihen lassen." Ibid., 38.

[11] "Interpretiert wird ja nicht nur, wo eine Schrift oder ein Video vorgelegt wird, sondern auch in den Gedanken, die jeder Mensch hat, der nicht taub und blind durch die Wirklichkeit wandert. Historiker und Literaten tun von Berufs wegen, was jeder tut, der sich in seiner Welt orientiert." Klüger, Ibid., 40–41.

[12] "Daß Literatur, die sich mit Geschichte befaßt, eine Form der Wirklichkeitsbewältigung ist" and "Kein Faktum wie kein Ding, ist, bei Lichte besehen, schatten- oder deutungslos. Nur verwechseln soll man das eine nicht mit dem anderen, das Ding mit der Deutung." Ibid., 50–52.

[13] "Was uns ein geliebtes oder auch ein nur anregendes Buch sagt, ist nicht dasselbe wie das, was 'der Dichter uns sagen will.' Wir haben jeder und jede unsere eigene Sprache, und diese Sprachen sind so unterschiedlich wie die Handschriften und die Fingerabdrücke. Die

Autoren sprechen *eine* Sprache, wir eine andere, sie sind gesättigt von ihren, wir von unseren Erfahrungen, sie werfen uns mit ihren Büchern ein Seil zu und ziehen an dessen einem Ende, wir am anderen, zwischen uns ist die Spannung." Klüger, *Katastrophen: Über deutsche Literatur* (Göttingen: Wallstein, 1994), 8.

[14] Efraim Sicher writes about the necessity of fantasy and the art of making up false stories in examples such as Jurek Becker's *Jakob der Lügner* (*Jacob the Liar*, 1975): "Fabrication and fairy tales are essential lies for us to believe in, giving courage to those who go to their deaths and leaving a memory when they are dead." Efraim Sicher, *The Holocaust Novel* (New York: Routledge, 2005), 28.

[15] Bachmann said in an interview in 1971 that dreams enabled her to write of the atrocities of violence and war: "In den Träumen weiß ich aber, wie ich es zu sagen hab'. Und für mich bin ich ganz sicher, daß in den Träumen alles drin steht, was an Furchtbarkeit in dieser Zeit geschieht, und daß wir alle ermordet werden." Ingeborg Bachmann, *Wir müssen wahre Sätze finden. Gespräche und Interviews*, ed. Christine Koschel and Inge von Weidenbaum (Munich: Piper, 1991), 70. Bachmann also said in an interview in 1963 that she was reading about the war in history books: "Was ich lese? Viele Sachbücher, Dokumentationen, die den letzten Krieg und die neuere Geschichte betreffen; überhaupt tendiert alles auf Fassen von Geschichte hin, auf Geschichtsphilosophie und Geschichtsschreibung." Ibid., 42.

[16] Graziella Hlawaty, *Die Stadt der Lieder* (Vienna: Zsolnay, 1995), back book cover. The novel was translated as *Broken Songs: An Adolescent in War-Torn Vienna*. Trans. Pamela S. Saur. Studies in Austrian Literature, Culture, and Thought (Riverside, CA: Ariadne, 2005).

[17] Many of the themes of childhood and coming of age during the war and the Holocaust in Austria are addressed in Klüger's 1992 and 2001 memoirs and reflect the themes discussed in this volume. An astounding number of scholarly works already attest to their place as the most significant postwar memoirs by an Austrian-Jewish author. Born in Vienna in 1931, Klüger writes of her difficult childhood and coming of age in the shadows of anti-Semitism and post-Anschluss violence. In 1942 Klüger and her mother were deported from Vienna on one of the last transports to Theresienstadt and from there to Auschwitz in 1944. They were then selected for forced labor at the Christianstadt camp, where they escaped a death march in 1945, afterwards settling briefly in Bavaria, Germany. Her father and half-brother were murdered in the Holocaust. In October 1947 Klüger and her mother emigrated to the United States, where Klüger went on to become a highly respected German scholar and

writer. She now lives in Göttingen, Germany, and Irvine, CA. Her memoirs examine her Austrian-Jewish heritage and identity, the reconstruction of memory, her ambivalent relationship to her native German language, her love of literature, her strained yet close relationship with her mother, and the difficulties and challenges of trying to come to terms with her past as a Holocaust survivor. One particular article on Klüger is of note as it addresses the importance of writing in her memoir *weiter leben*. Scholar Sandra Alfers examines the poems included in *weiter leben*, in which Klüger recalls "the process of creating poetry . . . as a means of maintaining her own voice and of surviving from one day to the next." Sandra Alfers, "Voices from a Haunting Past: Ghosts, Memory, and Poetry in Ruth Klüger's *weiter leben: Eine Jugend* (1992)," *Monatshefte* 100, no. 4 (2002): 521. Alfers discusses especially two of the eight poems from the memoir, "Auschwitz" and "Der Kamin" (The chimney), written when Klüger was thirteen years old while in the Auschwitz concentration and extermination camp. Klüger writes of the healing and soothing power of writing; she recalls the "poetic and therapeutic attempt to hold up a linguistic, whole rhymed entity in the face of this senseless and destructive circus, in which we were going under." ("ein poetischer Versuch, diesem sinnlosen und destruktiven Zirkus, in dem wir untergingen, ein sprachliches, ganzes Gereimtes entgegen zu halten . . ." (ibid., 521). Alfers notes of Klüger's memoir: "By interspersing that which happened (history) with that which is remembered of what happenend (autobiographical memory, common and deep memory), and with commentary on both, Klüger's autobiography calls attention to its own position between these categories." (ibid., 528.) See also further articles on Klüger's *weiter leben* and *Still Alive*: Dagmar C. Lorenz, "Memory and Criticism: Ruth Klüger's *weiter leben*," *Women in German Yearbook* 9 (1993): 206-224; Linda Schulte-Sasse, "*Living On* in the American Press: Ruth Klüger's *Still Alive* and Its Challenge to a Cherished Holocaust Paradigm," *German Studies Review* 27, no. 3 (October 2004): 469-475; Caroline Schaumann, "From *weiter leben* (1992) to *Still Alive* (2201): Ruth Klüger's Cultural Translation of Her 'German Book' for an American Audience," *The German Quarterly* 7, no. 3 (Summer 2004): 324-339; Frederik Lubich, "Surviving to Excel: The Last German Jewish Autobiographies of Holocaust Survivors Ruth Klüger, Marcel Reich-Ranicki, and Paul Spiegel," *Modern Judaism* 25, no. 2 (May 2005): 189-210.

[18] Trahan, for example, refers to statistics from a diary entry and to general statistics relating to the Jewish pogroms in Vienna. Elizabeth Welt Trahan, *Geisterbeschwörung: Eine jüdische Kindheit im Wien der Kriegsjahre*, trans. Elfriede Potyka (Vienna: Picus, 1996), 131. Trahan, born in 1925 in

Berlin, passed away in 2009 in Amherst, MA.

[19] See works by scholars Lawrence Langer, Berel Lang, James Young, and Efraim Sicher.

[20] James E. Young, *Writing and Rewriting the Holocaust: Narrative and the Consequence of Interpretation* (Bloomington: Indiana University Press, 1990), 132. Plath's poetry as it relates to Bachmann's prose is further discussed in my article "The Female Poet as Persecuted Jew: Gender (Mis)Representation in the Works of Ingeborg Bachmann and Sylvia Plath" in *After Postmodernism: Austrian Literature and Film in Transition*, ed. Willy Riemer, (Riverside, CA: Ariadne, 2000), 298–311, and in my book *Ingeborg Bachmann's Telling Stories: Fairy Tale Beginnings and Holocaust Endings* (Riverside, CA: Ariadne, 2002), 125–29.

[21] James E. Young, *Writing and Rewriting the Holocaust: Narrative and the Consequence of Interpretation* (Bloomington: Indiana University, 1990), 1.

[22] Sicher, xii.

[23] Ibid., 131.

[24] Ibid., 133.

[25] Ibid., xiii.

[26] Ibid., xvi–xvii.

[27] Ibid., xviii. Sicher reflects on Adorno's often-cited statement that to write after the Holocaust is barbaric, by adding that the philosopher intended to emphasize that "pleasure not be squeezed out of the screams of the victims." Ibid., xv–xvi.

[28] Ibid., xvi and x.

[29] "So ist die Literatur, obwohl und sogar weil sie immer ein Sammelsurium von Vergangenem und Vorgefundenem ist, immer das Erhoffte, das Erwünschte, das wir ausstatten aus dem Vorrat nach unserem Verlangen – so ist sie ein nach vorn geöffnetes Reich von unbekannten Grenzen." "Literatur als Utopie." Bachmann, *Werke IV*, 258.

[30] "Die Wahrheit nämlich ist dem Menschen zumutbar." Bachmann, "Die Wahrheit ist dem Menschen zumutbar," 275–77. The speech was given at the awarding of the Hörspielpreis der Kriegsblinden (Radio Play Prize of the War Blind) award ceremony in Bonn, Germany, in 1959.

[31] Sicher, 111.

[32] Ibid., 112.

[33] Ibid., 114.

[34] Ibid., 133.

[35] Ibid., 133.

[36] Thane Rosenbaum, as quoted in Sicher, 134. I would also argue that even those authors whose parents and grandparents did not

experience the Holocaust as victims were witnesses to its aftermath in society. Author Elisabeth Reichart, for example, was horrified to find that forced-labor and concentration camps such as Mauthausen had existed near her home and confronted the silence about the atrocities committed so close to home by members of her parents' and grandparents' generations in her 1984 novel *Februarschatten*.

[37] Sicher, 135.
[38] Ibid., 136-137.
[39] Ibid., 165.
[40] Ibid.,166.
[41] "Sie würden eine Kindheit haben und eine Jugend." Ruth Beckermann, *Unzugehoerig: Oesterreicher und Juden nach 1945* (Vienna: Löcker Verlag, 1989), 10.
[42] "There, where there is 'a future.'" (Dorthin, wo es 'eine Zukunft' gibt.) Ibid., 10.
[43] "Unsere Gefühle und Gedanken, unsere Identität als Kinder der Überlebenden, werden in diesem Land ignoriert und beleidigt." Ibid., 10.
[44] For example, in Beckermann's view, Alfred Hrdlicka's 1988 stone and bronze memorial on the Albertina Square in Vienna, "Mahnmal gegen Faschismus und Krieg" ("Warning against Fascism and War"), reinforces the stereotype of the victimized Jew as well as negative stereotypes of Jews. For Beckermann, the bronze sculpture of the kneeling Jewish man scrubbing the pavement says to her: "You lay in the dust. You slid on your stomachs. And this is our picture of you today. Fifty years later we form you according to this image, as pious elders. This moves the heart and pushes the victims away to a comfortable distance; it suggests that the Jews were a senile, elderly, sickly people whose natural death was close at hand. And you, who still live, we want to see you this way, outwardly and inwardly kneeling, that's how we let you live. And woe betide you if you fall out of that role." (Im Staub seid ihr gelegen. Auf dem Bauch seid ihr gerutscht. Und das ist heute unser Bild von euch. Fünfzig Jahre danach formen wir euch nach diesem Bild. Als frommen Alten. Das rührt ans Herz und rückt die Opfer gleichzeitig in angenehme Distanz; suggeriert es doch, daß die Juden ein seniles, alters-schwaches Volk waren, dessen natürlicher Tod kurz bevorstand. Und ihr, die ihr noch lebt, euch wollen wir so sehen, äußerlich und innerlich kniend, so lassen wir euch leben. Und wehe, wenn ihr aus der Rolle fallt.) Ibid., 14.
[45] "Zementierung der Opfer-Legende," "Darstellung einer Katastrophe ohne Täter und Opfer," "Umkehrung der historischen Täter- und Opferrolle," und "Rückkehr zu den gewohnten Feindbildern." Ibid., 47.
[46] Ibid., 29.

⁴⁷ Ibid., 26.
⁴⁸ "Whereas suicides were a rarity in concentration camps, they were part of everyday life after release." ("Waren Selbstmorde in den Konzentrationslagern Seltenheit, so gehörten sie nach der Befreiung zum Alltag.") Ibid., 71.
⁴⁹ Ibid., 73.
⁵⁰ Ibid., 80.
⁵¹ Ibid., 80.
⁵² Ibid., 99.
⁵³ Ibid., 99. Weiner reports a higher number of Austrian-Jewish survivors, 800, who hid in Vienna during the war. Rebecca Weiner, *The Virtual Jewish History Tour: Vienna*, Jewish Virtual Library, www.jewish virtuallibrary.org/jsource/vjw/Vienna.html, accessed February 11, 2010.
⁵⁴ Beckermann, *Unzugehoerig*, 99. Citing different numbers, Susanne Cohen-Weisz writes that, by April 1947, 700 Austrian Jews had returned from England, 800 from Shanghai, 200 from Palestine, and 350 from Karaganda in Russia. "From Bare Survival to European Jewish Vision: Jewish Life and Identity in Vienna," Working Papers, Institute For European Studies, The Hebrew University of Jerusalem, http://www.ef. huji. ac.il/publications/working.shtml, 5 (accessed June 8, 2010).
⁵⁵ Beckermann, 99.
⁵⁶ Cohen-Weisz, 6.
⁵⁷ Ibid., 23.
⁵⁸ Ibid., 99. Rebecca Weiner reports a much larger community of 15,000 Jews, "including unaffiliated Jews," consisting of "Eastern European refugees from the Holocaust era and their children, returning expatriates who lived abroad during World War II and Iranian Jews seeking asylum. Vienna has also served as a transit point for Jews leaving the Soviet Union en route to the United States or Israel." Weiner, *The Virtual Jewish History Tour Vienna*, *Jewish Virtual Library*, www.jewish virtuallibrary.org/jsource/vjw/Vienna.html, accessed February 11, 2010. Cohen-Weisz finds the Austrian-Jewish population to have been even higher than does Weiner. She writes that, in 2007, 7,014 Jews were registered in the IKG (Israelitische Kultusgemeinde) yet states that the "actual number of Jews living in Vienna is, however, assumed to be around 15,000-20,000." Cohen-Weisz, 8. Earlier in her working paper Cohen-Weisz declares that Vienna is home to 95 percent of today's Austrian Jewish population. Ibid., 2.
⁵⁹ Ibid., 3.
⁶⁰ Ibid., 21. Cohen-Weisz also comments on the changing identity of Austrian Jews: "An intra-Jewish discourse on the Austrian identity of the

Jews began and gathered momentum following the Waldheim affair, promoted on the one hand by the active dealing of the Austrian population with its own history and the place of the Jews in it, and on the other hand by the conscious desire of many members of the post-war Jewish generation to live in Vienna and build their future in the city as Viennese" (ibid., 32). She adds, "moreover, Viennese Jews' identity is Viennese rather than Austrian. . ." (ibid., 32). She continues, "European identity is more acceptable to Austrian Jews and to Jews abroad than Austrian identity" (ibid., 40). In the context of Cohen-Weisz's observations, I argue that the Austrian-Jewish memoirs and texts explored in this volume demonstrate the authors' unique, albeit at times ambivalent, Austrian heritage. I would also add that Ruth Klüger's memoirs display a more inclusive European Jewish identity, even a multi-national identity, in which she recognizes that she was born in Austria yet chooses to now live in both Germany and the United States.

[61] "Isolation" und "Niemandsland." Beckermann, 110 and 117.

[62] Ibid., 127.

[63] "Bald zwanzig Jahre sind seit Niederschrift dieses Textes vergangen. Viele Bücher erschienen zu dem Thema, neue Quellen wurden erschlossen, welche diesen schmalen Band ergänzen und erweitern, meine grundsätzlichen Analysen jedoch nicht verändern, sondern untermauern. Erstaunt war ich beim Durchlesen meines Essays wohl darüber, dass das Lebensgefühl der Unzugehörigkeit, in welcher ich ihn geschrieben hatte – durch die Ereignisse mal abgeschwächt, dann wieder bestärkt – Bestandteil jüdischen Lebens in diesem Land bleibt." (Beckermann, foreword to the 2005 edition of *Unzugehoerig*. Vienna, August, 2005, in: www.ruthbeckermann.com/biography/publications/unzugehoerig/index.php (accessed February 8, 2010).

[64] Sicher, 171. Following the German reunification in the 1990s, German neo-Nazi groups gained more followers due in part to high unemployment and economic strain in former East Germany. In Austria neo-Nazi groups, also tied to Nazi groups that continued to meet after World War II ended, were encouraged by the leadership of Jörg Haider and his right-wing political party, FPÖ, Freiheitliche Partei Österreichs, because of his populist, nationalist, anti-communist, and xenophobic rhetoric. In 2005 Haider left the FPÖ to form the new political party, BZÖ, Bündnis Zukunft Österreich, which he led until his death due to a traffic accident in 2008. The BZÖ's new head, Josef Bucher, and the FPÖ's leader, Heinz-Christian Strache, and FPÖ politician, Barbara Rosenkranz, revived heated political debates concerning Austria's role in the Holocaust and immigration reform, among other topics, in the

Austrian presidential elections of 2010. Debates over Holocaust memorials in Austria and Germany, designed and constructed in the late 1980s and early 1990s, have shaped public discourse concerning Holocaust remembrance. In Germany the Holocaust Memorial in Berlin, dedicated in 2005, provoked a heated debate over its design, location, and significance. Peter Carrier traces this debate about the "transmission and pedagogical function of history" in his volume *Holocaust Monument and National Memory: France and Germany since 1989* (New York: Berghahn Books, 2005), 47. Carrier examines the memorial's "central function of art in the attempted 'nationalism' of collective memory" (ibid., 47).

In Austria public debates over Vienna's Holocaust memorials focus largely on a general unease at confronting Austria's National Socialist past felt by some of Austria's citizens. Alfred Hrdlicka's Mahnmal gegen Krieg und Faschismus (Memorial against War and Fascism), constructed between 1988 and 1991, was the cause of much controversy. Some critics, such as Simon Wiesenthal, disagreed with the memorial's dedication to "all the victims of war," which included Wehrmacht soldiers as well as Jewish victims of the Holocaust, and others did not want to be reminded of Austria's role in the war and Holocaust, especially since the memorial is centrally situated, adjacent to Vienna's State Opera. Wiesenthal and other supporters therefore initiated the design and construction of a memorial dedicated solely to the murdered Jews. The memorial Mahnmal für die 65.000 ermordeten österreichischen Juden und Jüdinnen der Shoah, (Memorial to the 65,000 murdered Austrian Jews of the Shoah), or the Judenplatz Holocaust Memorial, also known as the Nameless Library, stands in the Judenplatz in the heart of Vienna. The memorial, designed by the British artist Rachel Whiteread, caused a heated debate before its dedication in 2000. Some critics believed that the reconstruction of a thirteenth-century synagogue discovered under the proposed site for the memorial would have been a more fitting memorial to Austria's murdered Jews. Again, other critics did not want to be reminded of Austria's role in the Holocaust. Now, the memorial shares the square with the Museum Judenplatz that houses the remains of the synagogue and a permanent exhibit on Jewish life in the Middle Ages.

[65] Ibid., 171.

[66] Ibid., 173.

[67] The exhibit resulted from the scholarship of Bachmann scholars Hans Höller, Helga Pöcheim, and Karl Solibakke, and was funded by the Verein zur Förderung von Werk- und Kunstverständnis Ingeborg Bachmann in Kooperation mit dem Bundesministerium für Auswärtige

Angelegenheiten, Austria.
  [68] Brinson, Dove, and Taylor, eds. "Immortal Austria"?, ix.

Chapter One

[1] Lawrence L. Langer, "Gendered Suffering. Women in Holocaust Testimonies" in *Preempting the Holocaust* (New Haven: Yale University, 1998), 45.
  [2] Daniela Gioseffi, *Women on War*, xxi.
  [3] Ibid., xxi–xxxvi.
  [4] Of those displaced, 75% were women and children, ten million of whom were under the age of eighteen. In 2007, a website of the UNHCR estimated that 20.8 million individuals fit the definition of a refugee, described as "owning to a well-founded fear of being persecuted for reasons of race, religion, nationality, membership of a particular social group, or political opinion, is outside the country of his nationality, and is unable to or, owning to such fear, is unwilling to avail himself of the protection of that country." The UNHCR more broadly defines refugees as "internally displaced persons, returnees, asylum seekers, resettled persons, and stateless people." www.ninemillion.org (accessed March 2, 2007). By 2010, the number of refugees internationally had increased to 32.8 million. http://www.ninemillion.org/index.php?/site/Sections/About/About-UNHCR (accessed June 14, 2010)
  [5] Since 1994, following the estimated 20,000–50,000 reported sexual assaults on girls and women during the conflict in Bosnia-Herzegovina, rape has been considered a war crime under the Geneva Conventions. Gioseffi states that, of the 500,000 child soldiers, many under ten years old, many girl soldiers are forced into sexual slavery. Gioseffi calls the 1989 Convention on the Rights of the Child, "the most important legal framework for the protection of children worldwide." Gioseffi's anthology is a cry for peace and for more international peace work, urging women and men to "celebrate the heroines and heroes of nonviolence instead of the false heroes of war," calling for "planetary citizenship" to end warfare and its destruction of the environment. Gioseffi, xxi–xxii, xxxiv, xxxix.
  [6] Joshua S. Goldstein, *War and Gender: How Gender Shapes the War System and Vice Versa* (Cambridge: Cambridge University, 2001), 407–12.
  [7] Ibid., 22, 27, and 407.
  [8] Ibid., 22.
  [9] Bachmann wrote, "war, real war, is just an explosion of this war that is peace." "Der Krieg, der wirkliche Krieg, ist nur die Explosion dieses

Kriegs, der der Frieden ist." Bachmann, *Wir müssen wahre Sätze finden*, 70. In 1946, Bachmann wrote in her diary that peace should be viewed as an essential condition, a "conditio sine qua non," and that "everyone, without distinction and forever, should be able to live and to work, and to eat and sleep without fear." (daß alle, ohne Unterschied und für immer, leben sollen und arbeiten sollen, dürfen, und essen und schlafen ohne Furcht, und weil dies die conditio sine qua non für sie ist, auch beharrlich verlangen dürfen, daß die Schwierigkeiten des Führens von Frieden keine leichtfertigen partiellen Lösungen finden, keine emphatischen und sentimentalen, keine langfristig gefährlichen und kurzfristig geflickten.) Bachmann, quoted from her diary, back cover of exhibit brochure, "Schreiben gegen den Krieg," (Vienna, Austria: Verein zur Förderung von Werk- und Kunstverständnis Ingeborg Bachmann in Kooperation mit dem Bundesministerium für Auswärtige Angelegenheiten, 2009).

[10] Goldstein, 9–10. Just some of the world's post-World War II women combatants include an estimated one-third of the Sandinista front's military; 4,000 women fighters, or six per cent, of the ZANLA forces in Africa; one-third of the rebel Tamil Tigers' force of 15,000 fighters; and women guerillas in Iraq in the late 1990s and in the Republic of Congo war in 1997. Goldstein's research shows that examples of women in guerilla warfare are not rare, unlike those in conventional war, and that these women have "added to the military strength of their units, and sometimes fought with greater skill and bravery than their male comrades." Yet Goldstein also observes that "whenever their forces seize power and become regular armies, women have been excluded from combat. Evidently, this exclusion is not based on any lack of ability shown by the women soldiers when they participated in the guerrilla phase of war." Ibid., 80–83.

[11] Ibid., 10.
[12] Ibid., 182.
[13] Ibid., 182.
[14] Ibid., 182.
[15] Ibid., 19.
[16] Ibid., 21.
[17] Ibid., 70.
[18] Ibid., 127.
[19] Ibid., 70.
[20] Ibid., 71.
[21] Ibid., 357-362.
[22] Ibid., 362.
[23] Ibid., 362.

[24] "Rapes in wartime apparently bear no relationship to the presence of prostitutes or other available women – showing that rape is not driven by sexual desire." Ibid., 363.
[25] Ibid., 34.
[26] Ibid., 39.
[27] Ibid., 47.
[28] Ingeborg Bachmann, *Werke 1*, ed. Christine Koschel, Inge von Weidenbaum, and Clemens Münster (Munich: Piper, 1993), 109 and 161.
[29] "Der junge Mann lächelte sie an. 'Noch eine, die nicht mitmacht. . . .' . . . "Wir konnten alle Bücher retten. Das Graurockgeschmiere haben wir auch mitgebracht. Was sollen wir damit machen? 'Verbrennen,' sagte Lois." Barbara Neuwirth, "Bücherverbrennung," in *In den Gärten der Nacht* (Frankfurt a. M.: Suhrkamp, 1990), 90.
[30] Elfriede Jelinek, "Der Wald," in *Schriftstellerinnen sehen ihr Land*, ed. Barbara Neuwirth (Vienna: Wiener Frauenverlag, 1993), 253. Much scholarship in German and English already exists on Jelinek's writing and her political activism, especially that written after she won the Nobel Prize for Literature. The following selected scholarly works illuminate Jelinek's writing, especially for English-speaking readers: Matthias Piccolruaz Konzett and Margarete Lamb-Faffelberger, eds., *Elfriede Jelinek: Writing Woman, Nation, and Identity: A Critical Anthology* (Madison, NJ: Fairleigh Dickinson University, 2007); Bettina Brandt, "The Challenging Writings of Elfriede Jelinek: An Austrian Feminist Wins the Nobel Prize in Literature," *The Women's Review of Books*, 22, no. 3 (December 2004): 1 and 4; Udo Borgert, *Women's Words, Women's Works* (Riverside, CA: Ariadne, 2001); Jorun B. Johns and Katherine Arens, eds., *Elfriede Jelinek: Framed by Language* (Riverside, CA: Ariadne, 1994); Allyson Fiddler, *Rewriting Reality: An Introduction to Elfriede Jelinek* (Oxford: Berg, 1994).
[31] Joan Ringelheim, "The Split Between Gender and the Holocaust," in *Women in the Holocaust*, ed. Dalia Ofer and Lenore J. Weitzman (New Haven: Yale University Press, 1998), 350.
[32] Sara R. Horowitz, "Women in Holocaust Literature: Engendering Trauma Memory" in Ofer and Weitzman, 366 and 371.
[33] Ibid., 366.
[34] Ibid., 366.
[35] Ibid., 366.
[36] Ibid., 374.
[37] Langer, *Preempting the Holocaust*, xix.
[38] Ibid., 44.
[39] Charlotte Delbo, *Auschwitz and After*, trans. Rosette C. Lamont (New Haven: Yale University Press, 1995), 267, in Lawrence L. Langer,

Preempting the Holocaust, 46.
[40] Langer, *Preempting the Holocaust*, 54.
[41] Ibid., 57.
[42] Ibid., 58.
[43] Baer and Goldenberg, xxviii.
[44] Ibid., xxviii.
[45] Ibid., xv–xvi.
[46] Ibid., xxx.
[47] Pascale Rachel Bos, "Women and the Holocaus: Analyzing Gender Difference," in Baer and Goldenberg, 25.
[48] Ibid., 30.
[49] Ibid., 30. Such arguments, as given by Bos, Baer, and Goldenberg, support Austrian-specific cultural readings of narratives in which Austrian culture informs identity, especially for those living outside of Austria in exile.
[50] Ibid., 31.
[51] Ibid., 33.
[52] Ibid., 31.
[53] Ibid., 35.
[54] Ibid., 37.
[55] Ibid., 261.
[56] Ibid., 261.
[57] S. Lillian Kremer, "Women in the Holocaust: Representation of Gendered Suffering and Coping Strategies in American Fiction," in Baer and Goldenberg, 274.
[58] Anita Brostoff, ed., *Flares of Memory: Survivors Remember Stories of Childhood During the Holocaust* (Oxford: Oxford University Press, 1998), xxxvi.
[59] Brostoff, 2.
[60] Edith Richter Levy, "The Aftermath," in Brostoff, 258–59.
[61] Ibid., 258–59.
[62] Brostoff, xxxix and xxxvii.
[63] Ibid., xxxvi–xxxvii.
[64] Langer, *Preempting the Holocaust*, 144–45.
[65] Ibid., 144–45.
[66] Some young women were unable to write of their traumatic war experiences, even in diary form. For example, a young woman of 16 in England, Joan Wyndham, writes in her diary of her inability to write of her trauma: "Sometimes I feel the significance of what is going on in the world, but even then I can't put it into words." Laurel Holliday, *Children in the Holocaust and World War II: Their Secret Diaries* (New York: Pocket

Books, 1995), 308.
[67] Brostoff, xxix.
[68] Holliday, xiv–xvi.
[69] Ibid., xix–xx.
[70] Ibid., xix–xx.
[71] Felix Pollak's poem "Wien 1967" describes such a painful relation to memory: "Despite the fact that my/ roots here/ are cut off/ they pain me/ like a scar/ when it rains." (Obwohl meine/ Wurzeln hier /abgeschnitten sind,/ schmerzen sie/wie eine/Narbe/wenn's regnet.) Felix Pollak, "Wien 1967," in *Ein Niemandsland, aber welch ein Rundblick! Exilautoren über Nachkriegs-Wien*, ed. Ursula Seeber (Vienna: Picus, 1998), 183.
[72] Brostoff, xxxiv.
[73] Ibid., xxxiv.
[74] "Die Wiener Dreißigerjahre, kurz bevor Hitler kam, erscheinen mir in diesen Widersprüchen, diesen Tänzen am Rand des Vulkans, recht deutlich gespiegelt." Hilde Spiel, *Die hellen und die finsteren Zeiten: Erinnerungen 1911-1946* (Munich: Paul List, 1989), 126.
[75] Hilde Spiel. *The Dark and the Bright: Memoirs 1911-1989*. Trans. Christine Shuttleworth. Riverside, CA: Ariadne, 116. "Es ist gräßlich und unerträglich. Die Eltern sitzen im Feuer. Der Teufel regiert." Spiel, *Die hellen und finsteren Zeiten*, 174–75. Spiel's parents managed to escape to London to live with their daughter and son-in-law; Spiel's father died a broken man shortly after his emigration. During her many visits to Austria following the war, Spiel states that she felt more like a guest, that she shared an affinity to the country of her birth but did not always feel a kinship to all of its people. Marcel Reich-Ranicki, "In den Lüften Europas," in Hilde Spiel, *Rückkehr nach Wien: Ein Tagebuch* (Munich: Amalthea, 1996), 15.
[76] Brigitte Bailer, "Frauen und Nationalsozialismus," *1938. NS-Herrschaft in Österreich*, eds. Brigitte Bailer, Elisabeth Klamper, and Wolfgang Neugebauer (Vienna: Bundesministerium für Inneres, 1998), 21.
[77] "Erst bei drei bis vier Kindern bleibt der Bestand des Volkes sichergestellt." Ute Benz, *Frauen im Nationalsozialismus. Dokumente und Zeugnisse* (Munich: Verlag C. H. Beck, 1993), 57.
[78] Kurt Cerwenka, *Die Fahne ist mehr als der Tod: Nationalsozialistische Erziehung und Schule in "Oberdonau" 1938-1945*. Edition Geschichte der Heimat (Franz Steinmaßl, Grünbach: 1996), 37.
[79] Ibid., 37.
[80] As an example of the number of women in the workforce, scholars

Irene Bandhauer-Schöffmann and Ela Hornung note the following percentages of women in the total labor force in Austria: 1910, 40%; during the war, 52%; and in 1961, 40%. Bandauer-Schöffmann and Hornung, "War and Gender Identity: The Experience of Austrian Women, 1945–1950," in *Austrian Women in the Nineteenth and Twentieth Centuries: Cross-Disciplinary Perspectives*, ed. David F. Good, Margarete Grandner, and Mary Jo Mayes (Providence: Berghahn Books, 1996), 215.

[81] Andreas Baumgartner, *Die vergessenen Frauen von Mauthausen* (Vienna: Mauthausen Komittee Österreich, 2006), 24.

[82] Ibid., 25.

[83] Bailer, "Frauen und Nationalsozialismus," 21.

[84] Elisabeth Klamper, "Die Verfolgung der österreichischen Juden" in Bailer, 37. Klamper points out that Jews were defined by the Nürnberg Laws as individuals who had three Jewish grandparents. Those with two Jewish grandparents were considered of "mixed race" (*Mischlinge*). Relationships between "mixed race" individuals were also forbidden. Klamper also notes that "race" was defined by religious affiliation only. Ibid., 37–38.

[85] In Aichinger's *Die größere Hoffnung*, Ellen describes the non-Jewish grandparents of her friends as the "wrong grandparents" (falsche Großeltern). Aichinger, *Die größere Hoffnung*, (Frankfurt. a. M.: Fischer, 1991), 28. While Aichinger's mother and the author went into hiding in Vienna, her twin sister was able to secure passage to England in 1939 on one of the last Kindertransport ships. The mother's younger siblings and the author's beloved grandmother, of whom she wrote, were deported to and murdered in Minsk. Ilse Aichinger, *Unglaubwürdige Reisen* (Frankfurt a. M.: S. Fischer, 2005), 10.

[86] Bailer, 21.

[87] Liliane Studer, ed. *Die Frau hinter der Wand: Aus dem Nachlaß der Marlen Haushofer* (Munich: Claassen, 2000), 140. Studer writers that Haushofer's friends could not understand why she volunteered but supposed that volunteering allowed her to leave home before beginning her studies in German in Vienna.

[88] "The inner mutual harmony between the housewife and the mother fixes all problems. Mother and housewife, that is the solution, and that should really be the title of this most important chapter." (Die innere wechselseitige Harmonie zwischen der Hausfrau und der Mutter löst alle Probleme. Mutter und Hausfrau, das ist die Lösung, und so muß die Überschrift dieses wichtigsten Kapitels in Wirklichkeit lauten!) Benz, 175.

[89] Bandhauer-Schöffmann and Hornung, 215.

[90] Ibid., 215.

[91] "Alle praktische Betätigung ist nur eine Brücke zwischen dem Studium und dem wirklichen Leben." Ibid., 213–14.

[92] Peter Malina, "Jugend im Nationalsozialismus," in Bailer, Klamper, and Neugebauer, 15.

[93] Cerwenka, 12.

[94] Ibid., 14–15.

[95] Ibid., 19–21, 40.

[96] Ibid., 52–53.

[97] Ibid., 70, 81.

[98] Ibid., 31.

[99] Ibid., 37.

[100] Ibid., 48.

[101] In April 25, 1933, the law "Reichsgesetz gegen die Überfüllung von Schulen und Hochschulen" was introduced by the National Socialist party. It limited admission to universities to only 1.5% of the Jewish population and to 10% of women. Anna Maria Sigmund, *Die Frauen der Nazis* (Munich: Wilhelm Heyne, 1998), 16.

[102] Baumgartner, 14-15.

[103] Benz, 196-98.

[104] "Die Ehe ist eine unmögliche Institution. Sie ist unmöglich für eine Frau, die arbeitet und die denkt und selber etwas will." Bachmann, *Wir müssen wahre Sätze finden*, 144.

[105] Heidemarie Uhl offers a good summary of events leading to the development of this term in her article "The Politics of Memory: Austria's Perception of the Second World War and the National Socialist Period," in *Austrian Historical Memory & National Identity*, ed. Gunther Bischof and Anton Pelinka (New Brunswick: Transaction Publishers), 1997, 66–80.

[106] Following the war, those Austrians who had been members of the Nazi party – 670,000 citizens – were not allowed to vote in the November 25, 1945, Austrian elections. Of those who were able to vote, 64% were women. A National Council (*Nationalrat*) was elected, consisting of 85 members of the Austrian People's Party (ÖVP, or Österreichische Volkspartei), 76 Socialists, and four Communists. The withdrawal of the right to vote was part of the de-nazification process that included the dismissal of 150,000 Austrian government functionaries and court trials of 13,000 former Nazis. Walter Göhring, Robert Machacek, and Friederike Stadlmann, *Aufbruch aus dem Nichts: Entstehung und Geschichte der 2. Republik Österreich* (Vienna: Verlag des Österreichischen Gewerkschaftsbundes, 1980), 18.

[107] The press and historians confirmed that Kurt Waldheim, president of Austria from 1986 to 1992, had been an intelligence officer in the

Wehrmacht during the Third Reich, although Waldheim continued to deny his active role in National Socialist crimes against humanity. Due to Waldheim's involvement in National Socialism, he and his wife were deemed "personae non gratae" by the United States and were officially denied permission to enter the country throughout his presidency. Waldheim was also not invited to visit other Western countries throughout his presidency.

108 The chapters are tellingly entitled "The Last Day of the Third Reich," "The End of the War: Liberation or Collapse?," "Hunger and Shortage," "Women Secure Survival: The Daily Fight for Food," "Changing Relations in Marriage and Family," and lastly, "The Short Days of Female Glory." The interviews were all conducted after the fiftieth anniversary of the Anschluss in 1988 and the surfacing of the "Waldheim affair." Bandhauer-Schöffmann and Hornung, 216.

109 Ibid., 217–19.

110 Ibid., 219.

111 Göhring, Machacek, and Stadlmann, 10.

112 Günter Unger, "Anmerkungen zur Herkunft von Hertha Kräftner," in *Hertha Kräftner: Das Werk*, ed. Franz Probst (Eisenstadt: Burgenländischer PEN-Club, 1977), 8.

113 Cohn is probably a Jewish surname. For Nöstlinger, the character of Cohn could be considered a positive depiction of a Jew and of a Russian soldier, also one who does not view her as representative of the Austrian perpetrators.

114 Bandhauer-Schöffmann and Hornung, 221.

115 Ibid., 222.

116 Göhring, Machacek, and Stadlmann, 19.

117 Ibid., 19.

118 Ibid., 19.

119 Ibid., 20.

120 Bandhauer-Schöffmann and Hornung, 225.

121 Göhring, Machacek, and Stadlmann, 22.

122 Bandhauer-Schöffmann and Hornung, 221-222.

123 Nöstlinger and Welsh also address how households were impacted by the bombings of Vienna by the Allies, as well as by the consequent deaths of family and friends and piles of rubble. During the last weeks of the war, fifty-two bombings were reported in Vienna, with approximately 9,000 civilians buried in rubble.

124 Bandhauer-Schöffmann and Hornung, 223.

125 Ibid., 223.

126 Ibid., 223 and 226.

[127] Ibid., 226.

[128] It is of note that American women journalists, reporting for American newspapers in Europe during World War II, focused largely on issues concerning the home front and the daily lives of women and family life during war. As Nancy Caldwell Sorel reports, "Barred from press briefings until late in the war, women reporters began by writing of the less combative side of the conflict – of the daily heroism of the medics, the miracles the doctors performed, how caring (even when bone-tired) the nurses were. They wrote of the young wounded far from home and of civilian victims close to home – families torn apart, old people cold and tired and homeless, mothers desperate for food for their children, children hungry and hurting and afraid." *The Women Who Wrote the War* (New York: Perennial, 2000), xiv.

[129] Bandhauer-Schöffmann and Hornung, 227. Younger women who were coming of age in families did not always carry the burden of laboring to survive, which gave them "a chance to enjoy some pleasures." Bandhauer-Schöffmann and Hornung, 228.

[130] Ibid., 229.

[131] Ibid., 229.

[132] Martha Maria Gehrke, *Das Donauland-Frauenbuch* (Vienna: Buchgemeinschaft Donauland, 1965), 425.

[133] Ibid., 425. In a section on how a woman should spend her time in the home, the handbook suggests an exhausting "schedule for the Hausfrau," which runs from 6 a.m. to 10 p.m. with only few breaks (ibid., 330–31). At the end of that section, the handbook comments on "working women" and reminds them to "wake up a half hour before that recommended schedule" since they have to "further care for the husband" (ibid., 341). Furthermore, the handbook states, "for the woman it is doubly important to rest briefly, in order to be fresh to cook and, especially, to meet the husband well rested and looking good" (ibid., 341).

[134] Bandhauer-Schöffmann and Hornung, 230

[135] Ibid., 230.

[136] Ibid., 220–21.

[137] Benz, 201–202.

[138] Sigmund's study of women who supported the Nazis as spouses, lovers, and friends, *Die Frauen der Nazis*, dedicates a chapter to Baldur's wife, Henriette von Schirach, who claimed after the war not to have known of the Jewish deportations that occurred daily and publicly. Following the Anschluss, Hitler named Baldur von Schirach *Gauleiter* (head of an administrative district), *Reichsstatthalter* (governor of the Reich), and *Oberbürgermeister* (mayor) of Vienna. Henriette, a follower of Hitler

who had been instrumental in promoting her husband's career, was elated to move with their three children to Vienna. Baldur von Schirach was ordered to plunder the Austrian Jews and have them deported, penniless, by 1940. Sigmund, 301. Following this, Dr. Löwenherz, the president of the Jewish religious community, the *Kultusgemeinde*, at the urging of Adolf Eichmann, traveled the world to seek a safe haven for Austrian Jews. When Dr. Löwenherz pleaded his case at a conference in Evian, 32 nations with "poor excuses" denied Austrian Jews refuge. Ibid., 301. Sigmund reports on Henriette's supposed ignorance about the facts that Jews were not allowed in the Vienna Woods, the Freudenau, or public gardens and baths and were forbidden to use trams and underground trains and to use public phones or send mail. During heavy American bombings of Vienna on September 10, 1944, the Schirach's villa was damaged, whereupon Henriette moved with the children to their country house in Bavaria. Following the war, after various trials of the couple, Baldur was sentenced to twenty years in prison in Spandau and Henriette was made to pay a financial penalty but did not have to serve a one-year probation. She later took on various jobs, divorced Baldur, and married a film producer, becoming in later years a controversial postwar author who maintained her positve attitude toward National Socialism until her death in 1992. In 1956 she published her memoir *Der Preis der Herrlichkei*t (the price of splendor) and in 1983 *Frauen um Hitler* (women surrounding Hitler). Baldur, whose ex-wife said of him in 1950, "he is not a war criminal, but rather an idealist and much too good for politics," published *Ich glaubte an Hitler* (I believed in Hilter) in 1967. Sigmund, 279–318.

[139] "Wenn früher die liberalen intellektualistischen Frauenbewegungen in ihren Programmen viele, viele Punkte enthielten, ihren Ausgang vom sogenannten Geiste nahmen, dann enthält das Programm unserer nationalsozialistischen Frauenbewegung eigentlich nur einen einzigen Punkt, und dieser Punkt heißt *das Kind*." Benz, 45.

[140] "Das Wort von der Frauen-Emanzipation ist ein nur vom jüdischen Intellekt erfundenes Wort, ..." Ibid., 42.

[141] "Als erstes steht für alle deutschen Frauen die Abteilung Mütterschulung and Mütterdienst." Ibid., 47.

[142] Ibid., 75.

[143] "Doch tröste Dich, Du liebes Muttchen, denn nur Du allein hattest neben meiner großen Liebe zum Vaterland einen Platz in meinem Herzen. Ein Idealist kämpft bis zum Tod." Ibid., 115–17.

[144] "The capital of a large multi-national empire under the German-speaking Habsburg dynasty for five centuries, Vienna after 1918 became the capital of the small Republic of Austria. With a population of 1.9

million, Vienna housed 28 percent of the country's entire population in 1934. In 1938, some 170,000 Jews lived in the city, as well as approximately 80,000 persons of mixed Jewish-Christian background. Including converts from Judaism, the Viennese Jewish population may have been as high as 200,000, more than 10 percent of the city's inhabitants." "Vienna," Holocaust Encyclopedia, United States Holocaust Memorial Museum, http://www.ushmm.org/wlc/article.php?ModuleId =10005452, (accessed March 2, 2010). Cohen-Weisz cites the official census of March 22, which shows that, in 1934, 191,481 registered Jews lived in Austria with 176, 034 Jews living in Vienna alone. Cohen-Weisz, 5.

[145] "Austria," Holocaust Encyclopedia, United States Holocaust Memorial Museum, http://www.ushmm.org/wlc/article.php?lang=en& ModuleId=10005447 (accessed March 2, 2010). Cohen-Weisz states that, following the Anschluss in 1938, "about 130,000 Austrian Jews had succeeded in emigrating and about 65,000 were deported, murdered or committed suicide." Cohen-Weisz, 5.

[146] Rebecca Weiner cites the deportation of 6,000 Jews from Austria. "The Virtual Jewish History Tour" (Vienna, Jewish Virtual Library) 2009, http://www.jewishvirtuallibrary.org/jsource/vjw/Vienna.html (accessed June 14, 2009). A further document states that on April 1, 1938, in Vienna, 60 Jews and on May 24, 1938, a further 50 Jews were deported to Dachau. Austrian Bundespressedienst, "Jüdisches Leben in Österreich," (Vienna: Österreich Dokumentation, 1994), 26.

[147] Information from *Jewish Vienna: Heritage and Mission* (Vienna: Vienna Tourist Board, 1995), 12–13; Bundespressedienst, Österreich-Dokumentation, *Jüdisches Leben in Österreich* (Vienna, 1994); *1938: NS-Herrschaft in Österreich: Texte und Bilder aus der gleichnamigen Ausstellung* (Vienna: Bundesministerium für Inneres, Dokumentationsarchiv des österreichischen Widerstandes, 1998); and *Frauenleben 1945 – Kriegsende in Wien.* (Sonderausstellung des Historischen Museums der Stadt Wien, September 21-November 19, 1995 (Vienna: Eigenverlag der Museen der Stadt Wien, 1995).

[148] Aichinger's twin sister was also sent to England by Kindertransport. Aichinger's family could only acquire one passage, and Aichinger felt that she was the stronger of the two sisters and therefore chose to remain in Vienna with her mother. The situation of a child's desperate measures to seek a safe haven and the image of a ship full of children sailing to safety is dealt with poetically in Aichinger's novel *Die größere Hoffnung*, which the author wrote as a young woman immediately after the war in 1948. Ilse Aichinger, conversation with author, Austria,

July 9, 2002.

¹⁴⁹ A few authors returned to Vienna after the war, such as Spiel, only to find that they no longer felt at home there. Spiel explored her conflicted attachment to her Austrian homeland in her 1990 memoir, *Welche Welt ist meine Welt? Erinnerungen. 1946-1989* (which world is my world? memoirs) (Munich: Paul List Verlag, 1990).

¹⁵⁰ Information from *Jewish Vienna: Heritage and Mission*, 12–13; Bundespressedienst, Österreich-Dokumentation: *Jüdisches Leben in Österreich; 1938: NS-Herrschaft in Österreich. Texte und Bilder aus der gleichnamigen Ausstellung*; and *Frauenleben 1945 – Kriegsende in Wien*, 205.

¹⁵¹ Seeber, ed. *Ein Niemandsland, aber welch ein Rundblick*, 208.

¹⁵² "Heute, sechzig Jahre nach dem März 1938, gilt die Beschäftigung mit dem lange verdrängten Thema Verfolgung und Exil, nicht zuletzt durch die Grundlagenarbeit einer jüngeren Generation von Forscherinnen und Forschern, als kulturpolitischer Auftrag und Teil offizieller Erinnerungsarbeit." Seeber, "Vorwort: Frauen in der Emigration: Eine 'überlesene' Geschichte wird ins Sichtfeld gerückt," in *Frauen aus Wien: Fotoband von Alisa Douer mit Texten von Ursula Seeber*, ed. Alisa Douer and Ursula Seeber (Vienna: Frauenförderung und Koordination von Frauenangelegenheiten, 1999), 9.

¹⁵³ Seeber, ed., *Ein Niemandsland, aber welch ein Rundblick*, 206.

¹⁵⁴ Ibid., 206.

¹⁵⁵ Ibid., 207.

¹⁵⁶ Ibid., 214.

¹⁵⁷ Hertha Pauli was born 1909 in Vienna and died 1973 in New York. "Schritt für Schritt geht man da auf doppeltem Boden. Ein Fuß steckt immer in der Vergangenheit, der zweite strebt in die Zukunft voraus, und wo sie einander schneiden, zergeht die Gegenwart im Wandel der Zeit." Hertha Pauli, "Wiener Variationen," in Seeber, ed.,163.

¹⁵⁸ "Die Sache ist die: Sie brauchen uns heute weniger, denn Europa erholt sich. . . . Sie haben Wurzeln. Wir sind Strandgut. Keine Amerikaner, aber auch keine Europäer mehr. Nicht Fisch und nicht Fleisch. Vielleicht sind sie es, die uns darin stören, in diesem Land ganz heimisch zu werden." Lili Körber, "Post aus Europa," in Seeber, ed., 132.

¹⁵⁹ "An der Aussprache erkennbar als Einheimische/aber im Ausdruck häufig als Fremde." Ruth Klüger, "Besuch der Exil-Touristinnen in Wien," in Seeber, ed., 205.

¹⁶⁰ Seeber, "Nachwort," 214.

Chapter Two

[1] Elizabeth Welt Trahan, *Walking with Ghosts. A Jewish Childhood in Wartime Vienna* (New York: Peter Lang, 1998), v.

[2] Although *Walking with Ghosts* was originally written in English, it was first published in Austria, translated into German. The German title, *Geisterbeschwörung: Eine jüdische Jugend im Wien der Kriegsjahre*, is not a literal translation of *Walking with Ghosts*; instead, it translates as "Conjuring up ghosts: A Jewish youth in Vienna during the war years." Trahan's memoir had been well received in Austria two years before being published in 1998 in its original English-language version. Quotations in English are taken from *Walking with Ghosts*.

[3] Elizabeth Welt Trahan, *Ten Dollars in My Pocket* (New York: Peter Lang, 2006), 3.

[4] Ibid., 4.
[5] Ibid., 199.
[6] Trahan, *Walking with Ghosts*, 9.
[7] Ibid., 237.
[8] Ibid., 96.
[9] Ibid., 1.
[10] Ibid., 69.
[11] Ibid., 1.
[12] Ibid., 2.
[13] Ibid., 67.
[14] Ibid., 68.
[15] Ibid., 118.
[16] Ibid., 142.
[17] Ibid., 145.
[18] Ibid., 112.
[19] Ibid., 112.

[20] Dagmar C. G. Lorenz, *Keepers of the Motherland: German Texts by Jewish Women Writers* (Lincoln: University of Nebraska Press, 1997), 275.

[21] Lorenz, xvi.
[22] Ibid., 291–92.
[23] Ibid., 292.
[24] Ibid., 275.
[25] Ibid., 275.
[26] Trahan, *Walking with Ghosts*, 226–27.
[27] Ibid., 70.
[28] Trahan, *Ten Dollars in my Pocket*, 34.
[29] Ibid., 115.

[30] Ibid., 268.
[31] Trahan, *Walking with Ghosts,* 211.
[32] Ibid., 211.
[33] Ibid., 3.
[34] Ibid., 3.
[35] Trahan, *Ten Dollars in my Pocket,* 279.
[36] Examples of such entries from *Ten Dollars in My Pocket* follow: "I found myself totally alone and lonely in midst of a crowd" (35); "Though my nerves are calm at the moment, they tend to slide back into a tense state at any provocation" (37); "I must pull myself together" (40); "Since coming here I seem not quite myself, am restless (71); "I feel myself lost" (85); "So why do I feel myself more as a stranger here" (99); "I am a stranger. The stranger" (114); "To go crazy cannot really be a sickness – it is just that utmost degree of loneliness that the body will bear" (207); "This is only a slight reverberation of the other great loneliness of the past" (207); "After weeks of unhappiness, insecurity and nervous restlessness I finally started out this last week on 'my' walk" (217).
[37] Trahan, *Ten Dollars in My Pocket,* 143.
[38] Ibid., 49.
[39] Ibid., 11.
[40] Ibid., 19.
[41] Ibid., 143.
[42] Ibid., 279.
[43] Trahan, *Walking with Ghosts,* 202.
[44] Trahan, *Ten Dollars in My Pocket,* 3.
[45] Ibid., 3.
[46] Ibid., 4.
[47] Ibid., 91.
[48] Ibid., 99.
[49] Ibid., 180.
[50] Ibid., 221.
[51] Ibid., 221.
[52] Ibid., 221.
[53] Ibid., 186.
[54] Ibid., 184–85.
[55] Ibid., 224.
[56] Ibid., 268.
[57] Ibid., 90.
[58] Ibid., 268.
[59] Ibid., 3.
[60] Ibid., 223.

[61] Ibid., 271.
[62] Ibid., 271.

Chapter Three

[1] "Schreib – an irgend etwas – erschaff was, das Leben neu, du fängst es neu an, mit einem neuen Blatt!" Dine Petrik, *Die Hügel nach der Flut. Was geschah wirklich mit Hertha K.?* (Salzburg: Otto Müller, 1997), 18.

[2] Joan Montgomery Byles, *War, Women, and Poetry, 1914-1945: British and German Writers and Activist*s (Newark, DE: University of Delaware Press, 1995), 176.

[3] Whereas the majority of literary critics heralded the new edition as long overdue and a celebration of a forgotten Austrian literary genius, some have criticized it as providing a skewed picture of the author's life and work, one that, with its inevitable ending in suicide, can only be read in the context of her depression and death. Scholars, such as Gerald Bisinger, have regarded the collection of Kräftner's work as "a posthumous novel," "a unique and complete work," and "a kind of novel, written by its main protagonist" Kräftner, *Kühle Sterne* (Klagenfurt: Wieser, 1998), 350. Literary critic Franz Haas of the *Neue Züricher Zeitung*, however, writes of *Kühle Sterne* that the "world will have to wait for a critical edition" of Kräftner's writings and laments the unexplained omissions in the letters and diaries. N. t., Zürich, October 4, 1997, 53-54, international edition.

[4] In Aichinger's short story "Mondgeschichte" (moon story), the female protagonist is pulled out of the river after attempting to drown herself. When she is asked why she no longer wants to live, the girl replies that she "is ugly," that she "was not beautfiul enough for one man." In *Märchen deutscher Dichter*, ed. Elisabeth Borchers (Frankfurt a. M.: Insel, 1972), 244. In Haushofer's short story "Wir töten Stella" ("Killing Stella"), the young woman Stella commits suicide after becoming pregnant by the middle-aged narrator's husband, in whose house she had been employed. Bachmann's protagonists from her novel cycle *Todesarten* are "murdered" by the society in which they live. The female protagonist in *Malina* symbolically disappears into a crack in the wall at the close of the novel, stating, "es war Mord" (it was murder), leaving only her male double Malina to tell her story. The protagonist Franza in Bachmann's novel fragment *Der Fall Franza* is psychologically and physically abused by her husband and unsuccesfully attempts to establish her sanity and self-worth throughout the novel. During a trip with her brother Martin to the Egyptian desert, Franza attempts to kill herself by begging an ex-Nazi

doctor to give her a lethal injection, to "eradicate her," as he had formerly done to the victims of euthanasia in the Holocaust. The doctor refuses, and Franza is instead raped and murdered at the end of the novel.

[5] Bachmann, *Werke: Todesarten: Malina und unvollendete Romane*, ed. Christine Koschel, Inge von Weidenbaum and Clemens Münster (Munich: Piper, 1993), 22-23.

[6] Montgomery Byles, 17.

[7] Ibid., 18.

[8] Ibid., 41.

[9] Ibid., 44.

[10] Ibid., 45.

[11] Ibid., 176.

[12] "Es hat mich nicht sehr berührt." Kräftner, *Kühle Sterne*, 357.

[13] "Früher oder später hätte ich es getan, ganz so wie mein Großvater," and "Es ist wahrscheinlich das Schicksal meines Großvaters, das in mir wiedergeboren wurde." Ibid., 340.

[14] Günter Unger described the attack on Kräftner as a "forcing" (*Bedrängung*): "[An officer] forced himself on the women who were there, among them the 17-year old Hertha Kräftner." ([Ein Offizier] bedrängte die anwesenden Frauen, darunter auch die 17 jährige Hertha Kräftner.) "Anmerkungen zur Herkunft von Hertha Kräftner," in Kräftner, *Das Werk*, 8.

[15] "Einmal nanntest Du mich fahrig und unausgeglichen. Eine fast vollkommene Definition. Aber ich war nicht immer so. Ich war einmal ein sehr ruhiges, klares Kind. Aber die Ereignisse am Kriegsende (Du weißt, was ich meine), der jähe Tod meines Vaters und manch anderes ließen mich so werden. Dann kam ein Erlebnis, das mich tief und heftig anrührte und mich schließlich ganz aus dem Gleichgewicht brachte. Da griff ich nach jenem Mantel und verschloß mich vor allem. Und ich lebte in meiner eigenen Welt, die wunderbar reich und schön war." Kräftner, *Kühle Sterne*, 26.

[16] "Sex," a translation of "Geschlecht," designates not so much the female gender but the sexual organ. "Nichts sagen. Nicht zu sagen. Unsäglich. Nichts gesagt vom Augenblick an wo dein Geschlecht barst." Petrik, 49.

[17] "Wien-Großbaustelle: Von Favoriten bis zur Universität zerbombte Fassaden. Gehen über Bomben. Besetzte Ämter. Kirchentreppen. Russen. Kein Aufhebens machen! Vergewaltiger. Hundsaugen. Schnell vorbei. Plünderer. Ein Trümmerhaufen, das Amalienbad. Leere Läden. Hunger. Heimkehrer. Schleichhandel." Petrik, 43.

[18] "And I lived in my own world that was wonderfully rich and beautiful." (Und ich lebte in meiner eigenen Welt, die wunderbar reich und schön war.) Kräftner, *Kühle Sterne,* 26.

[19] "Ich möchte immerfort Gedichte schreiben, aber zu viele Gedanken stürzen auf mich los." Ibid., 17.

[20] "Ich möchte mit der Abendröte gehn,/ tief mit dem Rot nach ferne./ Ich möchte in dem Abendrot vergehn,/ und möchte in den Winden wehn,/ die ohne Ziele rauschend gehn/ und steigen in die kühlen Sterne." Ibid., 31.

[21] "Nacht," "Melancholie," "Abschied," and "Abend." Ibid.

[22] "Der Weg zu deiner offnen Tür ist schwer/ durch die Gewißheit, daß die Wiederkehr/ mich nimmer so wird finden wie vorher." Ibid., 18.

[23] "Die Dämmerung kommt aus bleichem Land./ Ich fühle müd: sie bringt den Abschied mit./ Leb wohl . . . laß meine Hand . . . / Nein mach kein Licht./ Ich will im Dunkeln gehen." Ibid., 19.

[24] "Ich entdecke, daß ich zwiespältig bin. In mir vereinigen sich konträre Eigenschaften, die immer im Gleichgewicht bleiben. . . . Ich bin kalt u. brenne doch gleich einer roten Flamme." Ibid., 23.

[25] "Wunderbare Nächte schenkte – draußen auf dem weiten Meer, unterm Mond – Nächte u. Morgen ohne Küste, u. daß auch Du sie mir schenkst u. gerade so: Stunden ohne Küste." Ibid., 39.

[26] "Was weißt Du denn davon, was Mädchen denken, wenn sie nachts allein in ihrem Bette liegen? Wunderbare und schreckliche Nächte." Ibid., 39.

[27] Ibid., 365.

[28] Ibid., 366.

[29] "Und wenn ich mein Leben wiederleben müßte, würde ich nur die Zeit annehmen, in der ich Hertha traf, alles andere scheint unwichtig." Ibid., 367.

[30] "Ich fühle es: wenn ich liebe, dann liebe ich so sehr, daß es sonst nichts mehr für mich gibt." Ibid., 23.

[31] "Ich tue Dir damit weh und es tut mir leid, aber ich muß es trotzdem tun." Ibid., 341.

[32] "Leb wohl, ich habe Dich lieb gehabt." Ibid., 340.

[33] "Alles wäre ganz einfach gewesen, wenn ich Dich nicht so geliebt hätte, so ausgeliefert, so ohne Rettung, ohne Maß." Ibid., 339.

[34] "Ich habe Dich sehr geliebt." Ibid., 341.

[35] Kräftner describes her capacity and desire to love endlessly as "hours without a coast," in her diary entry, "Nights and mornings without a coast, and that you too give them to me, and just so: hours without a coast." (Nächte u. Morgen ohne Küste, u. daß auch Du sie mir schenkst

u. gerade so: Stunden ohne Küste.) Ibid., 39.

[36] "Mir tut niemand mehr leid. Ich bin nicht verzweifelt, nicht berauscht. Ich bin wie ein kaltes Reptil. Veronal. Sorgsam gesammelt, erschwindelt, oft am Abend betrachtet, manchmal die glatten Phiolen lange zwischen den Fingern gehalten, verborgen in meiner Seidenwäsche." Ibid., 325.

[37] "Trink Mohn und träume." Ibid., 341.

[38] "And I lived in my own world, that was wonderfully rich and beautiful." (Und ich lebte in meiner eigenen Welt, die wunderbar reich u. schön war.) Ibid., 26.

[39] "Doch ihre träumeblassen, zarten/ Hände müssen lange warten,/ bis einer kommt, der sie daraus befreit." Ibid., 18.

[40] "Seine Finger aber fühlen/ diese fast verblichenen Mädchenhände/ in noch nie gesagten Wünschen wühlen." Ibid., 20.

[41] "Noch nie fühlte ich die Bedeutung der Hände so sehr. Die Hände der Liebenden leben ein eigenes Leben. Und wenn der Mund der Rand der Seele ist, so sind die Hände der Liebenden die Schale, darin sie ruht. Und wenn ihre Hände sich berühren, so ist es, als ob der Inhalt zweier Schalen ineinander fließe. . . . Oh, Geliebter, ich liebe Dich in Deinen Händen." Ibid., 38.

[42] "Du bist nur noch ein weißes Tuch,/ das eine Hand, die ich vergaß,/ zu einem Abschied hob." Ibid., 51.

[43] "Ich gab dir meine Seele in die Hand,/ daß du ihr sagst: du bist in mir/ und aus mir hast du keine Tür./ Ich halte dich in einem sichern Rand." Ibid., 47.

[44] "Deine Hände kommen wie zwei Boote,/ um mich fortzutragen in ein Meer,/ aber mein Nicht-mit-gehn-Können ist viel mehr;/ denn ich bin schon eine Tote." Ibid., 62.

[45] "Handwerk – das ist Sache der Hände. Und diese Hände wiederum gehören nur einem Menschen, d. h. einem einmaligen und sterblichen Seelewesen, das mit seiner Stimme und seiner Stummheit einen Weg sucht. Nur wahre Hände schreiben wahre Gedichte. Ich sehe keinen prinzipiellen Unterschied zwischen Händedruck und Gedicht." . . . Wir leben unter finsterem Himmel, und es gibt wenig Menschen. Darum gibt es wohl auch so wenig Gedichte." Letter from Paul Celan to Hans Bender, Paris, May 18, 1960, in Harald Vogel and Michael Gans, *Rose Ausländer lesen*, Lesewege – Lesezeichen zum literarischen Werk: Leseportraits, Vol. 2 (Baltmannsweiler: Schneider Verlag Hohengehren, 1997), 212.

[46] Celan (Paul Antschel, 1920–1970), a Romanian German-speaking Jew who had physically survived the Holocaust in a work camp and

whose parents were murdered in Nazi death camps, lived in Vienna from 1947 to 1948, where he began his friendship with Ingeborg Bachmann. It is conceivable that Celan also met Kräftner during this time since she too moved to Vienna in 1947 and both were part of the tight-knit circle of postwar Viennese writers.

[47] "Vielleicht könnte ich einmal so werden, aber ich fürchte, Du wirst nicht Geduld haben, so lange zu warten." Kräftner, *Kühle Sterne*, 28.

[48] "Zum ersten Mal sah ich in der Ferne das Meer, ein heller blauer Streifen, darüber Abendrot. Das Meer. . . ich habe es so erwartet." Ibid., 112-113.

[49] "Durch eine Villenstraße kamen wir ans Meer, blau, weit, kühl." Ibid., 114.

[50] "Ich denke an eine Fähre, die uns immerfort über einen Strom hin und her fährt, aber wir merken es nicht und glauben, auf einem Meer zu sein, das nicht endet. Immer wieder erscheinen die gleichen Ufer, aber wir sehen sie nicht, weil wir einander ins Gesicht sehen." Ibid., 197.

[51] "Nun reicht es [das Wasser] mir bald bis zum Kinn. Ich denke viel an das Ende. Warum kam nur die Arche nicht?" Ibid., 247.

[52] "Wie gut, daß mein Vater tot ist. Ich hätte es nicht ertragen, ihn nicht mehr zu lieben. Wie böse, daß mein Vater tot ist. Er hätte mich nie gebraucht, er hätte mich immer geliebt. Und ich ihn. . . . ." Ibid., 138.

[53] "Das Gesicht meines toten Vaters,/ das meinem ähnlich sieht,/ wandelt in den Friedhofbäumen/ hin und her," and "Da ist mein Vater wieder gestorben." Ibid. 233.

[54] "Nun bin ich allein. Die Nacht ist wie aus großen schwarzen Stücken und alle fallen über mich. Irgendwo heult ein Hund vor Verlassenheit. Mein toter Vater ruft in mir." Ibid., 154.

[55] "Mein Vater ist tot, aber ich bin ihm nahe." Ibid., 155.

[56] "und da kommt an manchen Abenden/ mich mein Vater besuchen." Ibid., 243.

[57] "Ich kann vielleicht sagen: Oh, Melancholie! [Und] ein Gedicht auf weißes Papier schreiben mit blauer Tinte (ich liebe das sehr) . . . ." Ibid., 23.

[58] Kräftner writes, "Do you know that blue is the color of mourners?" (Weißt Du noch, daß Blau die Farbe der Trauernden ist?) Kräftner, *Das Werk*, 120. She also writes, "Where is the evening that gives me blue words . . . . (Wo ist der Abend, der mir blaue Worte schenkt . . . .) Kräftner, *Kühle Sterne*, 143. She writes twice of her "blue book" (das blaue Buch). Kräftner, *Kühle Sterne*, 159 and 169.

[59] Ibid., 146.

[60] "Beim Feueranmachen mit altem Papier verspürte ich mit einem

Mal die bekannte Lust, blau auf weißes Papier zu schreiben, ..." Ibid., 240.

[61] "Ich würde Büttenpapier und Ledereinband bevorzugen (ich hasse die forcierte Geste meiner Kollegen, mit der sie ihre Gedanken auf schlechtes Papier schmieren und dazu behaupten, die 'alte Form' gelte ihnen nicht), noch lieber aber würde ich mit Maschinenschrift auf weiches, rauhes Papier schreiben. Beides kann nicht sein." Ibid., 240.

[62] "Ich möchte eine grüne Mappe haben, in die ich jeden Tag ein Stück Papier lege, und außen soll stehen: 'Zu meinem Roman.'" Ibid., 242.

[63] "Niemals, niemals ist der Mond grün. Er ist weiß oder rot oder gelb, aber niemals grün." Ibid., 227.

[64] "Ich hütete mich, meine eigene Meinung zu befragen, und trachtete nach Objektivität. Aber was ist sie schon? Vertrat sie in diesem Fall der Leser oder der Redakteur?" Ibid., 229.

[65] "Niemals wird sich der Dichter dessen bewußt sein, was er entfesselt." Ibid., 231.

[66] "Sooft die schwarze Scheibe Mond/ mit Gelb sich füllt zum schmalen Bogen,/ wird ihm sein Blut von Zauberdrogen/ vergiftet." Ibid., 348.

[67] "Jeannie pudert sich die Nase und sagt halblaut über den Tisch zu mir: 'Stinkfad'. Weigel ist stolz und traurig zugleich (stolz, weil so viele gekommen sind, traurig, weil er alt wird). Und ich? Ich interessiere mich nicht mehr für Musik, nicht für Literatur, nicht für die Malerei, – ich flirte mit Kurt Moldovan." Ibid., 294.

[68] "sie schrieb die immer gleiche, krumme Zeile/ verbogner 'I' mit ungenauer Hand/ ins braun und lila Herbstzeitlosenland./." Ibid., 227.

[69] "... dieses dumme Doktorat." Ibid., 311.

[70] "Ich kann nicht kochen und selbst wenn ich es lerne, werde ich es nie gern tun. Haushalt ist etwas Gräßliches; natürlich kann ich mich überwinden und alles tun, was notwending ist, aber wer weiß, wie nervös es mich macht. Dann: Werde ich Arbeit finden und was für eine Art von Arbeit? ... Wird mir Zeit bleiben, neben aller Arbeit zu schreiben? Wirst Du mich anfeuern zu schreiben?" Ibid., 297.

[71] "In meinem Kopf ist ein riesiger Druck, ich spüre ihn bis in die Brauenhaare. Ich soll arbeiten! Ich soll meine Diss. schreiben, damit ich zu Dir kommen kann, ich soll eine Geschichte schreiben für einen Almanach, ich soll eine Novelle schreiben für eine Kleinbuchreihe, ich soll einen Roman schreiben, damit ich endlich von den Vorstellungen, die damit zusammenhängen, Ruhe habe. – Für einen normalen Menschen ist das durchaus nicht zuviel, aber ich sehe immer mehr, daß ich nicht so

belastbar bin wie. . . ." Ibid., 313-314.

[72] "Der Roman geht nicht weiter." Ibid., 318.

[73] "Mein Herz, vergiß nicht, daß ich nicht Deine Ehefrau (die über Wohnung, Wäschewaschen, Essenkochen schreibt) bin, sondern Deine Geliebte, die mit Vorliebe Sätze schreibt wie z. B.: 'Wenn Du nicht da bist, lege ich ein blaues Tuch um meinen Hals und male Dein Bild auf die Schattenwände der wachen Nächte.'" Ibid., 307.

[74] "Sie war schon tief im Tod gewesen, sie hatte von ihm her und zu ihm hin gelebt; . . . , und wenn wir Hertha Kräftners Tod nicht verstehen, ist das unsere Sache, nicht ihre." Hans Weigel, "Gedenkrede," in Kräftner, *Das Werk*, 5-6.

[75] In a 1989 article entitled "Aller Selbstmord: Flaschenpost der Toten" (All suicides: The dead's messages in bottles), Kräftner's biography is listed on a page along with other young male and female writers who took their lives, such as Otto Grabner (1952–1986), Friedemann Bayer (1944–1983), and Gerlinde Obermeier (1942–1984). The author Gerald Grassl prefaces his long list of well-known writers who celebrated death and suicide in their writing with the statement that Austria has one of the highest suicide rates in the world and that writers are especially well represented in this group. He believes that authors lead a substandard existence while attempting to uncover the "truth and the reality of society." The author contends that it is "one of the biggest cultural lies" that poets are inspired by their poverty; instead, he insists, "they are destroyed when writing no longer functions as a vehicle of resistance." Gerald Grassl, "Aller Selbstmord: Flaschenpost der Toten," *Volksstimme* (Vienna), November 1, 1989, 9.

[76] Wolfgang Broer, "Jedes Weltbild ist auch ein Seelenbild," *Kurier* (Vienna), March 18, 1978.

[77] "In each line, in each word the death drive is perceptible, romanticized, and on the border of kitsch, then again without illusion, almost forced. . . . Today's understanding would be that Hertha Kräftner must have suffered from the deepest depression, which paralyzed her so that she had only a partially fulfilled life but which at the same time became her motivating force. . . . Often artists shy away from relieving their suffering through psychotherapeutic help because they are afraid that their creativity will suffer. Probably, nobody thought of this in 1950, even though Kräftner intensively grappled with psychology, philosophy, and especially with Viktor E. Frankl." (In jeder Zeile, jedem Wort ist der Todestrieb spürbar, romantisiert, an der Grenze zum Kitsch, dann wieder illusionslos, beinahe zwingend. . . . Nach heutigem Verständnis muß Hertha Kräftner an schwersten Depressionen gelitten haben, die sie

lähmten, ein halbwegs erfülltes Leben zu führen, gleichzeitig aber auch ihre künstlerische Triebfeder waren. . . . Oft scheuen sich Künstler davor, ihren Leidensdruck etwa durch Inanspruchnahme psychotherapeutischer Hilfe zu lindern, aus Angst, dadurch ihre Kreativität einzubüßen. Soweit dachte 1950 wohl noch niemand, obwohl sich Kräftner intensiv mit Psychologie, Philosophie, insbesondere mit Viktor E. Frankl, auseinandersetzte." Klaus Vollmann, "Das schnelle Leben der Hertha K," *Prinz* (Vienna), November 1994, 100.

[78] "Weil er [Hirss] wohl sehr gut wußte, daß Herthas Gatte zugleich ihr Arzt sein muß." Kräftner, *Kühle Sterne*, 359.

[79] "Die wirkliche Ursache, warum der Tod einen trifft, zu wissen, ist niemals möglich; wirklich und ausschlaggebend ist nur, daß der Tod auch nach Teheran kommt." Ibid., 286.

[80] "Ein Mann, den ich nicht genug liebte, daß es mich im Leben gehalten hätte, sagte einmal: 'Sich töten?' – 'Wozu?' – 'Das führt doch zum nichts'. Das ist es: Es führt zum Nichts. Dort will ich hin. Ich konnte nicht alles haben, so will ich auch kein Etwas." Ibid., 325.

[81] It would not be the first time that an author whose work was controversial in the 1950s would finally find acceptance at the beginning of the twenty-first century and whose name would bring honor instead of raised eyebrows. Bachmann's work has inspired films such as *Malina* and *Ihr glücklichen Augen*, theatrical performances by Claus Peymann in the Burgtheater *Ingeborg Bachmann: Wer?*, dance performances, musical compositions, and even the highly sought-after literary Ingeborg Bachmann Prize; Bachmann's name has become an acceptable household word throughout Austria. A Carinthian secondary school in her home town of Klagenfurt has been renamed the Ingeborg Bachmann Gymnasium, and an InterCity (IC) train carrying passengers from Salzburg to Vienna bears her name.

[82] Peter Madler, *Books Abroad* (Norman: University of Oklahoma Press), Fall, 1964, no pages.

[83] Published by Schocken Books, New York.

[84] The collection of Kräftner's posthumous work is now housed in the Austrian Literature Archive (Österreichisches Literaturarchiv) at the Austrian National Library (Österreichische Nationalbibliothek), http://www.onb.ac.at/sammlungen/litarchiv/bestand/sg/nl/kraeftner.htm (accessed July 4, 2009). After writing this volume, and following renewed interest in Kräftner's work in Austria, a more recent scholarly work on Kräftner has been published in German: *Zum Dichten gehört Beschränkung: Hertha Kräftner – ein literarischer Kosmos im Kontext der frühen Nachkriegszeit*, ed. Evelyne Polt-Heinzl (Vienna: Edition Praesens, 2004). The translation of

the title is "Limitations are needed to write Poetry: Hertha Kräftner – A literary cosmos in the context of the early postwar period."
[85] "heft narrt krähe – hertha kräftner – literatur und bewegung" is a wordplay using the name "Hertha Kräftner" and words found in her poetry. Ruediger Engerth, *Salzburger Nachrichten*, October 1992, 7.
[86] *Burgenländische Freiheit* (Eisenstadt), May 29, 1996, 86.
[87] Ibid., 86.
[88] Photographs of the performance can be seen on Angelika Messner's website, http://angelikamessner.at/regie/kraeftner.shtml (accessed July 15, 2009).
[89] Kräftner wrote to fellow writer Herbert Eisenreich: "Jedes Seelenbild ist auch ein Weltbild. Selbst das realistischste Weltbild ist auch ein Seelenbild." Gerhard Altmann, "Nachwort," in Kräftner, *Kühle Sterne*, 353.

Chapter Four

[1] The word "unverschämt" could also be translated as "outrageous" or "insolent" instead of as "impudent." In her personal essay "Abschied von Weihnachten" (Farewell to Christmas), Aichinger recalls the Grimm fairy tale "The Goose Girl at the Well" (Die Gänsehirtin am Brunnen) from her childhood. The goose girl calls out to the prince, who is disguised as an old hunchbacked woman: "Old woman, you are becoming impudent!" (Alte, du wirst unverschämt!). For Aichinger and her sister Helga, this accusation became the catch phrase for all future exchanges of Christmas gifts. For Aichinger, using this sentence, which represents the "heart of her childhood" (Kern ihrer Kindheit), she "tries to stay on the trail of childhood." (Mit ihm [dem Satz] versuche ich bis heute der Kindheit auf der Spur zu bleiben.) It should be noted that, even though Aichinger's mother was Jewish, the family was a typical urban secular Viennese Jewish family who also celebrated traditional Austrian Christian holidays such as Christmas. Aichinger, "Abschied von Weihnachten," in *Unglaubwürdige Reisen*, 79.
[2] "Ich danke meinen Eltern, Freundinnen und Freunden, die mir mit Erzählungen und Schilderungen das Leben von damals näherbrachten." Eva Anna Welles, *Am Rande der Geschichte* (Vienna: Wiener Frauenverlag, 1990), 14.
[3] Aichinger said in a conversation that she resented that the publishers called *Die größere Hoffnung* a novel; instead, she felt that her narrative was based on reality. She said, "The war was the happiest time of my life because it showed what was true." (Der Krieg war die glücklichste

Zeit meines Lebens weil es sich gezeigt hat was wahr ist.) Ilse Aichinger, conversation with author, July 9, 2002.

4 "Die Kräfte der Kindheit hielten die Welt zusammen. Und die Küche meiner Großmutter lag mitten darinnen." Ilse Aichinger, "Kleist, Moos, Fasane," in *Kleist, Moos, Fasane* (Frankfurt a. M.: Fischer Taschenbuch, 1991), 13.

5 Simone Fässler, Vorwort to *Unglaubwürdige Reisen*, 10. In our conversation, Aichinger stated that her relationship with her grandmother was stronger than the one with her mother. She described her grandmother as embodying gentleness and silence and said that she was generous and less strict than her mother. Ilse Aichinger, conversation with author, July 9, 2002.

6 Aichinger began writing her novel at the small white kitchen table of the Welzls, family friends who took in Aichinger and her mother at the end of the war. On the way to the apartment, Aichinger had seen a dead horse, prompting her to begin her novel: "When Ellen crawled out of the cellar, she saw, on her left, a dead horse." (Als Ellen aus dem Keller kroch, sah sie linkerhand ein totes Pferd.) Aichinger, "Die Hoffnung in Odessa und Hernals," in *Unglaubwürdige Reisen*, 55.

7 "[Der Krieg] hatte ein langes zottiges schmutziges Fell, fast wie ein Wolf." Aichinger, *Die größere Hoffnung*, 140-141. The grandmother says, "It is possible that I will be taken tonight!" (Es ist möglich, daß ich heute nacht geholt werde!) Ibid., 133.

8 In the French variant by Perrault, the wolf devours both the grandmother and Little Red Riding Hood, and there is no passing hunter who saves them. Perrault's version closes with a moral that cautions young girls to watch out for strangers, especially those who seem charming and gentle but who are like wolves.

9 "Während Ellen eine Geschichte verlangte, verlangte sie von ihrer Großmutter und inmitten einer schwarzen, gefährlichen Nacht die Bereitschaft zu leben." Ibid., 138.

10 "In dieser Nacht war ein kleiner, verzweifelter Deserteur gegen zwei Uhr heimgekommen und am Morgen verhaftet worden." Ibid., 149.

11 "Habt ihr etwas schlecht gemacht?" "Die Großeltern. Unsere Großeltern sind schuld." Ibid., 27.

12 "Unsere Großeltern sind verächtlich, unsere Urgroßeltern bürgen nicht für uns." Ibid., 45.

13 "Schreiben kann man wie Beten eigentlich nur, anstatt sich umzubringen. Dann ist es das Leben selbst." Aichinger, *Kleist, Moos, Fasane*, 44.

14 Aichinger and her mother, a divorced Jewish doctor, survived the

war by hiding within Vienna at the homes of family and friends, while her twin sister Helga obtained passage on a Kindertransport ship to England. Aichinger and her mother had felt that Helga was too fragile to survive the war on the home front and therefore insisted that she be the one to take the single Kindertransport passage they had been able to obtain. Aichinger, conversation with author, July 9, 2002.

[15] "Die größere Hoffnung, unsere Hoffnung." Aichinger, *Die größere Hoffnung*, 218.

[16] "Du hast immer gesagt, wenn es finster wird, kommen die Räuber." Ibid., 134.

[17] "Damit habe ich leider recht behalten." Ibid., 134.

[18] Reichart expressed her fascination with the literary figure of the older woman who does not concern herself with convention or social expectations. Elisabeth Reichart, conversation with author, Vienna, June 2001.

[19] Reichart's narratives consider multiple forms of verbal and non-verbal communication, such as art, film, and theater, as well as the poetic language of fiction. These forms of communication, which stand apart from the misleading language of clichés and propaganda, are able to communicate truths, to forge bonds among people, and to heal the wounds of the past. Reichart's protagonists are aware of the limits of communication, and they do not always achieve the healing that is needed to overcome the past. In Reichart's works, being silent (*Schweigen*) is a non-verbal form of communication evident in facial expressions, in gestures, and in the absence of words; it is the conscious act of not speaking. Reichart shows that particularly women risk losing their voice and power, especially their capacity for artistic expression, and are socialized to practice this silence. Reichart uses the concept of silence in her works to explore the suppression of memories, shame, and denial, as well as the stillness that allows for artistic expression in contrast to overused, superficial, and commercial everyday language.

[20] Reichart, who grew up in Upper Austria, first learned of the events that occurred at Mauthausen from her grandmother, the only adult to share the truth with her. The German author Christa Wolf writes in the epilogue of *Februarschatten*: "Elisabeth Reichart grew up in Mühlviertel [Mauthausen]. Never, ever had she heard even one hint from the adults about that mass murder until she was herself almost an adult. That is when her grandmother spoke. We sat across from each other in a Viennese restaurant when she told me about it, hesitantly, as she writes here." Christa Wolf, Nachwort to *Februarschatten* by Elisabeth Reichart (Frankfurt a. M.: Fischer, 1989), 107.

[21] "Vergiß!" Reichart, *Februarschatten*, 26.
[22] "Ob erinnert oder vergessen. Der Unterschied liegt in den Schmerzen. Die Schmerzen beim Erinnern." Ibid., 29.
[23] "Everyone has abandoned me." (Alle haben mich verlassen.) Reichart, *Februarschatten*, 10, and "How I never earned being excluded." (Wie ich es nicht verdient habe, ausgeschlossen zu sein.) Ibid., 14.
[24] "Die Tochter hatte sich gegen die Eltern gestellt. Hatte geglaubt, sich für ihre Eltern schämen zu müssen. Hatte nicht gesehen, wie sehr sich die Eltern ihretwegen schämten." Ibid., 63.
[25] ". . . Bücherschreiben. Als ob das eine Lebensmöglichkeit für eine Frau wäre. Sie tut so, als gäbe es keine ungeschriebenen Gesetze für uns Frauen. Geht diesen Weg. . . . In ihren Papierbergen wird sie ersticken. Dann ist es zu spät. Für den richtigen Weg. Für den Weg aller Frauen." Ibid., 63.
[26] "Die Fragen der Tochter werden lästig. Wozu soll ich mich an meine Kindheit erinnern. Ich habe doch von klein auf gelernt: die einzige Möglichkeit zu überleben, ist zu vergessen." Ibid., 26.
[27] Ibid., 74.
[28] "Daß alles Erlebte, Erfahrene, einfach alles, in unserem Gehirn gespeichert wird." Ibid., 88.
[29] "'Ich kann dir nicht mehr erzählen. Ich konnte ihn doch nicht fragen: Warum bist du zum Baum gegangen.' Irgendwie ist alles auch sehr verschwommen. Zuerst gab es so viel Lärm darum. Dann durfte weder über Hannes, noch über seinen Tod geredet werden." Ibid., 49.
[30] "Bis zum Anfang meiner SCHULD." Ibid., 88. The capitalized letters emphasize Hilde's focus on her guilt.
[31] "'Jeder', sage er dann, 'der nichts gegen diese Menschenjagd tut, macht sich SCHULDIG." Ibid., 95. The capitalized letters emphasize Hilde's feelings of shame and guilt.
[32] "Warum auch wollte sie alles wissen. Warum auch hatte sie mein wichtigstes Wort nicht akzeptiert." Ibid., 103.
[33] "Was wirst du jetzt tun. Ich weiß es nicht." Ibid., 104.
[34] "Dein Interesse an diesen Frauen ist nicht normal!" Reichart, *Komm über den See* (Vienna: Deuticke, 2001), 39.
[35] In their study on Austrian women resistance fighters, the editors Karin Berger, Elisabeth Holzinger, Lotte Podgornik, and Lisbeth N. Trallori say of Austria's history, "Fascism and resistance have been successfully repressed chapters until today in the past of our country. This is especially relevant for the history of women." (Faschismus und Widerstand sind bisher erfolgreich verdrängte Kapitel in der Vergangenheit unseres Landes. Auf die Geschichte der Frauen trifft dies

in besonderem Maße zu.) *Der Himmel ist blau: Kann sein; Frauen im Widerstand; Österreich 1938–1945* [Heaven is blue: Could be; Women in the Resistance; Austria 1938–1945] (Vienna: Edition Spuren, Promedia, 1985), 6. The editors counter this silence and underrepresented history with documentation on women in the resistance during the Third Reich, including oral histories. While some women were relieved to finally tell their story, others kept their silence, still suffering from the fear of discrimination and persecution. Many surviving resistance fighters, at the time of publication in 1985, suffered from illness, from loneliness, and from having been forgotten. The editors note about the recollections shared by these women, "their memory is also resistance," 9. The editors demonstrate that reasons for resisting National Socialism ranged from believing in the workers' movement and helping people who were being persecuted to being patriotic toward their Austrian nation and working against Germany's "occupation" of Austria following the Anschluss. The authors additionally note that women were quite aware of the misogynistic propaganda of the Third Reich, which attempted to undermine and eliminate women's rights. The majority of the women interviewed had been imprisoned or sent to concentration camps, where they were often interrogated and tortured. Just as in Reichart's novel, in which Ruth's mother was threatened with harm to her daughter, the women in these camps were intimidated and tortured by Nazis who threatened to harm their husbands and children. Ibid., 240–63. It is of note that, while Reichart's Anna Zach is a fictional character based on the histories and experiences of Austrian resistance fighters, the former resistance fighters, the characters Mali F. and Hermine J., who were invited to speak at a school taught by the fictional Ruth are based on the real-life women resistance fighters Mali Fritz and Jursa Hermine, who walked back to Austria from their imprisonment at the concentration camp Ravensbrück after it was liberated by the Russian Army. Ibid., 263-264. Reichart highlights the omission of Fritz and Hermine's accomplishments from popular representations of Austrian history by eliminating their last names and giving just their initials in her novel.

[36] "Ich habe kaum etwas über Widerstandskämpferinnen gefunden, ihr Leben nur zwischen den Zeilen, keine hat zur Feder gegriffen, das Schreiben auch eine Geschlechterfrage, nach ihnen werde ich suchen." Reichart, *Komm über den See*, 92.

[37] "Später, sagt eine Frauenstimme, später wird es uns nicht gegeben haben." Ibid., 113.

[38] Ibid., 180.

[39] "Ein Schatten an der Wand, im Schein der Schreibtischlampe ein

Gesicht, langsam erkannte sie Anna Zach..." Ibid., 175.

[40] "Vorkriegskinder, Kriegskinder, Nachkriegskinder." Ibid., 14.

[41] "Nicht nur die Mutter, ganz Wien war ohne Gedächtnis. Wir Kinder nannten uns Trümmerkinder, aber woher die Trümmer kamen, wußten wir nicht." Ibid., 172.

[42] "I say only, we Eichmann's children." (Ich sage nur: Wir Eichmannskinder.) Reichart, *Nachtmär* (Salzburg: Otto Müller Verlag, 1995), 187. Nazi SS officer Adolf Eichmann was charged with the deportation and execution of Jews throughout Nazi-occupied Eastern Europe. German philosopher and political theorist Hannah Arendt, after having reported on the Eichmann trial in Israel for *The New Yorker*, published her controversial book *Eichmann in Jerusalem: A Report on the Banality of Evil* in 1963, thereby coining the phrase "the banality of evil" to describe the mindset of individuals such as Eichmann who commit horrific acts without thinking of their moral or ethical consequences. Arendt remarked that Eichmann was an ordinary person who demonstrated no signs of hatred or mental illness but who nonetheless committed horrific deeds because he believed he was merely following orders at the time and was acting within the laws of the Third Reich.

[43] "Überlebende, die nicht damit zurechtkamen, daß nur sie überlebt hatten." Reichart, *Nachtmär*, 105.

[44] As quoted in Reichart's novel from Wolfgang Borchert's 1947 play *Draußen vor der Tür* (*The Man Outside*): "Daß ich mir nicht das Leben nahm, das hat mich selbst entsetzt." Ibid., 105.

[45] "Ist es dir nicht aufgefallen, daß wir die gleiche Art haben, über uns zu reden: Bruchstücke, eingestreute Sätze, abcgebrochene Sätze, Episoden – eben Stückwerk." Ibid., 33.

[46] Ibid., 87.

[47] ". . . jeder in Gmunden wisse doch, daß die Frau Zach im Gefängnis gesessen sei – nein, eben nicht nur während des Nationalsozialismus, davon rede er nicht, wer redet denn noch davon, sondern wohlgemerkt auch unter den Amerikanern, und denen wolle sie doch hoffentlich nichts unterstellen." Ibid., 179.

[48] ". . . you had so many reasons to celebrate, every single deed was worth a party . . . ." (". . .ihr hattet doch so viele Gründe zu feiern, jede einzelne eurer Handlungen war ein Fest wert. . . .") Ibid., 181.

[49] "Freigelassen hat man sie, statt im See ertränkt." Reichart, *Komm über den See*, 79.

[50] "Was war in diesem Moment mit dem Wort Heimat geschehen, waren die Seen da noch blau, waren die Berge da noch weiß, ist Heimat diese Landschaft, genügt denn das." Ibid., 79.

[51] "Ist Heimat wirklich ein Ort für alle, für die Mörder wie für ihre Opfer?" Ibid., 152.
[52] "Wir sind zu früh geboren, mitten hinein in die Verbrechen, ohne eine Möglichkeit, uns dagegen zu schützen. Und doch hat jede versucht, sich gegen diese Wahrheit zu schützen, gegen die keine Blindheit hilft, . . . Der Alptraum ist in uns, er wiederholt sich in uns, sinnloser war noch keine Wiederholung." Reichart, *Nachtmär*, 185.
[53] "Bereits im Sommer 1945 stand es groß in der österreichischen Presse zu lesen: 'Vergessen wir die letzten sieben Jahre! Gemeinsam in die Zukunft!'" Reichart, *Komm über den See*, 162.
[54] "Es gibt uns nicht in der Realität dieses Landes. Es gibt uns nur auf den Friedhöfen der Namenlosen in unseren Wohnküchen oder in Altersheimen." Ibid., 162.
[55] "Es waren 'ihre Märchen.' Hier saß sie, wo Sie jetzt sitzen. Oma, sagte sie, Oma, erzähle. Am liebsten hörte sie die Geschichten aus den Bergen. Ganz genau wollte sie sie hören. Und immer wieder. Wehe mir, wenn ich etwas ausgelassen habe." (They were "her fairy tales. She [Granddaughter Anna] sat here, where you [Ruth] now sit. Oma, she said, Oma, tell the story. She loved to hear the stories of the mountains most of all. She wanted to hear them exactly. And over and over. Dear me, if I had left something out.) Ibid., 161.
[56] "Eines Tages wird Anna vielleicht erzählen." Ibid., 186.
[57] At times, *Nachtmär* reads like a drama composed of inner monologues grappling with the consequences of betrayal and regret. In the Brechtian style of the "Verfremdungseffekt" (alienation effect), Reichart layers the voices so that the reader is not able to identify with the protagonists and, instead, must observe how choices made in the past haunt the present and prevent a productive future within a community.
[58] "Ich konnte mir früher nie vorstellen, daß Wissen belastet. Aber seitdem ich weiß, daß ich Jüdin bin, ist mein erster Gedanke morgens: Eigentlich dürfte es mich nicht geben, wie es meine Eltern nicht geben dürfte. Dieser Zufall, einem absoluten Gesetz entkommen zu sein, macht mich verrückt. Andererseits, jetzt habe ich wenigstens eine monströse Geschichte, etwas zum Anhalten: Moses, die Bibel, die Diaspora, Pogrome, Auschwitz und die Zionisten. Irgendwo zwischen diesen Gedenksteinen wird wohl Platz für mich sein." Reichart, *Nachtmär*, 181-182.
[59] "Ich möchte nur wissen, was dich an diesen schauerlichen Nachgeburtsort der Verbrechen trieb, mitten *unter die Mörder und Irren*." Ibid., 182. The italicized portion forms the title of Bachmann's short story from 1961, "Unter Mördern und Irren" (Among Murderers and Madmen)

and questions the coexistence in the postwar era of those Austrian Nazis not punished for their crimes and collaborations and the victims of the Third Reich, such as Austrian Jews.

[60] "Soll ich mit den Opfern meiner Vorfahren prassen, aus ihrem Leid Kapital schlagen...?" and "Ihr habt ja meine Eltern nicht vertrieben oder den Herzinfarkt meines Großvaters verursacht." Ibid., 187.

[61] "Aber wir wissen nicht, ob wir es nicht getan hätten. Mit dieser Möglichkeit müssen wir leben, wie du mit der, wieder vertrieben werden zu können,...." Ibid., 187.

[62] "Als Rudolf davon sprach, daß es ein alter Fehler der Juden sei, immer nur von denen Hilfe und Opfer zu verlangen, die ohnedies auf ihrer Seite stünden, haben wir es nicht mehr gewagt, in ihre Richtung zu schauen." Ibid., 208.

[63] "Wir haben Esther nicht gesucht, wir haben nicht einen einzigen Tag nach ihr gesucht...." Ibid., 226.

[64] "Immer auf der Täterseite." Ibid., 208.

[65] Ingram's grandmother tells him that during the Third Reich she had thought it was a good idea to have her son, Ingram's uncle, have a relationship with Neva, who at the time was hiding in the family's attic. The grandmother now realizes that it was wrong to assume that romantic love was what Neva needed while hiding from the Nazis. Ibid., 141.

[66] "... die nichts mehr erschüttern kann...." Ibid., 18-19.

[67] Rudolf gives up his hopes of directing his own theater and returns to his job as a script editor. Paula is an assistant director who fulfills the visions of other directors but not her own. Marlen, who had hoped to be a writer of creative fiction, realizes that she has given up her own dreams for her husband Viktor, for whom she writes unsatisfactory plays. Instead of using the realm of theater as a challenging and creative platform for change and improvement, all four characters are mired in mediocrity and conformity.

[68] "... von dem kalten, künstlichen Auge begleitet,...." Ibid., 147.

[69] "Im Krieg waren nicht nur die Soldaten gefallen, sondern auch ihre Photos von den Wänden gekracht. Seine Kindheit war reich an solchen Geschichten, hatten ihn auf alles vorbereitet, außer auf ihre Idee, sich von ihrem Platz wegzubewegen und wieder die Eingangstür zu versperren." Ibid., 151.

[70] "abgeschnitten, aus," Ibid., 191.

[71] "Nach drei Generationen sind wir einander fremd und auf das Gedächtnis Fremder angewiesen." Ibid., 225.

[72] "Mich interessiert: Wohin geht's, und woher kommen wir. Lange Zeit war es die Vergangenheit, die mich beschäftigt hat, und jetzt fange

ich an, mich für unsere Zukunft zu interessieren. Also, wenn ich mein Werk anschaue, muß ich sagen, daß ich von der Vergangenheit in die Gegenwart und damit in die Zukunft gegangen bin. Ich denke, daß das auch notwendig ist, daß sich SchriftstellerInnen die Zukunft anschauen." (I am interested in where it is going and where we come from. For a long time it was the past that concerned me, and now I am beginning to care about our future. So, when I look at my work, I have to say that I went from the past to the present to the future. I think it's important that authors look to the future.) Karina Weber, "Vergessene Lächeln, verlorene Identität," interview with Elisabeth Reichart, *WeiberDiwan* (Vienna), January 12, 1998, 21.

[73] "Es ist schwierig mit der Sprache. Sie trennt und verbindet." Reichart, *Nachtmär*, 191.

[74] Eva Anna Welles, *Am Rande der Geschichte* (Vienna: Wiener Frauenverlag, 1990), 84.

[75] Ibid., 19.

[76] Ibid., 19.

[77] "The women did all the work that they got, cleaning, sewing, washing up, scrubbing floors, washing and ironing clothes." (Die Frauen machten jede Arbeit, die sie bekamen, putzen, nähen, aufwaschen, Böden reiben, Wäsche waschen und bügeln.) Ibid., 21.

[78] "Sowohl die Frauen als auch das Mädchen verrichteten mechanisch die Arbeit, und ihre Gedanken verliefen sich in Vergangenem, Zukünftigem und in Träumen." (The women as well as the girl completed their work mechanically, and their thoughts were scattered in the past, the future and in dreams.) Ibid., 37.

[79] "Aber sie wollte wie die Großmutter stark und unnachgiebig werden." (But she wanted to be strong and noncompliant like her grandmother.) Ibid., 35.

[80] "Die Großmutter war kritisch. Sie kannte eine Menge Leute und erfuhr immer alle Neuigkeiten. Sie schimpfte gerne auf die Reichen und die bestehenden sozialen Ungerechtigkeiten. Sie war der Meinung, daß man sich nichts gefallen lassen dürfe, obwohl sie wahrscheinlich nicht genau wußte, was sie eigentlich wollte. Mit dieser Einstellung vermittelte sie dem Kind jedoch, daß man sich mit Gegebenheiten nicht abzufinden brauchte. Es gab Mittel und Wege, Dinge zu ändern, wenn man die Macht besaß. Wie man an die Macht käme, wußte sie nicht, aber es schien zumindest ganz entfernt möglich zu sein, sie Erlangen zu können." Ibid., 35.

[81] "Einmal werde ich machen, was ich will, dachte sie." Ibid., 55.

[82] "Außerdem, wozu solln denn die Frauen sonst da sein, wenn ned

zum Heiraten und zum Kinderkriegen?" Ibid., 67.
 83 Ibid., 110.
 84 "Unaufhörlich kreisten ihre Gedanken. All die Jahre hatte der Mann von ihrer Substanz gezehrt, sie ausgehöhlt. Sie hatte sich nie dagegen gewehrt, weil ihr anerzogen war, den Mund zu halten und sich unterzuordnen. Sie hörte in Gedanken ihre Großmutter fragen, was sie denn sonst machen wolle, als heiraten. Nun, sie wußte mittlerweile genau, was sie lieber gemacht hätte." Ibid., 125.
 85 Ibid., 131.
 86 "Wir wollen keinen Krieg/ Wir brauchen keinen Sieg/Wir wollen unser freies Österreich/Und freuen uns auf die Hitlerleich!" Ibid., 145.
 87 "Sie hatte von Vergewaltigungen gehört, und sie erstarrte zuerst jedesmal innerlich, wenn sich ihr einer der Männer näherte. Es wurde auch in Gegenwart von Ehemännern und Kindern vergewaltigt, und Alter und Aussehen oder Schwangerschaft waren kein Grund, daß es nicht geschah." Ibid., 169.
 88 Ibid., 171. Christine Nöstlinger, whose children's novels discussed in chapter 7 are based on her own experiences as a child during World War II, likewise portrays Russian occupiers as soldiers who, although they have also suffered greatly in the war, are generous and kind.
 89 "Friedl hatte gehört, daß viele Juden das Land verließen, auch die Grätzers und Dr. Grünzweig waren über Nacht mit unbekanntem Ziel verreist." Ibid., 141.
 90 Ibid., 171.
 91 "Sie hätte härter arbeiten müssen als jeder Mann, hätte auf alles verzichten müssen, vor allem auf den Mann und das Kind, dann, vielleicht wäre es anders gekommen." Ibid., 182.
 92 Welles mentions, for example, Bertha von Suttner, who received the Nobel Peace Prize in 1905 for her book *Die Waffen nieder* (*Down with weapons*), and Gabriele von Possaner, who became a Doctor of "General Healing" ("Doktor der gesamten Heilkunde") in 1897.
 93 "Ich kann nicht aufhören zu berichten. Irgend etwas treibt mich an. Treibt mich. . . ." Ibid., 40.
 94 Johanna Nowak, *Gehorsam: Roman eines schuldhaften Lebens* (Vienna: Wiener Frauenverlag, 1994), 24.
 95 The protagonist explains that she has been taught by her mother to believe that a woman is sinful and must therefore be guided by a man: "Therefore she must be watched and guided by the stronger, and more rationally equipped man, and he has the power in church, state, family." (Daher muß sie vom stärkeren, verstandesmäßig besser ausgestatteten Mann beaufsichtigt und gelenkt werden, und diesem gehört die Herrschaft

in Kirche, Staat, Familie.) Ibid., 36.
[96] Ibid., 44–45.
[97] "Frausein heißt Selbslosigkeit." "Die Ehe zusammenzuhalten ist die moralische Verpflichtung der Frau, ein Scheitern der Ehe ihr Versagen, das Gebot der Unauflöslichkeit der Ehe ist das Geschenk Gottes an die Frau." Ibid., 64.
[98] "Männer müssen etwas leisten, Frauen müssen sie selbst sein, denn Frauen sind die Liebe." Ibid., 46.
[99] "Das Ziel aller weiblichen Erziehung hat unverrückbar die kommende Mutter zu sein." Ibid., 75.
[100] "Man sagt oft zu mir, ich wolle die Frauen aus den Berufen verdrängen. Nein, ich will nur auf größter Basis die Voraussetzung schaffen, eine Familie zu gründen und Kinder zu haben, weil unser Volk diese vor allem braucht." Ibid., 78.
[101] "Es erfordert elterliche Entschlossenheit, fest zu bleiben, wenn ein Kind Anordnungen nicht befolgen will." "Wenn Eltern nicht aufpassen, lernt auch ein Säugling bemerkenswert schnell, sie zu manipulieren." Ibid., 107.
[102] "Solches Geschreibsel ist schädlich für Mädchen." Ibid., 124.
[103] Ibid., 178.
[104] Ibid., 180.
[105] "Ich habe mein Leben im Griff." Ibid., 182.
[106] "... noch bevor sie zur Schule ging, saß sie an ihrem Schreibtisch und kritzelte Zettel um Zettel voll, zerknüllte sie wieder und warf sie weg. 'Ich schreibe Erzählungen. Etliche sind schon gedruckt worden, in Zeitungen und Büchern erschienen.'" Ibid., 179.
[107] "Die ungeschickte Renate hat sich später gegen ihr Schicksal aufgelehnt, Gaby, die Tüchtige, die Überlegene, sich unterworfen." Ibid., 178.
[108] "That is the child's duty, determined by God." "... Kindesplicht, vom Herrgott bestimmt." Ibid., 186
[109] "Gehorsam habe ich seine Vorschriften und Gebote befolgt, habe getan, was Er für richtig erklärt hat." Ibid., 186.
[110] "Gib acht, sonst endest du im Irrenhaus wie dein Onkel Anton." Ibid., 127.
[111] "Because Renate was crazy." (Denn Renate war verrückt.) Ibid., 146.
[112] "War sie endgültig verrückt geworden?" Ibid., 174.

Chapter Five

¹ "Es ist interessant, wie man sich zurückwünscht; dass man wieder sieht, wo man war als Kind. Und dann steht man dort und es ist natürlich nicht mehr da." Lore Segal, interviewed for documentary film, *Vielleicht habe ich Glück gehabt,* DVD, directed by Käthe Kratz (Austria: Extrafilm, 2003).

² *Into the Arms of Strangers: Stories of the Kindertransport,* DVD, directed by Mark Jonathan Harris and Deborah Oppenheimer (Burbank, CA: Warner Home Video, 2000).

³ "It's interesting how you wish you could go back, to see again where you were as a child. And then you stand there and it is of course not there anymore." (Es ist interessant, wie man sich zurückwünscht; dass man wieder sieht, wo man war als Kind. Und dann steht man dort und es ist natürlich nicht mehr da.) Lore Segal, interviewed for documentary film, *Vielleicht habe ich Glück gehabt.*

⁴ The German translations of the memoirs, which were published by the Viennese Picus press, as Martha Blend, *Ich kam als Kind: Erinnerungen* (Vienna: Picus, 1998) and Lore Segal, *Wo andere Leute wohnen* (Vienna: Picus, 2000), enable Austrian and other German-speaking readers to learn more about the underrepresented history of exiled Austrians.

⁵ Ibid., 11.
⁶ Ibid., 10.
⁷ *Into the Arms of Strangers: Stories of the Kindertransport,* DVD.
⁸ David Cesarani, Introduction to Harris and Oppenheimer, *Into the Arms of Strangers: Stories of the Kindertransport* by Mark Jonathan Harris and Deborah Oppenheimer (New York: Bloomsbury, 2000), 13.
⁹ Ibid., 82.
¹⁰ Ibid., 81.
¹¹ Ibid., 102.
¹² Segal, 38.
¹³ Even children who survived the Holocaust with their parents are often plagued by guilt about having been able to stay together as a family. Lilian Furst, for example, writes that she is haunted by her memory, "a sight [that] has remained engraved" in her mind, of seeing Kindertransport children on the train on which her father and she were traveling. She writes that they looked "miserable" and that they "already looked like the orphans most of them would become." She writes, "the faces of those children still haunt me, although these were the lucky ones, who did get away, and the majority of them were well received by their adoptive families." Desider Furst and Lilian R. Furst, *Home is Somewhere Else:*

Autobiography in Two Voices (Albany: State University of New York Press, 1994), 53–54.

[14] Information taken from Martin Gilbert, *Never Again: A History of the Holocaust* (New York: Universe Publishing, 2000), 44–45. Originally, two summer holiday camps were prepared to house incoming refugee children. However, due to flooding, the Pakefield camp was abandoned and the Dovercourt camp was "quickly filled to capacity with some 1,000 Jewish children and teenagers of all ages and backgrounds. Conditions at first were chaotic." Harris and Oppenheimer, 13.

[15] Segal, 45.

[16] Cesarani cites the example of the *Kind* Bertha Leverton, who was taken in as a maidservant and had the additional misfortune of having to constantly ward off the "unwanted attentions of her 'uncle.'" David Cesarani, Introduction to Harris and Oppenheimer, 10, and Leverton in Harris and Oppenheimer, 210.

[17] Ibid., 19.

[18] Ibid., 19.

[19] Ibid., 19.

[20] As an adult, Blend read testimonies of the Holocaust and visited with her aunt in Israel, where she learned that her father was murdered in Buchenwald. This information compelled her to research the fate of her mother, whose last known location was the internment camp of Opole, at the Polish-Czech border.

[21] Once in England, Segal writes about her sense of helplessness regarding the war: "And so it was clear to me without benefit of doubt that the grownups knew no more about it than I did, and were as powerless as I to prevent it, ..." Segal, 109.

American author Tracy Kidder, who has written on the human cost of war, calls the memories of survivors, "the cost of surviving." Kidder also describes a survivor as having "memories so fresh that he sometimes confuses past and present." Tracy Kidder describes the amazing story of Deogratias "Deo" Niyizonkiza who fled Burundi to the United States in 1993 and who recorded his memories in his book *Strength in What Remains*. Tracy Kidder, from the interview with Guy Raz, "From Poverty to the Ivy League: A Refugee's Story." *All Things Considered*, National Public Radio, August 29 and Sept. 1, 2009. http://www.npr.org/templates/story/story.php?storyId=112334064.

[22] Segal, 46.

[23] Ibid., 120.

[24] Ibid., 186.

[25] Ibid., 191.

[26] Blend, 33–60.
[27] Ibid., 11.
[28] Ibid., 14.
[29] Ibid., 123.
[30] Ibid., 108.
[31] Ibid., 123.
[32] Blend, "Eine eigene Geschichte" in *Ein Niemandsland, aber welch ein Rundblick,* ed. Seeber, 184.
[33] Segal, 40.
[34] Ibid., 62.
[35] Blend, 82.
[36] Ibid., 82.
[37] Ibid., 92.
[38] Ibid., 86-87.
[39] Ibid., 117.
[40] Ibid., 41.
[41] Ibid., 41.
[42] Ibid., 65.
[43] Ibid., 71.
[44] Segal, 56.
[45] Ibid., 60.
[46] Ibid., 61.
[47] Blend, 68.
[48] Ibid., 74.
[49] Ibid., 74.
[50] Segal, 162.
[51] Ibid., 163.
[52] Ibid., 172.
[53] Ibid., 69.
[54] Ibid., 193.
[55] As outlined in the Introduction, it was not until the early 1990s that Austria would confront its past and its complicity in National Socialism and the Holocaust. These complex issues regarding national responsibility are not addressed in Blend's or Segal's memoirs, since both authors capture their recollections of childhood, youth, and young adulthood in exile before such discussions were made popular.
[56] Ibid., 243.
[57] Ibid., 229.
[58] Ibid., 31-32.
[59] Ibid., 281.
[60] Ibid., 311.

[61] Ibid., 311.
[62] Blend, 4.
[63] Ibid., 111.
[64] Ibid., 12.
[65] Ibid., 12.
[66] Ibid., 14.
[67] Ibid., 15.
[68] Ibid., 58.
[69] Ibid., 72.
[70] Ibid., 75.
[71] Ibid., 105.
[72] Ibid., 143.
[73] Ibid., 149.
[74] Segal, 46.
[75] Ibid., 150.
[76] Blend, 8.
[77] Ibid., 76-77.
[78] Ibid., 103.
[79] Ibid., 106.
[80] Ibid., 165.
[81] Segal, 312. This "calamity" refers to the Cold War.
[82] Helen Hilsenrad, *Brown Was the Danube* (New York: Thomas Yoseloff, 1966), 292.
[83] Ibid., 348
[84] Ibid., 349.
[85] Ibid., 385.
[86] Ibid., 413.
[87] Ibid., 413.
[88] Ibid., 424.
[89] Ibid., 425.
[90] Ibid., 425.
[91] Ibid., 486.
[92] Ibid., 489-92.
[93] Mona Golabek and Lee Cohen, *The Children of Willensden Lane: Beyond the Kinderstransport. A Memoir of Music, Love, and Survival* (New York: Warner Books, 2002), x.
[94] Ibid., 17.
[95] Ibid., 23.
[96] Ibid., 31.
[97] Ibid., 28.
[98] Ibid., 221.

[99] Ibid., 253 and 265.
[100] Ibid., 265, 266-267.
[101] Ibid., x.
[102] Melissa Hacker, *My Knees Were Jumping. Remembering the Kindertransports*. Independent Film Channel and Docurama, 1996.
[103] Ibid., 261 and 272.
[104] Ibid., 273. The first reunion of the Kindertransport *Kinder* was organized by Bertha Leverton in 1989. It is here that the *Kinder* "began to understand how the tragedy had shaped them." Ibid., 18.
[105] Ibid., 274.
[106] Ibid., 274.
[107] Robert Krell, "Recollections" in *Never Again: A History of the Holocaust* by Martin Gilbert (New York: Universe Publishing, 2000), 103.

Chapter Six

[1] Vivan Jeannette Kaplan, *Ten Green Bottles: The True Story of One Family's Journey from War-Torn Austria to the Ghettos of Shanghai* (New York: St. Martin's Press, 2004), 188.

[2] The German-speaking Jewish refugees in Shanghai called themselves "Shanghailanders," as can be found in Kaplan's memoirs: ". . . Shanghailanders as we called ourselves." Kaplan, 188. For an overview of the history of German-speaking Jews in Shanghai, visit www.ushmm.org/wlc/article.php?lang=en&ModuleId=10007091 (accessed January 25, 2010).

[3] *The Port of Last Resort: Zuflucht Schanghai*, DVD, directed by Joan Grossman and Paul Rosdy (Vienna/New York: A co-production of Pinball Films, Vienna/New York, and Extrafilm, Vienna, 1998.).

[4] Ernest G. Heppner, *Shanghai Refuge: A Memoir of the World War II Jewish Ghetto*. (Lincoln & London: University of Nebraska Press, 1995); and, Ernest G. Heppner, "The Relations between the Western European Refugees and the Shanghai Resident Jews: A Personal Memoir." in *The Jews of China*, Vol. 2, *A Sourcebook and Research Guide*, ed Jonathan Goldstein (Armonk, NY: M. E. Sharpe, 1999), 57–69; and Illo L. Heppner, "Shanghai: A Woman's Eyewitness Report." in Goldstein, ed., 49–56.

[5] A brief overview of twenty-first century refugees provides a sociohistorical context for the situation of Austrian and German Jews in China during World War II. In 2000 there were an estimated 20.8 million refugees in the world, 9 million of whom were children under the age of 18. The United Nations defines refugees as "internally displaced persons,

returnees, asylum seekers, resettled persons," and "stateless people." According to the United Nation High Commission for Refugees, a refugee is a "person who owing to a well-founded fear of being persecuted for reasons of race, religion, nationality, membership of a particular social group, or political opinion, is outside the country of his nationality, and is unable to or, owing to such fear, is unwilling to avail himself of the protection of that country." www.ninemillion.org, (accessed July 13, 2009). The agency that once supported and ensured the survival of the German-speaking Jews in China, the American Jewish Joint Distribution Committee (JDC), strives to ensure "that overseas Jewish communities have the resources they need to help their most vulnerable children and families." Today the JDC has programs worldwide that help "empower women" from "the former Soviet Union to Israel." www.jdc.org (accessed July 13, 2009).

[6] See the film's website for more information: www.shanghaighetto.com/index.html.

[7] In Welles' post-World War II film noir, the protagonist known as both Rosalie and Elsa, born in Shanghai to White Russian exiles, lives in the U.S. with her shady, wealthy husband. After falling in love with the Irish-American Mike O'Hara, she is shot to death in a love triangle at the end of the film. Rosalie's belief that one "can't win" reflects the aftermath and hopelessness faced by war refugees. Rosalie says early in the film, "You need more than luck in Shanghai." For viewers, her past as a child of refugees remains a mystery – one that clearly marks her fate and leads to her tragic death. Novelists, such as the emigré writer Vicki Baum in her 1940 novel *Shanghai '37*, also imagined the fate of European exiles in Shanghai during the war. Baum writes of their fate, "The nothingness in which the exile lived became black and dense and impenetrable as never before. The foreign city swallowed them up." Vicki Baum, *Shanghai '37*, trans. Basil Creighton (New York: The Book League of America, 1940), 90. The novel begins with a Chinese proverb: "Better a dog in peace than a man in war," inviting readers into a world of refugees whose lives intersect at the Shanghai Hotel on Nanking Road, halfway between the Bund and the English race course. Baum's novel details the fictional lives of the people who converge there, including the German political refugee Kurt Planke and the German Jew Dr. Emanuel Hain, who flee to Shanghai together during the war.

[8] "Aber es ist eine versunkene Welt, genauso wie die des alten Österreich-Ungarn oder der jüdischen Städte und Dörfer im europäischen Osten. Eine Welt, die nur mehr durch die Erzählungen der Menschen, die sie erlebt und geschaffen haben, lebendig gehalten wird." Franziska

Tausig, *Shanghai Passage: Emigration ins Ghetto* (Vienna: Milena, 1987), 13.

⁹ Tausig comments that some long-standing Shanghai restaurants today still serve typical Austrian dishes such as Schnitzel and Strietzel, as they did when Austrian refugees frequented them during World War II. Helmut Opletal, who wrote a foreword for the translation of Tausig's *Shanghai Passage: Emigration to the Ghetto*, notes that former Austrian President Thomas Klestil visited the "Ghetto" of Shanghai in 1995 and that this interest shows that Austria is officially engaged in the history of Austrian exiles. Since 1994 there has been a plaque in Huoshan Park that memorializes the "thousands of Jews" who fled to Shanghai during the war. Opletal mentions, however, that the plaque does not mention that these Jews were largely Austrian and German. Opletal, Foreword, to Tausig, 13, 17-18.

¹⁰ Documents and memoirs cite numbers of German-speaking Jewish refugees ranging from more than 17,000 to 18,000. Miller counts 18,000 European Jews and of those 17,000 German Jews. Frieda Miller, *Shanghai: A Refuge During the Holocaust; A Teacher's Guide* (Vancouver, BC: Vancouver Holocaust Education Centre, 1999), 1 and 18. www.vhec.org/images/pdfs/Shanghai%20Teachers%20Guide.pdf (accessed January 26, 2010). The United States Holocaust Memorial Museum Encyclopedia counts 17,000 German-speaking Jews in Shanghai. "German and Austrian Jewish refugees in Shanghai," www.ushmm.org/wlc/article.php?lang=en&ModuleId=10007091 (accessed January 26, 2010).

¹¹ Miller, 18.

¹² Former refugee Ernest Heppner explains what almost prevented his attempt to escape from Nazi terror: "It was not difficult to get out; it was the free world that would not give us a place." *The Port of Last Resort.*

¹³ Ibid.

¹⁴ David Kranzler, *Japanese, Nazis and Jews: The Jewish Refugee Community of Shanghai, 1938-1945* (Hoboken, NJ: KTAV Publishing House, Inc., 1988), 38 nn 21 and 22.

¹⁵ Professor Irene Eber from Hebrew University in Jerusalem, interviewed in *Shanghai Ghetto*, states that Austrian Jews were "encouraged" to leave the country in the following way: the Nazis arrested Jewish men, deported them to camps, then told their families that the only way to get their men back was to leave the country, giving them deadlines of between twenty-four hours to as much as one month. In the summer of 1938, President Roosevelt called for an intergovernmental conference to be held in Evian, France. The failure of the nations that attended the conference to help the Jews showed the world, as well as refugees like Kranzler, that "Hitler didn't give a damn." Kranzler,

interviewed in *Shanghai Ghetto*.
[16] *Port of Last Resort.*
[17] Kranzler, 24.
[18] Ibid., 44.
[19] Miller, 18-19.
[20] Kaplan, ix.
[21] Ibid., ix.
[22] Ibid., ix.
[23] Ibid., ix.
[24] Ibid., *Acknowledgements*.
[25] Ursula Bacon, *Shanghai Diary: A Young Girl's Journey from Hitler's Hate to War-Torn China*. (Milwaukie, OR: M Press, 2004), Foreword.
[26] Ibid., Foreword.
[27] Ibid., 255.
[28] Bacon writes: "I snuggled up against her [Bacon's nanny, Fraulein Amanda], closed my eyes, and told myself a story." Rena Krasno, *Strangers Always: A Jewish Family in Wartime Shanghai* (Berkeley, CA: Pacific View Press, 1992), 12. In a later passage, Bacon writes: ". . . I doubted I would ever go to sleep. . . . I tried to shut out the busy noises around me and forced my mind to create the same dream world I had been able to conjure up ever since I was a little girl, lonely for someone to tell me a story." Ibid., 40. Whereas Bacon describes her personal account of exile to China as a "story," Krasno, in her memoir about her life in Shanghai from 1923 to 1949, stages her own experiences as part of a collective historical experience that authenticates and validates her recollections. Krasno, born into a stateless Russian family working in Shanghai, witnessed the Japanese occupation of China and the arrival of Jewish refugees from Central and Eastern Europe. She asserts that her "account is entirely factual," yet adds that it is her "personal perspective." Ibid., xiv. Although Krasno had "been avidly reading literature about Shanghai," she turned to her own diaries and historical documents to capture this time period, as she writes, "The paucity of material turned me back again and again to these diaries and various documents I saved along with them, finally inspiring me to gather them together and publish them in the form of this journal, in the hope of recapturing those momentous days and sharing them with others." Ibid., xiv. Krasno's perspective on her coming of age as a German-speaking Jew in Shanghai gives an account of the lives of exiles who joined the already established Jewish population living in Shanghai. In writing with the intent of informing others of her experience, Krasno, like other writers of memoirs, provides testimony while confronting and reconstructing her past.

[29] Kaplan, 1.
[30] Ibid., 2 and 5.
[31] Ibid., 5 and 9.
[32] Ibid., 24.
[33] Ibid., 24.
[34] Ibid., 26.
[35] Ibid., 40.
[36] Ibid., 44.
[37] Ibid., 46.
[38] Ibid., 50.
[39] Ibid., 61-2.
[40] Ibid., 87.
[41] Ibid., 115.
[42] Ibid., 114.
[43] Ibid., 118.
[44] Ibid., 119.
[45] "Mein Mann war ungarischer Rechtsanwalt. Seine Heimat gab es nicht mehr. Dieser Teil von Ungan war an Rumänien gefallen, ein Land, dessen Sprache und Gesetze ihm völlig unbekannt waren. Er konnte also seinen Beruf nicht mehr ausüben. Mein Vater hatte ein großes Unternehmen und stellte ihn als Mitarbeiter ein. . . . Wir hatten wieder von ganz vorne beginnen müssen, mein Mann in einem neuen Beruf. Im Jahre 1922 bekam ich einen Sohn, einen echten Wiener. Zwanzig Jahre lebten wir in Wien ein arbeits- und erfolgreiches Leben." Tausig, 42.
[46] "Nach 20 Jahren wurden wir wieder einmal mit Stumpf und Stiel entwurzelt." Ibid., 47.
[47] "Die Religionszugehörigkeit erwies sich als untragbar in den Augen der neuen Machthaber." Ibid., 47.
[48] "Es wäre wert, ihr ein Denkmal zu setzen. Ein Topf heißer Tee, wenn du frierst, ein Bett, in dem du ausschlafen kannst, dein Gewand, das neben dem Ofen trocknet, das kann dir den Mut zum Überleben geben. Sie war viel älter als wir und lebt bestimmt nicht mehr, und ich möchte hier für sie einen Kranz niederlegen." Ibid., 63.
[49] "Nur an zu Hause durfte man nicht denken." (Only one could not think of home.) Ibid., 70.
[50] "Mit dem Brief wollte er uns trösten und beruhigen, aber die Trauer um die verlorene Heimat, die Sehnsucht nach dem verlorenen Zuhause war zwischen den Zeilen zu lesen." (He wanted to comfort and calm us with the letter, but the mourning for the lost homeland, the longing for the lost home, could be read between the lines.) Ibid., 89.
[51] Bacon, 11.

52 Ibid., 13.
53 Ibid., 22.
54 *Shanghai Ghetto.*
55 Ibid.
56 "Sie [die Emigration] sollte neun bittere Jahre dauern." (It [the emigration] would last nine bitter years.) Tausig, 93. "Die Jahre in Shanghai waren bittere Jahre." (The years in Shanghai were bitter.) Ibid., 99. Tausig wrote about her voyage and about her time in China and published newspaper articles after her return to Austria following her exile. In 1948, Tausig received a letter from a reader of one of her articles about her voyage to China. The writer stated that he had worked on board the ship on which she had traveled and that the crew had been ordered to do the grim task of "liquidating" the Jewish passengers if they could not drop them off on shore. Ibid., 94.
57 "Sie waren wie ein Kelch, randvoll mit einem grausamen Schicksal angefüllt, den ich bis zum letzten Tropfen leeren musste." Ibid., 99.
58 "German and Austrian Jewish Refugees in Shanghai," *Holocaust Encyclopedia*, United States Holocaust Memorial Museum, www.ushmm.org/wlc/article.php?lang=en&ModuleId=10007091 (accessed January 25, 2010).
59 *Port of Last Resort.*
60 Ibid., 97.
61 Ibid., 283–84.
62 *Shanghai Ghetto.*
63 Kaplan, 141.
64 Ibid., 148.
65 I. Heppner, "Shanghai: A Woman's Eyewitness Report," 50.
66 Ross, 135.
67 Ibid., 209.
68 Tausig, 100.
69 "Demel" is one of the most famous Viennese coffeehouses and pastry shops. Ibid., 117, 121, and 124.
70 Kaplan, 212.
71 Ibid., 212.
72 Ibid., 177.
73 Ibid., 212.
74 Ibid., 212.
75 Ibid., 240.
76 "Diese schönen Mädchen waren die unglücklichsten Geschöpfe auf der Welt. Die ungeheure Tragik so eines Schicksals erfuhr ich durch einen Zufall." (These beautiful girls were the unhappiest creatures in the

world. I learned of the horrible tragedy of such a fate by chance.) Tausig, 109.

77 "Das sind so Vergleiche, die man gewöhnlich als übertrieben bewertet. Je länger aber unser Leben dauert, umso unwirklicher erscheint es uns. Je kleiner das Scherzel von unserem Lebensbrot wird, umso winziger wird das Leben und umso größer die Zahl der Erinnerungen. Viele von uns leben nur mehr von ihren Erinnerungen. Und die werden von der Abnützung nicht trübe. Im Gegenteil, je mehr man sie abnützt, umso glänzender und glitzernder werden sie." Ibid., 113.

78 Ibid., 141.
79 Ross, 153.
80 Ibid., 142–43.
81 Bacon, 66–67.
82 *The Port of Last Resort.*
83 Ibid.
84 I. Heppner, 52.
85 Kaplan, 172.
86 Bacon, 43.
87 Ibid., 46.
88 Ibid., 64 and 67.
89 Ibid., 67.
90 Ibid., 85. After waiting in long lines to get a work permit to leave the Hongkew Ghetto, Bacon writes, "I had turned my mind back, way back, to the beautiful pictures and grand moments of the past that occupied my nights." Ibid., 172.
91 Ibid., 121.
92 Ibid., 175.
93 Ibid., 229.
94 Ibid., 175.
95 Ibid., 189.
96 Ibid., 192.
97 I. Heppner, 53.
98 Physician Dr. Sam Didner, an Austrian refugee in Shanghai, reported that he performed abortions on prostitutes and young married women "who felt they could not afford to raise children in the deteriorating conditions in Shanghai." James R. Ross, *Escape to Shanghai: A Jewish Community in China* (New York: The Free Press, 1994), 7. Didner says he performed an average of two abortions a week, even though abortions were illegal in Shanghai at the time. While he tried to discourage women from having abortions, "he understood that many of the women had no choice." Ibid., 72.

Bacon's memoir recalls the staggering number of victims of infanticide who filled garbage cans in the alleyways. They were mostly the unwanted babies of destitute and desperate Chinese mothers. In her memoir, Bacon recalls finding a baby Chinese girl who was crying in a pile of garbage. She retrieved the infant, took her to a hospital, and was assured that she would be cared for in an orphanage. Bacon, 223–25.

[99] Kaplan, 258.
[100] *Shanghai Ghetto.*
[101] Miller, 22.
[102] *The Port of Last Resort.*
[103] Ibid. Illo Heppner describes this show as having a "bitter irony" for those watching who later learned that six million Jews had been persecuted and murdered during the Holocaust.
[104] Kaplan, 221.
[105] *The Port of Last Resort.*
[106] Ibid.
[107] Ibid.
[108] Kaplan, 200–208. Kaplan describes the relocated refugees as "abandoned," "desolate," "grim and frightened," and "dejected and fatigued." Ibid., 203–205
[109] "Zwerg mit der eisernen Faust." Tausig, 131.
[110] I. Heppner, 52. Illo's husband, Ernest Heppner, describes Ghoya: ". . . the ghetto was governed by a very brutal, sadistic Japanese named Ghoya. He was paranoid, he was a psychopath, and he called himself the 'king of the Jews.' . . . I could talk an hour about Ghoya, what he did. He was so. . . he had such an inferiority complex. . . . And if he didn't like you, he would jump on the desk and slap you. And if it really got bad, he would send you for one night into the bunker [punishment barracks]. . . ." www/ushmm.org/wlc/media_oi.php?lang=en&ModuleId=10006236&MediaId=2608 (accessed January 26, 2010).
[111] Bacon, 243.
[112] Ibid., 231.
[113] Walter Manes, *Personal Papers, 1918–1999.* NB007, NB008. Robert Wiener Library, London, England.
[114] Bacon, Foreword.
[115] Ibid., 231.
[116] Ibid., 232.
[117] Ibid., 232.
[118] Ibid., 229.
[119] Ibid., 239.
[120] Ibid., 251.

[121] Kaplan, 253–54.
[122] "Es musste doch schon viele Jahrhunderte her sein, dass unser Volk so herumzigeunert ist. Wir hatten vergessen, dass wir mit dem Wanderstab geboren sind. Vielleicht weil wir es nicht wahrhaben wollten, steckten wir immer wieder den Kopf in den Sand." Tausig, 173.
[123] Bacon, 261.
[124] Ibid., 263.
[125] Ibid., 264.
[126] Ibid., 264.
[127] "Entschuldigung, gnädige Frau . . . sind Sie vielleicht meine Mama?" Tausig, 192.
[128] "einem neuen Lebensabschnitt in der Heimat." Ibid., 192.
[129] "Nur ich war noch da, der Einzige, in dessen Schicksal sie noch eingreifen konnte. Und der wehrte sich dagegen." Ibid., 197.
[130] Second-generation Austrian-Jewish writer Ruth Beckermann provides an example of this in her 1989 personal essay "Wir möchten sie los sein" (We want to be rid of them). Past events that affected her family and her identity as an Austrian Jew inform her present identity and her present views of Austrian culture. In her bitter critique of Austria's handling of returning Jews and refugees after World War II, she writes that Jews were treated as "unwanted strangers." Beckermann, 71. She describes how those returning from camps or exile had to prove that they were victims of Nazi terror in order to receive financial support. The 5,700 returning Jews were "too much" for the city of Vienna, Beckermann writes. 852 Austrian Jews who planned to return to Austria after their exile in Shanghai were only allowed entry after exhausting negotiations and the financial support of local and international Jewish organizations. Ibid., 74. Beckermann reports two further incidents that underscore her assessment of Austria's response to displaced persons. In the Stafa and Flott movie theaters, the news program *Wochenschau* reported on the return of the Austrian Jews from Shanghai. The show's commentary emphasized that Jews were returning to "help with the rebuilding of the homeland," yet Beckermann writes that the public responded, "Gas them." Ibid., 78. She concludes that the newspaper *Arbeiter Zeitung* from August 21, 1946, expressed the public's sentiment in their first-page headline, "We want to be rid of them!" (Wir möchten sie los sein!). Ibid., 84.
[131] Kaplan, 275.
[132] Ibid., 279.
[133] Ibid., 285.
[134] "Shpann" would more likely be spelled with "sch" in German;

therefore, this spelling may have been invented for an English-speaking readership.
[135] Lois Ruby, *Shanghai Shadows* (New York: Holiday House, 2006), 3.
[136] Ibid., 5–6.
[137] Ibid., 94.
[138] Ibid., 35.
[139] Ibid., 75.
[140] Ibid., 75 and 83.
[141] Ibid., 48.
[142] Ibid., 68.
[143] Ibid., 14.
[144] "Aber der einzige unserer Freunde, der die Flucht dorthin erhoffte, ist noch weniger ein echter Shanghaier geworden, als es ihm je gelang, ein echter Wiener zu werden." Aichinger, "Erlebnisgarantie für Wiener in Shanghai," in *Unglaubwürdige Reisen*, 161.
[145] While the travel guide Aichinger reads advises tourists to "plan the short time carefully," she comments bitingly that her family friend, Dr. Weisselberg, "had no chance to plan his time" and notes that his "ending in one of the many death camps" makes his "friendly, almost obsequious smile a warning." (Dr. Weisselberg hatte keine Möglichkeit, seine Zeit zu planen, sie gehörte ihm so wenig, wie ein Belastungszeuge sich gehören kann.) She concludes, (Aber das Ende des Dr. Weisselberg in einem der vielen Vernichtungslager macht sein freundliches, fast devotes Lächeln zum Menetekel.) Ibid., 164.
[146] Aichinger, Vorwort to *Unglaubwürdige Reisen*, 10.
[147] Ingrid Jacoby, *My Darling Diary: A Wartime Journal – Vienna 1937-39, Falmouth 1939-44* (Penzance, Cornwall: United Writers: 1998), 11.
[148] Ibid., 14.

Chapter Seven

[1] Lisl Weil, *To Sail a Ship of Treasures* (New York: Atheneum, 1984), 1.
[2] Annemarie Klinger, "Kinderliteratur von Exil-Schriftstellern," *Neue Zeit* (Graz) (December 14, 1997), 38.
[3] Ibid., 38.
[4] Lobe's work demonstrates that outsiders are included and that those who are deemed "foreign" must discover freedom for themselves: ". . . the power of that certainty, of which Mira Lobe's work always reminds us: he who is excluded must be included; he who has experienced injustice must experience justice; he who is deemed 'other' must become free for himself." (. . . die Kraft jener Gewißheit, an die uns das Werk von

Mira Lobe immer von neuem erinnert: Wer ausgegrenzt wird, muß einbezogen werden; wem Unrecht widerfährt, muß Recht geschehen; wer fremdbestimmt wird, muß frei werden für sich selbst.) *Freiheit ist besser als Speck: Texte für Mira Lobe* (Vienna: Verlag Jungbrunnen, 1993), 19.

[5] A june bug is also called a cockchafer.

[6] Such examples include the Austrian variant "Tuchent" of the German standard word "Federdecke." Christine Nöstlinger, *Zwei Wochen im Mai* (Weinheim: Beltz Verlag, 1988), 65.

[7] Thanks to Dr. Al Gurganus of The Citadel in Charleston, SC, for identifying the images of tracer shells and for noting the overexposed June bugs on the book cover.

[8] "Außerdem ist ein Schiff mit Zucker noch auf hoher See unterwegs." Nöstlinger, "Postlude," *Zwei Wochen im Mai*, 206.

[9] Weil, 1.

[10] Ibid., 28.

[11] "Maikäfer flieg! Der Vater ist im Krieg" and "Pulverland ist abgebrannt." Ibid., 5. The Austrian term "powder land" (Pulverland) suggests the German "Pommerland," or the region of Poland under siege during World War II. "Pulverland" refers to an area at war during World War II.

[12] "Doch die Maikäfer waren nie schuld, wenn Pulverland abbrannt; auch vor fünfundzwanzig Jahren nicht." Ibid., 5.

[13] "Die Geschichte, die hier erzählt wird, ist eine Pulverlandgeschichte, und sie ist wirklich passiert." Ibid., back cover.

[14] "Es war Krieg. Es war schon lange Krieg. Ich konnte mich überhaupt nicht daran erinnern, dass einmal kein Krieg gewesen war. Ich war den Krieg gewohnt und die Bomben auch." Nöstlinger. *Maikäfer, flieg!: Mein Vater, das Kriegsende, Cohn und ich* (Weinheim: Beltz & Gelberg, 1996), 7.

[15] "Der mit dem Schleifstein war der Blöde in der Klasse. Hildegard war die Lehrerin. Ich übernahm die Stimmen sämtlicher Zwergschüler. Meine Lieblingsrolle war der Blöde mit dem Schleifstein." Ibid., 68-69.

[16] "Die Zeiten, die werden langsam wieder normal werden, und wenn dann die Schule anfängt, kann sie doch nicht so reden!" Ibid., 172-73.

[17] "'Dann wird sie schon aufhören damit!' murmelte mein Vater. Ich schwor mir, nie damit aufzuhören und nie mehr in die Schule zu gehen und alles zu tun, dass die Zeiten nicht mehr normal würden. Ich beschloss, nie mehr normale Zeiten zu wollen." Ibid., 172-73.

[18] "Das 'An-welchen-Onkel-denke-ich-Spiel' war kein leichtes Spiel. Die Onkel sahen sich sehr ähnlich. Sie hatten alle hellblaue Glotzaugen und einen Bart und abstehende Ohren und eine Halbglatze." Ibid., 36-37.

[19] "[Father] ripped pages out of a book that he had found on the desk of Mrs. von Braun. On the cover was a big, black swastika. The book had speeches by the Fuehrer printed in it." ([Der Vater] riss dazu die Seiten aus einem Buch, das er im Schreibtisch der Frau von Braun gefunden hatte. Auf dem Buchdeckel war ein großes schwarzes Hakenkreuz. Im Buch waren Führer-Reden abgedruckt.) Ibid., 38.

[20] ". . . die Frauen zerstückeln, und dann schmeißen sie sie in Fässer und salzen sie ein!" Ibid., 32.

[21] "Die Russen schneiden Frauen die Busen ab und erschießen die Kinder und rauben die Häuser aus und zünden alles an und alle verbrennen." Ibid., 32.

[22] "Für mich war [Cohn] der erste hässliche, stinkende, verrückte Mensch, den ich je geliebt habe." Ibid., 104.

[23] "Ich liebte den Koch, weil er kein Krieg war. Nichts an ihm war Krieg, gar nichts. . . . Er war ein Feind und hatte eine sanfte, tiefe Schlafstimme. Er war ein Sieger und bekam Tritte, dass er quer durch die Lufthausküche flog." Ibid., 105.

[24] "Die Russen tun selten etwas Böses." Ibid., 192.

[25] "Mir fiel der Berger Schurli aus unserem zerbombten Haus ein. Der hatte trotz ausgehängter Todesanzeige nicht geglaubt, dass sein Vater tot war, sooft ich es ihm auch erklärt hatte. . . . Ich sagte: 'Kann alles sein! Vielleicht ist dein Vater zur Untergrundbewegung gegangen und kämpft jetzt gegen die letzten Nazis!' Das gefiel Gerald." Ibid., 133.

[26] Ibid., 8.

[27] "Die Frau Brenner hatte schon ein paar Mal gesagt, dass solche Frauen wie meine Großmutter bei der Gestapo angezeigt gehören." Ibid., 10.

[28] "Ich erzählte ihm, wie bös und wie wild die Großmutter werden konnte, und übertrieb dabei gewaltig." Ibid., 154.

[29] "wurde die Großmutter von Tag zu Tag größer und dicker und wilder." Ibid., 158.

[30] "Ich erzählte viel, erzählte lang, und wenn ich nicht immer bei der Wahrheit geblieben bin, so nur deshalb, damit es meine Mutter lustig und freundlich fand." Ibid., 211.

[31] "Meine Großmutter gab es wirklich nicht mehr. Sicher, so wild und so groß und so herrlich, wie ich sie Cohn geschildert hatte, war die Großmutter nie gewesen, aber so klein und so zittrig und jämmerlich wie die Alte, die da in der Puppenküche stand, war meine Großmutter nicht." Ibid., 187.

[32] "Aber damals hat alles angefangen, was es heute noch gibt." Ibid., 5.

[33] "Den Krieg hatte ich gut gekannt, im Krieg hatte ich mich ausgekannt. Den Frieden musste ich erst lernen, und ich war keine gute Schülerin im Frieden-Lernen, denn was ich da lernen sollte, hatte so gar nichts mit dem zu tun, was sich mein Kriegs-Kinder-Glaube unter "Frieden" vorgestellt hatte. Und die Erwachsenen waren keine sehr ehrlichen Lehrer. Weil sie das heute oft auch nicht sind, ist meine alte Geschichte vielleicht immer noch passend." Nöstlinger, *Zwei Wochen im Mai*, 5.

[34] "Ich sah mich und den Hansi auf dem Friedhof zwischen den umgefallenen Grabsteinen im Gras hocken und mit ihm Latein lernen." Ibid., 157.

[35] "Zuerst waren [seine Lippen] kalt und schmeckten nach Schnittlauch." Ibid., 185.

[36] "Aber das glaubte ich nicht. Bis heute glaube ich es ihm nicht. Er hat es einfach nicht ausgehalten, dass ich jemand anderen genauso stark liebe wie ihn. Nur das hat er nicht zugelassen." Ibid., 203.

[37] "Und gar so weit her mit dieser Ehrlichkeit, das wusste ich, war es bei den erwachsenen Leuten nicht. Nach dem Krieg, da hatten die meisten gestohlen. Lebensmittellager hatten sie ausgeräumt. Aus den Wohnungen, wo Leute geflohen waren, hatten sie Sachen geholt. Und aus den Kellern hatten sie sich gegenseitig den letzten Kübel Kohlen gestohlen." Ibid., 184.

[38] "Nur jemanden, der weniger hat als man selber ... darf man unter gar keinen Umständen etwas wegnehmen. Wo man den anderen etwas wegnehmen darf ... muss man von Fall zu Fall entscheiden." Ibid., 184-185.

[39] "Graust dir denn nicht?" Ibid., 185.

[40] All translations are mine. A selection of German subtitles are "Anfang," "Abschied," "Heimweh," "Krank," and "Angst."

[41] Renate Welsh, "Zeitgeschichtlicher Überblick," in *Johanna* (Reinbek by Hamburg: Rohwohlt, 1998), 185.

[42] Ibid., 187.

[43] Ibid., 144.

[44] "Weil jede Diktatur dieselbe Art von Menschen braucht, egal, was für eine Diktatur es ist. Und schöne Wörter können sie alle machen." Ibid., 144-45.

[45] "Fast alle Leute sagten, die Juden seien an allem schuld. An der Arbeitslosigkeit, an den hohn Preisen. Manche behaupteten, die Juden regieren die Welt." Ibid., 164.

[46] "Ich und mein Kind, wir müssen uns einen eigenen Platz suchen. Vielleicht mit Peter, vielleicht ohne ihn." Ibid., 182.

[47] "Wie du deinen Bauch vor dir hertragst." Ibid., 183.

[48] "Damals hatte sie beschlossen, sich Dieda zu nennen, sie hatte einfach nicht geantwortet, wenn man sie mit ihrem alten Namen ansprach." (She decided then to call herself her-over-there, she just didn't answer when she was called by her old name.) Welsh, *Dieda oder das fremde Kind* (Hamburg: Verlag Friedrich Oetinger, 2002), 44.

[49] "'My whole life I have never seen such an obstinate, stubborn, headstrong, defiant child,' said the old man one evening to his wife. . . . 'That girl is dangerous, mark my words.'" ('In meinem ganzen Leben habe ich kein derart halsstarriges, dickköpfiges, eigenwilliges, trotziges Kind gesehen,' sagte der Alte eines Abends zu seiner Frau. . . . 'Das Mädchen ist gefährlich, denk an meine Worte.') Ibid., 10.

[50] Ibid., 80.

[51] "Hunger and sadness feel so similar." (Hunger und Traurigkeit fühlten sich so ähnlich an.) Ibid., 116.

[52] "In Wien sind die Russen! Sei froh, dass wir hier sind." Ibid., 83.

[53] "And the Russians came and the women smeared ash on their faces, even the old ones, and then she, Annemarie, just stepped forward and made a curtsy and folded her hands, and the Russians stroked her curls and went away, and everyone said it was a miracle." (Und als die Russen kamen und die Frauen sich alle Asche ins Gesicht schmierten, auch die alten, das sei sie, Annemarie, einfach vorgetreten und habe einen Knicks gemacht und die Hände gefaltet, und die Russen hätten ihre Locken gestreichelt und wären abgezogen, und alle hätten gesagt, es sei ein Wunder.) Ibid., 142.

[54] Ibid., 84 and 87.

[55] "Lügen, lauter erbärmliche Lügen!" (Lies, nothing but miserable lies!) Ibid., 92.

[56] "Sometimes, however, a word dropped innocently, a name of a place like Ebensee, Mauthausen, or Hartheim; then shadows fell on faces and fingers cramped up. Dieda resolved to ask Mrs. Fischer when they were alone sometime what it meant, but then she became afraid of the shadows and ate what Mrs. Fischer put in front of her in silence." (Manchmal allerdings fiel ein Wort, das ganz harmlos daherkam, ein Ortsname wie Ebensee, Mauthausen oder Hartheim, dann fielen Schatten über die Gesichter und die Finger verkrampften sich. Dieda nahm sich vor, Frau Fischer zu fragen, wenn sie einmal allein waren, was das bedeutete, aber dann bekam sie Angst vor den Schatten und aß schweigend, was Frau Fischer vor sie hinstellte.) Ibid., 94.

[57] "Der arme Mann, . . . schon wieder eine Tochter. So ein netter Mensch, und hat schon wieder Pech gehabt." Ibid., 150.

58 "Ein Mäderl kann auch ein Glück sein." Ibid., 150.
59 "Pech gehabt. Pech gehabt. Ich bin das erste Pech, und jetzt hat er das zweite." Ibid., 151.
60 "Mädchen sind genauso viel wert. Manche Leute wissen's nur nicht." Ibid., 154.
61 "Weil die Leute blöd sind. . . . Und die blödesten sind die Frauen, weil sie mitmachen . . . . " "Lass dir nie einreden, dass du weniger wert bist als andere . . . ." Ibid., 154.
62 A first version of the novel *Geh heim und vergiß alles* was published by Herder in 1964 under the title *Das Schattennetz* (*The shadow net*).
63 In an interview, Recheis states that she is happy to have written *Lena* because young people write to her saying that they now have a better understanding of Austrian history during and after the war. (Käthe Recheis, Interview with Agathe Gansterer, "Mit Kindern über den Krieg reden," *Die Furche*, no. 11 (March 13, 2008), 1.
64 Ibid., 1.
65 Ibid., 1.
66 Käthe Recheis, *Lena: Unser Dorf und der Krieg* (Vienna: Herder, 1987), 301.
67 Ibid., 302.
68 Ibid., 301.
69 "Heute waren wir alle keine Helden, und in ganz Österreich werden nicht viele gewesen sein, die es waren. Das ist keine Wahl, bei der man noch etwas ändern kann. . . . Willst du denn, daß sie deinen Vater einsperren?" Ibid., 74.
70 Ibid., 283.
71 "Ich sagte mir, daß wir immer dagegen gewesen waren und es nie gewollt hatten, aber es nützte nichts. Ich begann mich mitschuldig zu fühlen." Ibid., 283.
72 "Immerzu wurden wir aufgefordert, so tüchtig wie die Preußen zu werden! Wir hatten nichts gegen die Preußen, aber wir hatten sehr viel dagegen, daß sie uns als Vorbild hingestellt wurden. Der Führer, der doch selber ein Österreicher war, schien von seiner Heimat nicht viel zu halten. Sogar der Name Österreich wurde verboten." Ibid., 76.
73 Recheis, interview with Gansterer, 1.
74 "Dem Tagebuch vertraute ich alles an, die Begeisterung für die Flieger, die Begeisterung für Großdeutschland, das siegen sollte." Ibid., 121.
75 "Zur Zeit der Blitzkriege, als Zwölfjährige, war ich wie so viele andere verführt von einer Ideologie, die uns junge Menschen mit lügnerischen Idealen köderte." Ibid., 301.

[76] Lena says "Aber wir haben ihnen doch nichts getan!" and Christoph replies "Darauf kommt es nicht an. Im Krieg – da sind eben alle Feinde." Ibid., 101.

[77] "Sie wissen recht gut, was im Schloß Hartheim geschieht. Sie wollen es nur nicht wahrhaben." Ibid., 92.

[78] "Nein, das will ich nicht wahrhaben, weil es nicht wahr ist. Weil es eine Verleumdung ist. Der Führer würde so etwas nie zulassen." Ibid., 93.

[79] "Der Onkel sagte, im Lager habe er Kinder gesehen, nicht einmal so alt wie Christoph und die Lena, manchmal sogar ganz kleine Kinder." Ibid., 131.

[80] "Mit Orden, die jemand dafür bekam, weil er andere Menschen getötet hatte, wollte ich nichts mehr zu tun haben." Ibid., 178.

[81] "Die armen Kinder!" Ibid., 288.

[82] Ibid., 186.

[83] Ibid., 196.

[84] Ibid., 196.

[85] "Und wenn alles vorbei ist, werden sie uns fragen, warum wir es zugelassen haben. Weil niemand, der es nicht selber erlebt hat, begreifen wird, wie hilflos man unter so einer Regierung ist." Ibid., 196.

[86] "The war was over. It was peace. But it would take a long time until we could forget the war." "Der Krieg war aus. Es war Frieden. Aber es würde lange dauern, bis wir den Krieg vergessen konnten." Ibid., 296.

[87] "Die Kinder, die jetzt geboren werden, kennen den Krieg und die Diktatur nur noch aus den Geschichten, die wir ihnen erzählen. Und vielleicht werden sie nie ganz begreifen, was Friede und Freiheit damals für uns bedeutete." Ibid., 300.

[88] "It seems much more important to me to recognize the mechanisms that can lead a people to commit crimes and to inhumanity." (Viel wichtiger erscheint mir, daß wir alle uns die Mechanismen klar machen, die ein Volk ins Verbrechen und in die Unmenschlichkeit führen können.) Ibid, 303.

[89] "Daß jede Intoleranz gegen Menschen, die anders sind als wir, schon die Wurzel kommenden Unrechts in sich trägt." Ibid., 303.

[90] "My parents taught me that a person's freedom and dignity are threatened in every dictatorship." (Meine Eltern lehrten mich, daß Freiheit und Würde des Menschen in jeder Diktatur bedroht sind.) Käthe Recheis, *Geh heim und vergiß alles: Roman* (Plöchl, Austria: Bibliothek der Provinz, 1964), 7.

[91] "Ich habe es vergessen. Es gibt nichts mehr, was mich daran erinnert." "Plötzlich erinnere ich mich. Und da weiß ich auf einmal: Ich habe es nicht vergessen." Ibid., 9.

[92] Ibid., 9.
[93] Ibid., 94.
[94] "Als ich nach dem Lichtschalter griff, wußte ich plötzlich, daß alles nur eine Täuschung gewesen war, der friedliche Garten und das friedliche Haus. Das Lager war mir nachgefolgt, es erfüllte das Zimmer, es erfüllte das ganze Haus." Ibid., 29.
[95] "Zum ersten Mal fühlte ich mich mit den kranken, leidenden Männern verbunden, ich war ihnen auf seltsame Weise ähnlich geworden, als sei auch ich krank, gequält, verlassen und hilflos wie sie." Ibid., 41.
[96] "War ich wirklich hübsch?" Ibid., 61.
[97] "Ich war kaum erwachsen, meine Kleider waren mir zu groß, und ich mußte alte Männerschuhe tragen. . . . Aber [Imre] küßte meine Hand, wie man einer Dame die Hand küßt." Ibid., 65.
[98] "Alles, was früher geschehen war, vor jener Nacht mit dem Kommandanten, schien mir klar und scharf getrennt von meinem jetzigen Leben zu sein. Ich sah auf meine Schuhe. Es war mir gleichgültig, daß ich Männerschuhe tragen mußte. Ich würde deshalb nie mehr verlegen oder schüchtern werden." Ibid., 97-98.
[99] Ibid., 71.
[100] "Mein Vater war tot. Er wäre nicht tot, hätte der Kommandant früher geholfen. Ich wußte jetzt, warum er es nicht getan hatte. Seine Eltern, seine Frau, seine Kinder, seine ganze Familie wurden in einem KZ-Lager getötet." Ibid., 120.
[101] Recheis, interview with Gansterer, 1.

Conclusion

[1] "Das ich erinnere, wenn die Zeit kommt." In this poetic context, the verb "erinnere" could even translate as "remind" or "commemorate." Petra Ganglbauer, *Der Himmel wartet* (Vienna: Milena, 2006), 7. In this novel, a montage of related narrative passages, Ganglbauer examines how media culture and mass culture play out in individual memory and desire.
[2] "Alles, was ich hier über dieses Geschriebene sagen könnte, kann man natürlich besser erfahren, indem man es liest." Elfriede Jelinek, Vorwort, "Das flüchtige jetzt," in *Flüchtlingskinder: Erinnerungen* by Claire Felsenburg, ed. Rosemarie Schulak and Konstantin Kaiser (Vienna: Verlag der Theodor Kramer Gesellschaft and Aktionsradius Augarten, 2002), 11.
[3] Gioseffi is hopeful that women and men can work together for a more peaceful future: "Only humanitarian diplomacy and a kinder, gentler commitment to a global community can end international terrorism. Only steps to promote greater economic justice, fair labor practices, and sound

environmental policies can move us toward a safe and peaceful world." Gioseffi, *Women on War,* xx. Goldstein's study shows that it is war that causes injustice and that "ultimately, in little ways, we all participate in the war system and we all shape its evolution." Goldstein, 414. These observations lead him to conclude, "if you want justice (gender and others), work for peace." Goldstein, 424.

[4] Klüger, *Dichter und Historiker,* 51.

[5] ". . . auch jede glückliche Wende." Aichinger, "Das Ende des Wohnens" (The end of living/residing), in *Unglaubwürdige Reisen,* 85. Whereas Aichinger's grandmother's deportation and murder are worked through by way of a literary fairy tale in Aichinger's novel, her personal essays confront these crimes in a painfully straightforward manner. In her 2002 essay "Aus der Geschichte der Trennungen" (Out of the story of separations), for example, Aichinger writes that her aunt, who escaped to England before the war, saved clothes for her mother, Aichinger's beloved grandmother. Aichinger writes: "During the war 'Auntie' bought clothes for her. She saved these clothes until her own death. After the 6th of May, 1942, when the deportation train drove off to Minsk, nobody would have been able to wear them anymore." Ibid., 69. In an earlier essay, "Sonntagsglück in Hetzendorf" (Sunday happiness in Hetzendorf), Aichinger tells of the apartment in which her grandmother was able to live for two years before her deportation: "Both years in which my grandmother lived there stayed as they were, no shadow of a future." Ibid., 45. In a third essay from 2004, "Hills and gentle Cardinals" (Hügel und sanfte Kardinäle), Aichinger begins, "It was a Tuesday in May 1942, . . . when she heard somewhat rushed words: 'The area in which your people live is dangerous this afternoon,'" and at the end of the essay she describes this place "of her people" as the one "from which they were deported." Ibid., 131. She calls the twentieth century "this time when little children were ripped from the arms of their mothers," "a time when a god-forsaken horde became of the 'people of God.'" Ibid., 131.

[6] Klüger, "Die Ödnis eines entlarvten Landes" in *Katastrophen: Über deutsche Literatur* 80.

[7] ". . . in Aichinger's book Austria has shrunk into the private hell of a child. It is no longer a place where a minority fights for its civil rights; it is a place where a child clings to straws on the way to death, the mother in exile, the father an enemy." (. . . in Aichingers Buch ist Österreich zu der privaten Hölle eines Kindes zusammengeschrumpft. Es ist nicht mehr ein Ort, wo eine Minderheit um ihre Bürgerrechte kämpft, es ist ein Ort, wo ein Kind sich an Strohhalme klammert auf dem Weg in den Tod, die Mutter im Exil, der Vater ein Feind.) Ibid., 81.

8 "... an Austria that abandons or devours its own children." (... ein Österreich, das seine eigenen Kinder aussetzt oder verschlingt.) Ibid., 81.

9 "... it is the ghosts that haunt me, me, who am not even religious. Ghosts are the unresolved, unredeemed past." (es sind die Gespenster, die mich heimsuchen, mich, die ich doch gar nicht gläubig bin. Gespenster sind die ungelöste, unerlöste Vergangenheit.) Ruth Klüger, *Unterwegs verloren: Erinnerungen* (Vienna: Paul Zsolnay Verlag, 2008), 228.

10 "Gespenster unterscheiden kaum zwischen Kleinigkeiten und Enormitäten, sie sind für beides zuständig. Wie die Lebenden nehmen sie, was sie kriegen können." Ibid., 228.

11 "Was unterwegs verloren geht, bist immer du selbst, und der nächste Ankunftsort besteht, wie die vorigen, aus dem Jetzt und dem Damals, es gibt keinen neuen Anfang, nur Fortsetzungen auf einem Weg, der zusehends schmaler wird." Ibid., 235.

12 Dagmar Lorenz, in her volume on German-speaking Jewish women authors, has observed that "the theme of persecution pervades German-Jewish literature." *Keepers of the Motherland*, 319. Lorenz demonstrates that literary works by authors such as Grete Weil, Ronnith Neumann, Ruth Klüger, Esther Dischereit, and Katja Behrens examining historical events of the 1980s and 1990s, broaden "the basis for a new Jewish women's literature." Ibid., 275. Lorenz also comments on authors who experienced World War II and the Holocaust firsthand and describes the authenticity that writers such as Klüger offer readers: "what distinguishes Klüger's writing from that of exile writers and the younger generation of Jewish authors is the fact that she was at the places that they try to imagine. Hence, Klüger does not search for her lost culture and the death camps. Having survived and left the country of her oppressors, she knows that memory transcends time and space." Ibid., 293.

13 "Nicht Abklatsch der Wirklichkeit, sondern ihre Interpretation." Klüger, *Unterwegs verloren*, 171.

Bibliography

Documentary Films:
Into the Arms of Strangers. DVD. Written and directed by Mark Jonathan Harris and produced by Deborah Oppenheimer. 2000; Warner Brothers Pictures and Sabine Films, Burbank, CA. 2005.
My Knees Were Jumping. Remembering the Kindertransports. DVD. Produced and directed by Melissa Hacker. 1996; Independent Film Channel. 2003.
Shanghai Ghetto. DVD. Produced and directed by Dana Janklowicz-Mann and Amir Mann. Rebel Child Productions. 2002; Menemsha Entertainment, Los Angeles, CA. 2005.
Tangled Roots. DVD. Produced and directed by Heidi Schmidt Emberling. New Day Films. Oxygen Media in association with Spirit Productions, Harriman, NY. 2001.
The Port of Last Resort. Zuflucht Schanghai. DVD. Directed by Joan Grossman and Paul Rosdy. 1998; A co-production of Pinball Films, Vienna/New York and Extrafilm, Vienna. 2006.
Vielleicht habe ich Glück gehabt. Film/ORF Production. Directed by Käthe Kratz. 2002; Produktion Extrafilm, Vienna. 2003.

Primary Texts:
Aichinger, Ilse. *Die größere Hoffnung.* Frankfurt. a. M.: Fischer, 1991.
———. *Herod's Children.* Translated by Cornelia Schaeffer. New York: Atheneum, 1963.
———. "Mondgeschichte," *Märchen deutscher Dichter.* Edited by Elisabeth Borchers. Frankfurt a. M.: Insel, 1972.
———. *Unglaubwürdige Reisen.* Frankfurt a. M.: S. Fischer, 2005.
Bachmann, Ingeborg. *Werke.* Volumes I-IV. Edited by Christine Koschel and Inge von Weidenbaum. 1978. Munich: Piper, 1993.
———. *The Thirtieth Year: Stories.* Translated by Michael Bullock. New York: Holmes & Meier, 1987.
———. *Wir müssen wahre Sätze finden.* Munich: Piper, 1983.
Baum, Vicki. *Shanghai '37.* Translated by Basil Creighton. New York: Book League of America, 1940.
Blend, Martha. *A Child Alone.* London: Vallentine Mitchell, 1995.

———. *Ich kam als Kind: Erinnerungen.* Translated by Karin Hanta. Vienna: Picus, 1998.
Boin, Lilly H. *My Story.* Lincoln, Nebraska, NB: Contact Center, 1989.
Canetti, Veza. *Die Schildkröten.* Munich: Carl Hanser, 1999.
———. *The Tortoises.* Translated by Ian Mitchell. New York: New Directions, 2001.
———. *Die gelbe Strasse.* Munich: Carl Hanser, 1990.
———. *The Yellow Street.* Translated by Ian Mitchell. New York: New Directions Publishing, 1991.
Felsenburg, Claire. *Flüchtlingskinder: Erinnerungen: Vorwort von Elfriede Jelinek.* Edited by Rosemarie Schulak and Konstantin Kaiser. Vienna: Verlag der Theodor Kramer Gesellschaft and Aktionsradius Augarten, 2002.
Freundlich, Elisabeth. *Finstere Zeiten: Vier Erzählungen.* Mannheim: persona, 1986.
———. *Die fahrenden Jahre: Erinnerungen.* Salzburg: Otto Müller, 1992.
———. *The Traveling Years.* Translated by Elizabeth Pennebaker. Riverside, CA: Ariadne, 1999.
———. *Der Seelenvogel: Roman.* Vienna: Zsolnay, 1986.
Furst, Desider and Lilian R. *Home is Somewhere Else: Autobiography in Two Voices.* New York: State University of New York Press, 1994.
Ganglbauer, Petra. *Der Himmel wartet.* Vienna: Milena, 2006.
Geiser, Katharina. *Vorübergehend Wien.* Vienna: Zsolnay, 2006.
Golabek, Mona, and Lee Cohen. *The Children of Willesden Lane: Beyond the Kinderstransport: A Memoir of Music, Love, and Survival.* New York: Warner Books, 2002.
Grossberg, Mimi. *Eine österreichische Exilautorin in New York.* Begleitbuch zur Ausstellung der Österreichischen Exilbibliothek im Literaturhaus. *Zirkular* (Vienna). Sondernummer, 54, 1999.
Haidegger, Christine. *Zum Fenster hinaus: Eine Nachkriegskindheit; Roman.* Reinbek: Rowohlt, 1979.
———. *Mama Dear. Memoir of a Postwar Childhood in Europe.* Translated by Heidi J. Petermichl. Riverside, CA: Ariadne, 2002.
Haushofer, Marlen. *Die Wand.* 1968. Munich: Deutscher Taschenbuch Verlag, 1991.
———. *The Wall.* Translated by Shaun Whiteside. San Francisco: Cleis, 1990.
Heppner, Ernest G. *Shanghai Refuge: A Memoir of the World War II Jewish Ghetto.* 1993. Lincoln, NB: University of Nebraska Press,

1995.

———. "The Relations between the Western European Refugees and the Shanghai Resident Jews: A Personal Memoir." In Jonathan Goldstein, ed., *The Jews of China. Volume Two, A Sourcebook and Research Guide*. Armonk, NY: M. E. Sharpe, 1999. 57-69.

Heppner, Illo. "Shanghai: A Woman's Eyewitness Report." In Jonathan Goldstein, ed., *The Jews of China. Volume Two, A Sourcebook and Research Guide*. Armonk, NY: M. E. Sharpe, 1999. 49-56.

Hilsenrad, Helen. *Brown Was the Danube: A Memoir of Hitler's Vienna*. New York: Thomas Yoseloff, 1966.

Hlawaty, Graziella. *Die Stadt der Lieder*. Vienna: Zsolnay, 1995.

———. *Broken Songs. An Adolescent in War-Torn Vienna*. Translated by Pamela Saur. Riverside, CA: Ariadne, 2005.

———. *Erzählungen*. Vienna: Edition Atelier, 1999.

Ivanji, Ildi. *Wetten am Tor: Erzählungen*. Vienna: Picus, 2000.

Jacoby, Ingrid. *My Darling Diary: A Wartime Journal – Vienna 1937-39, Falmouth 1939-44*. Penzance, Cornwall: United Writers, 1998.

Jelinek, Elfriede. *Die Ausgesperrten*. 1980. Reinbek bei Hamburg: Rowohlt, 2000.

———. *In den Alpen: Drei Dramen*. Berlin: Berlin Verlag, 2002.

———. *Wonderful, Wonderful Times*. Translated by Michael Hulse. London: Serpent's Tail, 1990.

———. *Die Kinder der Toten*. Reinbek bei Hamburg: Rowohlt, 1995.

Kaplan, Vivian Jeanette. *Ten Green Bottles: The True Story of One Family's Journey From War-Torn Austria to the Ghettos of Shanghai*. New York: St. Martin's, 2002.

Kaus, Gina. *Was für ein Leben*. Hamburg: Albrecht Knaus, 1979.

———. *Die Unwiderstehlichen: Kleine Prosa*. Edited by Hartmut Vollmer. Oldenburg: Igel, 2000.

———. *Von Wien nach Hollywood*. Frankfurt: Suhrkamp, 1990.

Kerschbaumer, Marie-Thérèse. *Der weibliche Name des Widerstands*. Klagenfurt: Wieser, 1980.

———. *Woman's Face of Resistance: Seven Reports*. Translated by Lowell A. Bangerter. Riverside, CA: Ariadne, 1996.

Klüger, Ruth. *weiter leben: Eine Jugend*. Göttingen: Wallstein, 1992.

———. *Still Alive: A Holocaust Girlhood Remembered*. New York: The Feminist Press, 2001.

———. *unterwegs verloren: Erinnerungen*. Vienna: Zsolnay, 2008.

Kräftner, Hertha. *Kühle Sterne*. Klagenfurt: Wieser, 1998.

———. *Das Werk: Gedichte; Skizzen; Tagebücher*. Edited by Franz Probst.

Eisenstadt: Burgenländischer PEN-Club, 1977.
Krasno, Rena. *Strangers Always: A Jewish Family in Wartime Shanghai*, Berkeley, CA: Pacific View, 1992.
Kurzweil, Edith. *Briefe aus Wien: Jüdisches Leben vor der Deportation*. Vienna: Verlag Turia & Kant, 1999.
Lachs, Minna. *Zwischen zwei Welten: Erinnerungen 1941-1946*. Foreword by Julian Schutting. Vienna: Löcker Verlag, 1992.
Leverton, Bertha and Shmuel Lowensohn, eds. *I Came Alone*. Sussex: Book Guild, 1990.
Martel, Yann. *Life of Pi*. Edinburgh: Canongate, 2002.
Neuwirth, Barbara. "Bücherverbrennung," *In den Gärten der Nacht*. Frankfurt a. M.: Suhrkamp, 1990.
———. *Über die Thaya*. Vienna: Edition Koenigstein, 2000.
———. *Escaping Expectations: Stories by Austrian Women*. Riverside, CA: Ariadne, 2001.
Nöstlinger, Christine. *Maikäfer, flieg!* 1973. Weinheim: Beltz, 1996.
———. *Zwei Wochen im Mai: Mein Vater, der Rudi, der Hansi und ich*. 1981. Weinheim: Beltz, 1988.
Nowak, Johanna. *Gehorsam: Roman eines schuldhaften Lebens*. Vienna: Wiener Frauenverlag, 1994.
Perko, Gudrun, ed. *Mahlzeit: Frauen zwischen 70 und 100 erzählen aus ihren Erinnerungen*. Vienna: Milena, 2000.
Petrik, Dine. *Die Hügel nach der Flut: Was geschah wirklich mit Hertha K.?* Salzburg: Otto Müller, 1997.
Recheis, Käthe. *Geh heim und vergiß alles: Roman*. Plöchl, Austria: Bibliothek der Provinz, 1964.
———. *Lena: Unser Dorf und der Krieg*. Munich: Deutscher Taschenbuch Verlag Junior, 1987.
Reichart, Elisabeth. *Februarschatten*. Frankfurt a. M.: Fischer, 1989.
———. *February Shadows*. Translated by Donna Hoffmeister. Riverside, CA: Ariadne, 1989.
———. *Komm über den See*. Vienna: Deuticke, 2001.
———. *Nachtmär*. Vienna: Müller, 1995.
Rosenkranz, Erika. *Und ich fand es herrlich: Erinnerungen einer Vertriebenen*. Vienna: Czernin, 2001.
Rotenberg, Stella. *Gedichte*. Tel Aviv: Olamenu, 1972.
———. *Die wir übrig sind*. Darmstadt: J.G. Bläschke, 1978.
———. *Meine wahre Heimat*. Edition Mnemosyne, Band 8, Klagenfurt: Alekto, 1999.
Ruby, Lois. *Shanghai Shadows*. New York: Holiday House, 2006.
Saville, Annette. *Only a Kindertransportee*. Northolt, Middlesex: New

Millennium, 2002.
———. *Little Grass Orphan Annie*. London: self-published, 1994.
Shedd, Charlotte. *Thank You America*. Riverside, CA: Ariadne: 1997.
Seeber, Ursula, ed. *Ein Niemandsland, aber welch ein Rundblick! Exilautoren über Nachkriegs-Wien*. Vienna: Picus, 1998.
Segal, Lore. *Other People's Houses*. 1964. New York: New York Press, 1994.
———. *Wo andere Leute wohnen: Roman*. Translated by Sabina Illmer. Vienna: Picus, 2000.
Spiel, Hilde. *Rückkehr nach Wien: Ein Tagebuch*. Munich: Amalthea, 1996.
———. *Return to Vienna. A Journal*. Translated by Christine Shuttleworth. Riverside CA: Ariadne, 2011.
———. *Die hellen und die finsteren Zeiten: Erinnerungen 1911-1946*. Mu-nich: List, 1989.
———. *The Dark and the Bright: Memoirs 1911-1989*. Translated by Christine Shuttleworth. Riverside, CA: Ariadne, 2007.
Tausig, Franziska. *Shanghai Passage: Emigration ins Ghetto*. Vienna: Picus, 2008.
Trahan, Elizabeth Welt. *Geisterbeschwörung: Eine jüdische Kindheit im Wien der Kriegsjahre*. Translated by Elfriede Potyka. Vienna: Picus, 1996.
———. *Walking with Ghosts: A Jewish Childhood in Wartime Vienna*. New York: Peter Lang, 1998.
———. *Ten Dollars in My Pocket: The American Education of a Holocaust Survivor: A Memoir in Documents*. New York: Peter Lang, 2006.
Weil, Lisl. *To Sail a Ship of Treasures*. New York: Atheneum, 1984.
Welsh, Renate. *Johanna*. 1979. Reinbek bei Hamburg: Rowohlt Taschenbuch, 1998.
———. *Dieda oder Das fremde Kind*. Hamburg: Verlag Friedrich Oetin-ger, 2002.
Welles, Eva Anna. *Am Rande der Geschichte*. Vienna: Wiener Frauenverlag, 1990.

Secondary Texts:
Achberger, Karen. *Understanding Ingeborg Bachmann*. Columbia, SC: University of South Carolina Press, 1995.
Alfers, Sandra. "Voices from a Haunting Past: Ghosts, Memory, and Poetry in Ruth Klüger's *weiter leben: Eine Jugend*." *Monatshefte* 100, no. 4 (2008): 519-533.
Auschwitz filmen oder die Darstellbarkeit der Geschichte. Mitteilungen des

Instituts für Wissenschaft und Kunst 4. Vienna: Institut für Wissenschaft und Kunst, 1995.
Baer, Elizabeth R. and Myrna Goldenberg, eds. *Experience and Expression: Women, the Nazis, and the Holocaust.* Detroit: Wayne State University Press, 2003.
Bailer, Brigitte, Elisabeth Klamper, and Wolfgang Neugebauer, eds. *1938: NS-Herrschaft in Österreich.* Vienna: Bundesministerium für Inneres, 1998.
Bakos, Eva. *Wilde Wienerinnen: Leben zwischen Tabu und Freiheit.* Vienna: Ueberreuter, 1999.
Bandhauer-Schöffmann, Irene and Ela Hofnung, eds. *Wiederaufbau weiblich: Dokumentation der Tagung "Frauen in der österreichischen und deutschen Nachkriegszeit."* Vienna: Geyer-Edition, 1992.
Baumgart, Reinhard and Thomas Tebbe, eds. *Einsam sind alle Brücken: Autoren schreiben über Ingeborg Bachmann.* 1992. Munich: Piper, 2001.
Baumgartner, Andreas. *Die vergessenen Frauen von Mauthausen: Die weiblichen Häftlinge des Konzentrationslagers Mauthausen und ihre Geschichte.* Vienna: Mauthausen Komitee Österreich, 2006.
Beckermann, Ruth. *Unzugehoerig: Oesterreichische Juden nach 1945.* Vienna: Löcker Verlag, 1989.
Behrend, Hannah. "An Austrian Refugee in Wartime Manchester." In *This Working World: Women's Lives and Cultures in Britain 1914-1945*, edited by Sybil Oldfield, 133-137. London: Bristol, PA: Taylor & Francis, 1994.
Berger, Karin, Elisabeth Holzinger, Lotte Podgornick, and Lisbeth N. Trallori. *Der Himmel ist blau: Kann sein; Frauen im Widerstand; Österreich 1938-1945.* Vienna: Promedia Verlag (Edition Spuren), 1985.
Berger, Franz Severin and Christian Holler. *Trümmerfrauen: Alltag zwischen Hamstern und Hoffen.* Vienna: Ueberreuter, 1994.
Benz, Ute. *Frauen im Nationalsozialismus: Dokumente und Zeugnisse.* Munich: Verlag C. H. Beck, 1993.
Bischof, Gunther and Anton Pelinka, eds. *Austrian Historical Memory & National Identity.* New Brunswick: Transaction Publishers, 1997.
Bischof, Gunther, Anton Pelinka, and Erika Thurner, eds. *Women in Austria.* Contemporary Austrian Studies. Volume 6. Piscataway, NJ: Transaction Publishers, 1998.
Borgert, Udo. *Women's Words, Women's Works.* Riverside, CA: Ariadne, 2001.

Brandt, Bettina. "The Challenging Writings of Elfriede Jelinek: An Austrian Feminist Wins the Nobel Prize in Literature," *Women's Review of Books*, 22, no. 3 (December, 2004): 1 and 4.

Brinker-Gabler, Gisela, and Markus Zisselsberger. *"If We Had the Word": Ingeborg Bachmann; Views and Reviews.* Riverside, CA: Ariadne, 2004.

Brinson, Charmian, Richard Dove, and Jennifer Taylor, eds. *"Immortal Austria?" Austrians in Exile in Britain.* The Yearbook of the Research Centre for German and Austrian Exile Studies, London. Vol. 8. Amsterdam: Rodopi, 2007.

Broer, Wolfgang. "Jedes Weltbild ist auch ein Seelenbild." *Kurier* (Vienna), March 18, 1978.

Brostoff, Anita, ed. *Flares of Memory: Survivors Remember Stories of Childhood During the Holocaust.* Oxford: Oxford University Press, 1998.

Cargnelli, Christian, and Michael Omasta, eds. *Aufbruch ins Ungewisse.* Vienna: Wespennest, 1993.

Cerwenka, Kurt. *Die Fahne ist mehr als der Tod: Nationalsozialistische Erziehung und Schule in "Oberdonau" 1938-1945.* Edition Geschichte der Heimat. Grünbach Austria: Franz Steinmaßl, 1996.

Cohen-Weisz, Susanne. "From Bare Survival to European Jewish Vision: Jewish Life and Identity in Vienna." Working Papers. Institute For European Studies. Hebrew University of Jerusalem. http://www.ef.huji.ac.il/publications/working.shtml (accessed June 8, 2010).

Critchfield, Richard. "Hilde Spiel and the Problem of Cultural Identity." *Modern Austrian Literature* 32, no. 3 (1999): 52-65.

DeMerrit, Linda. "*Lebkuchenherz* and Cultural Identity: Elisabeth Reichart's *Nachtmär*." *Modern Austrian Literature* 32, no. 3 (1999): 85-100.

Diner, Hasia R. *We Remember with Reverence and Love: American Jews and the Myth of Silence after the Holocaust, 1945-1962.* New York: New York University Press, 2009.

Dokumentationsarchiv des österreichischen Widerstandes. *Widerstand und Verfolgung in Wien 1934-1945.* 3 vols. Vienna: Dokumentationsarchiv des österreichischen Widerstandes, 1975.

Dombrowski, Nicole Ann. *Women and War in the Twentieth Century.* New York: Garland, 1999.

Douer, Alisa, Ursula Seeber, and Edith Blaschitz, eds. *Wie weit ist Wien: Lateinamerika als Exil für österreichische Schriftsteller und*

Künstler. Vienna: Picus, 1995.
Douer, Alisa, and Ursula Seeber, eds. *Frauen aus Wien: Fotoband von Alisa Douer mit Texten von Ursula Seeber*. Vienna: Frauenförderung und Koordination von Frauenangelegenheiten, 1999.
Eibeshitz, Jehoshua, and Anna Eilenberg-Eibeshitz. *Women in the Holocaust: A Collection of Testimonies*. Vol.1. New York: Remember, 1993.
Elshtain, Jean Bethke. *Women and War*. Chicago: University of Chicago Press, 1995.
Fiddler, Allyson. *Rewriting Reality: An Introduction to Elfriede Jelinek*. Oxford: Berg, 1994.
——, ed. *"Other" Austrians: Post-1945 Austrian Women's Writings. Proceedings at the Conference Held at the University of Nottingham from 18-20 April 1996*. Bern: Lang, 1998.
Frauenleben 1945: Kriegsende in Wien. Vienna: Historisches Museum der Stadt Wien, 1995.
Gehrke, Martha Maria. *Das Donauland-Frauenbuch: Ein moderner Ratgeber für Heim und Familie*. Vienna: Buchgemeinschaft Donauland, 1965.
Gilbert, Martin. *Never Again: A History of the Holocaust*. New York: Universe, 2000.
Gilman, Sander L., and Jack Zipes, eds. *Yale Companion to Jewish Writing and Thought in German Culture 1096-1996*. New Haven: Yale University Press, 1997.
Giorgio, Adalgisa, ed. *Writing Mothers and Daughters: Renegotiating the Mother in Western European Narratives by Women*. Oxford: Berghahn, 2002.
Gioseffi, Daniela, ed. *Frauen über den Krieg: Eine Sammlung bedeutender Stimmen gegen den Krieg*. Vienna: Wiener Frauenverlag, 1992.
——. *Women on War: An International Anthology of Women's Writings from Antiquity to the Present*. 1988. New York: Feminist Press at the City University of New York, 2003.
Göhring, Walter, Robert Machacek, and Friederike Stadlmann. *Aufbruch aus dem Nichts: Entstehung und Geschichte der 2. Republik Österreich*. Vienna: Verlag des Österreichischen Gewerkschaftsbundes, 1980.
Goldstein, Joshua S. *War and Gender: How Gender Shapes the War System and Vice Versa*. Cambridge: University of Cambridge Press, 2001.
Goldstein, Jonathan, ed., *The Jews of China*. Vol. 2, *A Sourcebook and Research Guide*. Armonk, NY: M. E. Sharpe, 1999.
Good, David, Margarete Grandner, and Mary Jo Maynes, eds.

Austrian Women in the Nineteenth and Twentieth Centuries: Cross-Disciplinary Perspectives. Providence, RI: Berghahn Books, 1996.

Grassl, Gerald. "Aller Selbstmord: Flaschenpost der Toten." *Volksstimme* (Vienna), November 1, 1989, 9.

Gürtler, Christa, and Sigrid Schmid-Bortenschlager. *Erfolg und Verfolgung: Österreichische Schriftstellerinnen 1918-1945; Fünfzehn Porträts und Texte*. Salzburg: Residenz, 2002.

Hackl, Erich. *Abschied von Sidonie*. Zurich: Diogenes, 1989.

———. *Materialien zu Abschied von Sidonie*. Zurich: Diogenes, 2000.

Hahnl, Hans Heinz. *Vergessene Literaten: Fünzig österreichische Lebensschicksale*. Vienna: Österreichischer Bundesverlag, 1984.

Harris, Mark Jonathan, and Deborah Oppenheimer. *Into the Arms of Strangers: Stories of the Kindertransport*. New York: Bloomsbury, 2000.

Heinemann, Marlene. *Gender and Destiny: Women Writers and the Holocaust*. New York: Greenwood, 1986.

Herrberg, Heike, and Heidi Wagner. *Wiener Melange: Frauen zwischen Salon und Kaffeehaus*. Berlin: Edition Ebersbach, 2002.

Hödl, Klaus. *Jüdische Identitäten: Einblicke in die Bewußtseinslandschaft des österreichischen Judentums*. Innsbruck: Studien, 2000.

Höller, Hans. *Ingeborg Bachmann*. Reinbek: Rowohlt, 1999.

Holliday, Laurel. *Children in the Holocaust and World War II: Their Secret Diaries*. New York: Pocket Books, 1995.

Jenk, Gabriele. *Steine gegen Brot: Trümmerfrauen schildern den Wiederaufbau in der Nachkriegszeit*. Bergisch-Gladbach: Lübbe, 1988.

Johns, Jorun B., and Katherine Arens, eds. *Elfriede Jelinek: Framed by Language*. Riverside, CA: Ariadne, 1994.

Kahn Keimowitz, Hazel, and Wolfgang Mieder, eds. *The Jewish Experience of European Anti-Semitism*. Burlington, VT: Center for Holocaust Studies at the University of Vermont, 1995.

Ketzer, Adrienne. *My Mother's Voice: Children, Literature, and the Holocaust*. Toronto: Broadview, 2002.

Rittner, Carol, and John K. Roth, eds. *Women and the Holocaust: Different Voices*. New York: Paragon House, 1993.

Klüger, Ruth. *Katastrophen: Über deutsche Literatur*. Göttingen: Wallstein, 1994.

———. *Dichter und Historiker: Fakten und Fiktionen*. Vienna: Picus, 2000.

———. "Growing up in the Eye of the Firestorm: A Jewish Childhood under the Nazis." In *Facing Fascism and Confronting the Past: German Women Writers from Weimar to the Present*. Edited by Elke P. Frederiksen and Martha Kaarsberg Wallach. New York: SUNY

Press, 2000.

———. *Gelesene Wirklichkeit: Fakten und Fiktionen in der Literatur.* Göttingen: Wallstein, 2006.

Klusacek, Christiane, Herbert Steiner, and Kurt Stimmer, eds. *Dokumentation zur österreichischen Zeitgeschichte 1938-1945.* Vienna: Jugend und Volk Verlag, 1971.

Kranzler, David. *Japanese, Nazis and Jews: The Jewish Refugee Community of Shanghai, 1938-1945.* Hoboken, NJ: KTAV Publishing House, Inc., 1988.

Kreis, Gabriele. *Frauen im Exil: Dichtung und Wirklichkeit.* Düsseldorf: Claassen, 1984.

Kremer, S. Lillian. *Women's Holocaust Writing: Memory and Imagination.* Lincoln, NB: University of Nebraska Press, 1999.

Konzett, Matthias Piccolruaz, and Margarete Lamb-Faffelberger, eds. *Elfriede Jelinek: Writing Woman, Nation, and Identity; A Critical Anthology.* Madison, NJ: Fairleigh Dickinson University Press, 2007.

Köppen, Manuel, ed. *Kunst und Literatur nach Auschwitz.* Berlin: Erich Schmidt, 1993.

Kopetzky, Helmut. *Die andere Front: Europäische Frauen im Krieg und Widerstand, 1939 bis 1945.* Cologne: Pahl-Rugenstein, 1983.

Langer, Lawrence. *Preempting the Holocaust.* New Haven: Yale University Press, 1998.

———. *The Holocaust and the Literary Imagination.* New Haven: Yale University Press, 1975.

Lauber, Wolfgang. *Wien: Ein Stadtführer durch den Widerstand 1934-1945.* Vienna: Böhlau, 1987.

Lennox, Sara. *Cemetery of the Murdered Daughters: Feminism, History, and Ingeborg Bachmann.* Amherst, MA: University of Massachusetts Press, 2006.

Lezzi, Eva. *Zerstörte Kindheit: Literarische Autobiographien zur Shoah.* Cologne: Böhlau, 2001.

Lorenz, Dagmar C. G. *Keepers of the Motherland: German Texts by Jewish Women Writers.* Lincoln, NB: University of Nebraska Press, 1997.

———. "Memory and Criticism: Ruth Klüger's *weiter leben.*" In *Women in German Yearbook* 9 (1993): 206-224.

Losenicky, Daniela. "Frauenarbeit und Krieg am Beispiel Österreich." Hochschulschrift, Diplom-Arbeit. University of Vienna, Austria, 1998.

Lubich, Frederick. "Surviving to Excel: The Last German Jewish Autobiographies of Holocaust Survivors Ruth Klüger, Marcel

Reich-Ranicki, and Paul Spiegel." *Modern Judaism* 25, no. 2 (May 2005): 189-210.

Madler, Peter. *Books Abroad*. Norman, OK: University of Oklahoma Press, 1964.

Macdonald, Sharon. *Images of Women in Peace and War*. Basingstoke: Macmillan, 1988.

Marsiske, Hans-Arthur, ed. *Zeitmaschine Kino*. Marburg: Hitzeroth, 1992.

Matthews, Jenny. *Women and War*. Ann Arbor, MI: The University of Michigan Press, 2003.

Miller, Frieda. *Shanghai: A Refuge During the Holocaust;. A Teacher's Guide*. Vancouver, BC: Vancouver Holocaust Education Centre, 1999.

Mittauer, Michael, and Reinhard Sieder. *Frauen in Österreich nach 1945*. Vienna: Geyer Edition, 1985.

Montgomery Byles, Joan. *War, Women, and Poetry, 1914-1945: British and German Writers and Activists*. Newark, DE: University of Delaware Press, 1995.

Neuwirth, Barbara, ed. *Schriftstellerinnen sehen ihr Land: Österreich aus dem Blick seiner Autorinnen*. Vienna: Wiener Frauenverlag, 1995.

Ofer, Dalia, and Lenore J. Weitzman, eds. *Women in the Holocaust*. New Haven: Yale University Press, 1998.

Österreicher im Exil: Großbritannien 1938-1945. Vienna: Dokumentationsarchiv des österreichischen Widerstandes, 1992.

Phillips, Zlata Fuss. *German Children's and Youth Literature in Exile: Biographies and Bibliographies*. München: Saur, 2001.

Pelz, Monika. *Eine Frau heiratet sowieso und kriegt Kinder: Ein Frauen-Report*. Vienna: Jungbrunnen, 1990.

Plainl, Gill. *Women's Fiction of the Second World War*. Edinburgh: Edinburgh University, 1996.

Reisdorfer, Kathryn H. "Seeing Through the Screen: An Examination of Women in Soviet and German Popular Cinema in the Inter-War Years." PhD diss., University of Minnesota, 1993.

Remmler, Karen. *Waking the Dead: Correspondences between Walter Benjamin's Concept of Remembrance and Ingeborg Bachmann's Ways of Dying*. Riverside, CA: Ariadne, 1996.

Reynoldson, Fiona. *Women and War*. Hove: Wayland, 1993.

Riemer, Willy, ed. *After Postmodernism: Austrian Literature and Film in Translation*. Riverside, CA: Ariadne, 2000.

Rosenberger, Nicole. *Poetik des Unbefugten: Zur Darstellung von Krieg und Verfolgung in Ilse Aichingers Roman "Die größere Hoffnung."* Vienna:

Braumüller, 1998.

Ross, James R. *Escape to Shanghai: A Jewish Community in China*. New York: Free Press, 1994.

Sage, Lorna. *Women in the House of Fiction: Post-War Women Novelists*. Basingstoke, Hampshire: Macmillan, 1992.

Sarris, Andrew. *Politics and Cinema*. New York: Columbia University Press, 1978.

Schaumann, Caroline. "From *weiter leben* (1992) to *Still Alive* (2001): Ruth Klüger's Cultural Translation of her 'German Book' for an American Audience." *The German Quarterly* 77, no. 3 (Summer 2004): 324-339.

Schlicht, Michael, ed. *Geschichte: Grundlagen und Hintergründe; Szenische Geschichtsdarstellung*. Marburg: Hitzeroth, 1989.

Schmidjell, Christine. *Marlen Haushofer: 1920-1970. Zirkular*. June 22, 1990. Vienna: Dokumentationsstelle für neuere österreichische Literatur, 1990.

Schmidlechner, Karin M. *Kriegsende und Nachkriegszeit in der Steiermark*. Vienna: Döcker, 1997.

Schulte-Sasse, Linda. "'Living On' in the American Press: Ruth Klüger's *Still Alive* and its Challenge to a Cherished Holocaust Paradigm." *German Studies Review* 27, no. 3 (October 2004): 469-475.

Schwarz, Daniel. *Imagining the Holocaust*. New York: St. Martin's, 1999.

Schweiger, Waltraud. *Friedensausbruch: Frauenleben in den Nachkriegsjahren*. Graz: die Edition, 1990.

Seeber, Ursula, and Evelyne Polt-Heinzl, eds. *Die Zeit gibt die Bilder: Schriftsteller, die Österreich zur Heimat hatten; Fotografiert von Alisa Douer*. Vienna: Dokumentationsstelle für neuere österreichische Literatur, 1992.

Seeber, Ursula, ed. *Ein Niemandsland, aber welch ein Rundblick: Exilautoren über Nachkriegs-Wien*. Vienna: Picus, 1998.

Sicher, Efraim. *The Holocaust Novel*. New York: Routledge, 2005.

Sigmund, Anna Maria. *Die Frauen der Nazis*. München: Wilhelm Heyne, 1998.

Sheldon, Sayre P., ed. *Her War Story: Twentieth-Century Women Write about War*. Carbondale, IL: Southern Illinois University Press, 1999.

Sorel, Nancy Caldwell. *The Women Who Wrote the War*. 1999. New York: Perennial, 2000.

Strigl, Daniela. *Marlen Haushofer: Die Biographie*. Munich: Claassen, 2000.

Studer, Liliane, ed. *Die Frau hinter der Wand: Aus dem Nachlaß der Marlen Haushofer.* Munich: Claassen, 2000.

Szepansky, Gerda. *"Blitzmädel" "Heldenmutter" "Kriegerwitwe": Frauenleben im Zweiten Weltkrieg.* Frankfurt a. M.: Fischer Taschenbuch Verlag, 1986.

Taucher, Franz. *Damals in Wien.* Vienna: Europaverlag, 1981.

Thüminger, Rosemarie. *Bis der Herbst kommt.* Vienna: Dachs, 1991.

Tidl, Maria. *Frauen im Widerstand: Frauen im Kampf gegen Faschismus und Krieg.* Vienna: Bund Demokratischer Frauen Österreichs, 1978.

Totten, Samuel, ed. *Teaching Holocaust Literature.* Needham Heights, MA: Allyn & Bacon, 2001.

Vansant, Jacqueline. *Against the Horizon: Feminism and Postwar Austrian Women Writers.* New York: Greenwood, 1988,

Veigl, Hans, and Sabine Derman. *Alltag im Krieg: 1939-1945.* Vienna: Ueberreuter, 1998.

Vice. Sue. *Holocaust Fiction.* London: Routledge, 2000.

Vocelka, Karl. *Trümmerjahre: Wien 1945-1949.* Vienna: Jugend und Volk, 1985.

Vogel, Harald, and Michael Gans. *Rose Ausländer lesen: Lesewege – Lesezeichen zum literarischen Werk; Leseportraits.* Vol. 2. Baltmannsweiler: Schneider Verlag Hohengehren, 1997.

Walter, Ingrid. *Dem Verlorenen nachspüren: Autobiographische Verarbeitung des Exils deutschsprachiger Schriftstellerinnen.* Edition Wissenschaft. Traunstein: Driesen, 2000.

Waxman, Zoë Vania. *Writing the Holocaust: Identity, Testimony, Representation.* Oxford Historical Monographs. Oxford: Oxford University Press, 2006.

Weedon, Chris, ed. *Postwar Women's Writing in German.* Providence, RI: Berghahn Books, 1997.

Weigel, Sigrid. *Ingeborg Bachmann: Hinterlassenschaften unter Wahrung des Briefgeheimnisses.* Vienna: Zsolnay, 1999.

Weiner, Rebecca. "The Virtual Jewish History Tour Vienna," *Jewish Virtual Library.* A Division of the American-Israeli Cooperation Enterprise. 2008. http://www.jewishvirtuallibrary.org/jsource/vjw/Vienna.html (accessed January 18, 2010).

Weinzierl, Ulrich, ed. *Österreichs Fall: Schriftsteller berichten vom "Anschluß"* Vienna: Jugend und Volk, 1988.

Young, James E. "Holocaust Documentary Fiction: The Novelist as Eyewitness." In *Writing and the Holocaust.* Edited by Berel Lang. New York: Holmes & Meier, 1988.

——. *Writing and Rewriting the Holocaust: Narrative and the Consequence of Interpretation*. Bloomington: Indiana University Press, 1990.

Zeman, Herbert. *Das 20. Jahrhundert. Band 7. Geschichte der Literatur in Österreich von den Anfängen bis zur Gegenwart*. Graz: Akademische Druck- und Verlagsanstalt, 1999.

Ziegler, Meinrad, and Waltraud Kannonier-Finster. *Österreichisches Gedächtnis: Über Erinnern und Vergessen der NS-Vergangenheit*. Vienna: Böhlau, 1997.

General Index

Abortion, 30, 39, 152, 245n, 246n
Aichinger, Ilse, 5, 6, 13, 22, 24, 30, 35, 40, 42, 47, 67, 69, 79, 83-88, 161, 162, 164, 188-190, 193n, 207n, 212n, 213n, 216n, 224n-226n, 248n, 256n; *Die größere Hoffnung* (*Herod's Children*), 13, 40, 47, 84-88, 164, 189, 190, 207n, 213n, 224n-226n; *Kleist, Moos, Fasane* (Kleist, moss, pheasants), 225n, 226n; "Mondgeschichte" (Moon story), 216n; *Unglaubwürdige Reisen*, 83, 161, 162, 189, 207n, 224n, 225n, 248n, 256n
Annexation of Austria, *See also* Anschluss.
Anschluss, 6, 23, 38-41, 43, 51, 70, 105, 106, 113, 136, 141-143, 164, 173-175, 178-181, 192n, 195n, 211n, 228n
Austrian-Jewish experience, 10, 14, 16, 19-23, 30, 31, 38, 39, 43, 47, 49-66, 85-87, 97, 99, 112-163, 175, 181, 185, 189, 190, 193n-196n, 198n-201n, 207n, 208n, 211n-213n, 224n-226n, 230n, 231n, 233n, 235n-248n, 252n, 256n
Austro-Fascism. *See also* National Socialism.
Austro-Hungarian Empire, 6, 38, 136, 142, 143, 174, 192n, 193n, 212n, 241n
Bachmann, Ingeborg, 6, 13, 16-17, 22, 26, 29, 30, 42, 47, 67, 68, 79, 98-99 164, 195n, 197n, 201n-203n, 208n, 216n, 217n, 220n, 223n, 231n; *Das dreißigste Jahr* (*The Thirtieth Year: Stories*), 16-17; *Der Fall Franza* (*Franza's Case*) 216n, 217n; "Die Wahrheit ist dem Menschen zumutbar" ("It Is Reasonable for Humankind to Expect the Truth"), 17, 197n; "Literatur als Utopie" ("Literature as Utopia"), 17; *Malina*, 13, 29, 76, 216n, 223n; *Todesarten* (*Death Styles*), 47, 68, 216n, 217n; "Unter Mördern und Irren" ("Among Murderers and Madmen"), 231n; *Wir müssen wahre Sätze Finden. Gespräche und Interviews* (We have to find true sentences. Conversations and interviews), 195n, 202n, 203n, 208n; poetry by, 29
Bacon, Ursula, 50, 139, 140, 144, 145, 151, 152, 155-158, 162, 242n, 244n-247n; *Shanghai Diary: A Young Girl's Journey from Hitler's Hate to War-Torn China*, 50, 139, 140, 144, 145, 151, 152, 155-158, 162, 242n, 244n, 245n-247n
Baer, Elizabeth R., 30, 33; *Experience and Expression: Women, the Nazis, and the Holocaust*, 30, 33
Baum, Vicki, 50, 136, 240n, 241n; *Shanghai '37*, 136, 240n, 241n
Beckermann, Ruth, 8, 18-21, 189, 198n, 199n, 200n, 247n, 248n; *Unzugehoerig: Oesterreicher und Juden nach 1945* (Not belonging: Austrians and Jews after 1945), 18-21, 198n, 199n, 200n, 247n, 248n
Behrens, Katja, 60
Benz, Ute, 47, 206n, 211n; *Frauen im*

Nationalsozialismus (Women in National Socialism), 47, 206n, 211n
Bernhard, Thomas, 6, 43, 193n
Bernhold, Monika, 9, 10, 194n; "Representations of the Beginning: Shaping Gender Identities in Written Life Stories of Women and Men," 9, 194n
Blend, Martha, 35, 36, 50, 112-123, 125-128, 131, 164, 168, 188, 235n-239n; *A Child Alone* (*Ich kam als Kind*), 50, 112, 113, 115-128, 131, 134
Breicha, Otto, 80; *Warum Hier? Warum heute?*, 80
Brostoff, Anita, 35-37, 205n, 206n; *Flares of Memory: Stories of Childhood during the Holocaust*, 35-37, 205n, 206n
Byles, Joan Montgomery, 67, 69, 216n; *War, Women, and Poetry, 1914-1945*, 67, 69, 216n
Canetti, Veza, 38, 50; *Die Schildkröten* (*The Tortoises*), 38
Celan, Paul, 13, 68, 74, 220n
China, 24, 50, 135-163, 188, 239n-248n
Concentration camps, 7, 11, 14, 15, 17, 20, 25, 30-38, 44, 45, 49, 51, 60, 88-92, 93-95, 105, 116, 137, 156-158, 175, 177-179, 181, 182, 184-186, 188, 195n, 196n, 198n, 212n, 220n, 226n-231n, 236n, 247n, 248n, 252n-256n
Cohen-Weisz, 20, 21, 199n, 212n
Delbo, Charlotte, 25, 205n; *Auschwitz and After*, 25, 205n
Dischereit, Esther, 18, 60
Dor, Milo, 77
Ebner, Jeannie, 67, 77, 79, 80, 221n
Ehrlich, Bettina, 165
Éluard, Paul, 68

Emigration. *See also* Exile.
Exile, 6, 7, 18-21, 23, 24, 35, 38, 49-52, 56, 62-64, 86, 87, 97, 99, 112-164, 168, 188, 190, 193n, 195n, 212n, 213n, 235n-248n
Fairy tale, 11, 13, 76, 86, 88, 96, 121, 224n, 225n, 230n, 256n
Feld, Friedrich, 165
Feminism, 28-30, 48, 61
Finkelgrün, Peter, 18
Freundlich, Elisabeth, 50, 51
Fleischmann, Lea, 18
Furst, Lilian, 61, 235n, 236n; *Home is Somewhere Else*, 61, 235n, 236n
Ganglbauer, Petra, 188, 255n; *Der Himmel wartet*, 188, 255n
Gender, 9-11, 25-27, 30-34, 47, 61, 84, 89, 92, 106, 107, 160, 161, 176, 177, 190, 256n
Gioseffi, Daniela, 25, 26, 28, 192n, 202n, 256n
Golabek, Mona, 112, 131-134, 238n; *The Children of Willensden Lane: Beyond the Kindertransport: A Memoir of Music, Love, and Survival*, 112, 131-134, 238n
Goldenberg, Myrna, 30, 33; *Experience and Expression: Women, the Nazis, and the Holocaust*, 30, 33
Goldstein, Joshua S., 26-29, 202n, 256n; *War and Gender: How Gender Shapes the War System and Vice Versa*, 26-29, 202n, 203n, 256n
Grandmother, 24, 85-111, 170, 176, 188, 225n, 226n, 232n, 250n, 251n, 256n
Grimm Brothers, 86, 224n; "Goosegirl at the Well, The" (Die Gänsehirtin am Brunnen), 224n; "Little Red Riding Hood" (Rotkäppchen) 86, 225n
Grossberg, Mimi, 51

Grossman, Joan, 135, 239n, 241n, 242n, 244n, 245n; *The Port of Last Resort*, 135, 146, 239n, 241n, 242n, 244n, 245n
Gruppe 47 (Group 47), 77
Gürtler, Christa, 23; *Erfolg und Verfolgung: Österreichische Schriftstellerinnen 1918-1945* (Success and persecution: Austrian women writers 1918-1945), 23
Hacker, Melissa, 133, 134, 239n; *My Knees Were Jumping*, 133, 134, 239n
Hakel, Hermann, 80
Handke, Peter, 6, 193n
Harris, Mark Jonathan, 18, 134, 235n; *Into the Arms of Strangers*, 18, 112, 134, 235n
Haushofer, Marlen, 22, 29, 48, 49, 68, 164, 193n, 207n, 216n; *Die Wand* (*The Wall*), 29; *Wir töten Stella* (*We Kill Stella*), 49, 216n
Heppner, Ernest, 50, 135, 239n, 241n; *Shanghai Refuge: A Memoir of the World War II Jewish Ghetto*, 50, 239n
Heppner, Illo, 50, 135, 145, 147, 150, 152, 155, 239n, 244n-246n
Heym, Georg, 68, 73
Hilsenrad, Helen, 112, 128-129, 238n; *Brown Was the Danube*, 112, 128-130, 238n
Hlawaty, Graziella, 14, 193n, 195n; *Die Stadt der Lieder* (*Broken Songs: An Adolescent in War-Torn Vienna*), 14, 195n
Holliday, Laurel, 35, 206n; *Children in the Holocaust and Word War II: Their Secret Diaries*, 35, 206n
Holocaust, 6, 8, 14, 15-22, 30-40, 43, 49-51, 54, 57, 59, 60, 61, 65, 66, 68, 83, 85-89, 97-101, 105, 106, 111-163, 175, 178, 179, 181, 182, 184-191, 195n-197n, 201n, 212n, 224n-231n, 235n-248n, 252n-254n, 256n
Honigmann, Barbara, 18
Höller, Hans, 22, 201n
Ivanji, Ildi, 193n
Jacoby, Ingrid, 161-162, 148n; *My Darling Diary: A Wartime Journal – Vienna 1937-39, Falmouth 1939-1944*, 162, 148n
Janklowicz-Mann, 136, 240n-242n, 244n-246n; *Shanghai Ghetto*, 135, 136, 145, 240n-242n, 244n-246n
Jelinek, Elfriede, 21, 22, 29, 30, 47, 188, 193n, 194n, 204n, 255n, 256n; "Das flüchtige Jetzt" (The fleeting now), 188, 255n, 256n; *Die Kinder der Toten* (*The Children of the Dead*), 47; "Der Wald" (The forest), 29, 30, 204n; *In den Alpen* (In the Alps), 29, 30
Kafka, Franz, 68
Kaplan, Vivian Jeannette, 50, 135, 138-141, 147, 151-153, 156-159, 162, 164, 188, 239n, 244n-248n; *Ten Green Bottles: The True Story of One Family's Journey from War-Torn Austria to the Ghettos of Shanghai*, 50, 138-142, 144, 147, 148, 150-159, 162, 239n, 244n-248n
Kaus, Gina, 50
Kindertransport, 18, 24, 49, 50, 112-135, 143, 144, 162, 163, 213n, 226n, 235n-239n
Körber, Lili, 52, 213n
Kosiner, Gerda, 138-141, 145, 147-153, 156-159, 162, 188
Klüger, Ruth, 8, 12-14, 16, 30, 52, 60, 164, 189, 190, 193n-196n, 214n, 256n; "Besuch der Exil-Touristinnen in Wien" (Visit of the exile tourists in Vienna), 52,

214n; *Dichter und Historiker: Fakten und Fiktionen* (Poets and historians: Facts and fictions), 12, 13, 194n, 256n; *Katastrophen: Über deutsche Literatur* (Catastrophes: About German literature), 195n; *Unterwegs verloren: Erinnerungen* (Lost along the way: Memories), 190, 196n, 256n; *weiter leben: eine Jugend (Still Alive: A Holocaust Girlhood Remembered)*, 14, 52, 190, 196n
Kräftner, Hertha, 22, 24, 44, 67-83, 188, 209n, 216n- 224n; *Kühle Sterne* (cool stars), 68-82, 216n-224n; *Notizen zu einem Roman in Ich-Form* (Notes to a novel in the first person), 68, 73, 76, 79
Krasno, Rena, 242n, 243n
Kratz, Käthe, 113, 235n; *Vielleicht habe ich Glück gehabt (Maybe I was lucky)*, 113, 235n
Labor camps. See also Concentration camps.
Lang, Berel, 197n
Langer, Lawrence L., 15, 30, 197n, 202n, 205n; *Preempting the Holocaust*, 30, 32, 33, 202n, 205n
Lasker-Schüler, Else, 68, 73
Lobe, Mira, 165
Lorenz, Dagmar, 23, 60, 61, 214n; *Contemporary Jewish Writing in Austria*, 23; *Keepers of the Motherland: German Texts by Jewish Women Writers*, 23, 60, 61, 214n
Lustiger, Gila, 18
Manes, Walter, 155, 156, 246n
Mann, Amir, 136, 240n-242n, 244n, 246n; *Shanghai Ghetto*, 135, 136, 145, 240n-242n, 244n, 246n
Martel, Yann, 5, 192n; *Life of Pi*, 5, 192n
Mauthausen, 44, 88-92, 177, 182, 184-186, 207n, 226n, 227n, 252n, 253n, 255n
Menasse, Robert, 21
Mental health issues, 10, 24, 39, 53, 60, 63, 65-83, 87, 89-92, 94, 95, 97-100, 108, 110, 111, 114, 115, 117, 119, 120, 125, 127, 138, 140, 144-146, 150, 152, 158, 161, 165, 168, 171, 181, 184-188, 190, 222n, 228n, 229n
National Socialism, 6, 19-23, 28, 38-52, 54, 56, 57, 59, 62, 85-89, 91-101, 105-110, 112-163, 168-171, 173-185, 192n, 200n, 201n, 208n, 209n, 210n, 228n-231n, 233n-235n, 237n, 250n, 252n-256n
Neumann, Ronnith, 60
Neuwirth, Barbara, 23, 29, 204n; *In den Gärten der Nacht* (In the gardens of night). 29, 204n; *Schriftstellerinnen sehen ihr Land: Österreich aus dem Blick seiner Autorinnen* (Women writers see their country: Autria from the perspective of its women writers), 23; *Über die Thaya* (Over the Thaya), 29
Nöstlinger, Christine, 12, 24, 35, 36, 44, 46, 164-173, 176, 178, 183, 187, 189, 192n, 193n, 209n, 233n, 249n-251n; *Maikäfer, flieg! (Junebug, fly!)*, 44, 46, 165-171, 173, 249n-251n; *Zwei Wochen im Mai (Two weeks in May)*, 46, 165-167, 171-173, 249n, 251n
Nowak, Johanna, 24, 84, 85, 107-111, 170, 188, 233n-235n; *Gehorsam: Roman eines schuldhaften Lebens* (obedient: Novel of a guilt-ridden life), 84, 85, 101, 107-111, 170, 233n-235n
Ofer, Dalia, 30; *Women in the Holocaust*, 30, 31

Okopenko, Andreas, 80
Oppenheimer, Deborah, 18, 134, 235n; *Into the Arms of Strangers*, 18, 112, 134, 235n
Pauli, Hertha, 52, 165, 213n
Perrault, Charles, 225n
Petrik, Dine, 67, 71, 216n, 218n; *Die Hügel nach der Flut: Was geschah wirklich mit Hertha K?* (The hills after the flood: What really happened to Hertha K.?), 67, 71, 216n, 218n
Prostitution, 148, 149, 161, 245n
Rabinovici, Doron, 21
Rape, 10, 26, 27, 30, 34, 43, 44, 70, 71, 105, 152, 169, 170, 175, 204n, 217n, 218n, 233n, 250n, 252n
Recheis, Käthe, 12, 24, 35, 36, 61, 164-167, 178-189, 253n-255n; *Geh heim und vergiß alles* (Go home and forget everything), 165, 178, 183-187, 253n-255n; *Lena: Unser Dorf und der Krieg* (Lena: Our village and the war), 165, 166, 178-183, 187, 253n, 254n
Reichart, Elisabeth, 5, 8, 11, 22, 24, 30, 42-44, 47, 84, 88-101, 110, 111, 170, 177, 193n, 198n, 226n-231n; *Februarschatten* (February Shadows), 11, 42, 44, 45, 47, 84, 88-92, 97, 100, 101, 111, 198n, 226n-232n; *Komm über den See* (Come across the lake), 47, 84, 88, 92-97, 100, 101, 111, 227n-230n; *Nachtmär* (Nighttale), 47, 84, 88, 92, 97-101, 170, 229n-232n
Resistance Movement, Austria, 22, 25, 26, 28, 29, 38, 39, 42, 49, 84, 86, 87, 91-97, 99, 101, 102, 110, 160, 170, 178, 179, 181-183, 188, 191, 228n, 229n, 230n
Rich, Adrienne, 5, 192n; "Dark Fields of the Republic: Six Narratives," 5, 192n
Rosdy, Paul, 135, 239n, 241n, 242n, 244n-247n; *The Port of Last Resort*, 135, 146, 239n, 241n, 242n, 244n-247n
Rotenberg, Stella, 50
Ruby, Lois, 159-161, 248n; *Shanghai Shadows*, 159-161, 248n
Rühm, Gerhard, 77
Salten, Felix, 165
Schindel, Robert, 21
Schirach, Baldur von, 42, 48, 211n
Schirach, Henriette von, 42, 48, 211n
Schmid-Bortenschlager, Sigrid, 23; *Erfolg und Verfolgung: Österreichische Schriftstellerinnen 1918-1945* (Success and persecution: Austrian women writers 1918-1945), 23
Seeber, Ursula, 23, 50, 52, 213n, 214n; *Ein Niemandsland, aber welch ein Rundblick! Exilautoren über Nachkriegs-Wien* (A no-man's land, but what a view! Exile authors on postwar Vienna), 23, 50, 52, 213n
Segal, Lore, 35, 36, 50, 112-128, 131, 164, 168, 188, 235n-239n; *Other People's Houses* (*Wo andere Leute wohnen*), 50, 112, 113, 115-128, 131, 134, 235n-239n
Shanghai. See also China.
Shedd, Charlotte, 8, 193n; *Thank You America*, 8, 193n
Shoah. See also Holocaust.
Sicher, Efraim, 15-18, 21, 22, 195n, 197n, 200n; *The Holocaust Novel*, 15-18
Sigmund, Anna Maria, 47, 48; *Die Frauen der Nazis* (Women of the Third Reich), 47, 48
Spiegelman, Art, 16; *Maus I*, 16; *Maus II*, 16

Spiel, Hilde, 38, 50, 51, 206n, 213n; *Die hellen und die finsteren Zeiten. Erinnerungen 1911-1989 (Hilde Spiel – the Dark and the Bright: Memoirs 1911-1989)*, 38, 206n; *Rückkehr nach Wien: ein Tagebuch*, 206n; *Welche Welt ist meine Welt? Erinnerungen. 1946-1989*, 213n

Steinthaler, Evelyn, 23; *Frauen 1938 (Women 1938)*, 23

Tausig, Franziska, 136, 138, 139, 142-145, 147-149, 154, 157, 158, 162, 188, 241n, 243n-248n; *Shanghai Passage: Emigration ins Ghetto* (Shanghai passage: Emigration to the Ghetto); 136, 138, 142-145, 148, 149, 157, 158, 162, 241n, 243n-248n

Third Reich. See also National Socialism.

Trahan, Elizabeth Welt, 8, 11, 14, 16, 22-24, 36, 53-66, 67, 83, 164, 188, 193n, 196n, 197n, 214n. 215n, 216n; *Walking with Ghosts (Geisterbeschwörung: Eine jüdische Jugend im Wien der Kriegsjahre)*, 11, 14, 23, 53-66, 188, 196n, 197n, 214n, 215n, 216n; *Ten Dollars in my Pocket*, 23, 24, 53-66, 188, 214n, 215n, 216n

Trakl, Georg, 68, 73

Trauma. *See also* Mental health.

Waldlager Gunskirchen, 178

Waxman, Zoë Vania, 30; *Writing the Holocaust: Identity, Testimony, Representation*, 30

Weigel, Hans, 77, 78, 80, 221n, 222n

Weigel, Sigrid, 6, 7, 22; *Ingeborg Bachmann: Hinterlassenschaften unter Wahrung des Briefgeheimnisses*, 193n

Weil, Grete, 60

Weil, Lisl, 164, 167, 248n, 249n; *To Sail a Ship of Treasures*, 164, 167, 248n, 249n

Weitzman, Lenore J., 30, 31; *Women in the Holocaust*, 30, 31

Welles, Eva Anna, 24, 83-85, 101-107, 110-111, 170, 188, 193n, 225n, 232n, 233n; *Am Rande der Geschichte* (at the edge of history), 83, 84, 101-107, 110, 111, 170, 225n, 232n, 233n

Welsh, Renate, 12, 24, 35, 36, 164-167, 173-178, 183, 187, 189, 192n, 193n, 209n, 251n-253n; *Dieda oder das fremde Kind* (Her, over there or the strange child), 165, 176-178, 252n, 253n; *Johanna*, 165, 173-175, 178, 251n, 252n

Wiesel, Elie, 16, 17

Wiesenthal, Simon, 201

Work camps. *See also* Concentration camps.

World War I, 67, 69, 101, 103-107, 142, 174

World War II, 5, 6, 8-11, 13-25, 27, 28, 30-53, 59-62, 65, 66, 68, 69, 74, 75, 82-89, 91-95, 99-103, 105-107, 111-164, 166-191, 194n-203n, 207n-213n, 217n, 218n, 220n, 225n, 233n, 235n-248n, 249n, 253n-256n

Young, James, 14-16, 197n